STEVE
KERR

STEVE
KERR

A Life

SCOTT HOWARD-COOPER

wm
WILLIAM MORROW
An Imprint of HarperCollinsPublishers

Grateful acknowledgment is made to the following for the use of the photographs that appear in the art insert: Ronald Reagan Presidential Library (page 1); John Storey/Getty Images (page 2, top); Golden Eagle Distributors (page 2, bottom left and right); David E. Klutho/Getty Images (page 3); Manny Millan/Getty Images (pages 4–6); Nathaniel S. Butler/Getty Images (pages 7 and 8, top right); Keith Allison (page 8, top left); and Pete Souza (page 8, bottom).

HarperCollins books may be purchased for educational, business, or sales promotional use. For information, please email the Special Markets Department at SPsales@harpercollins.com.

FIRST EDITION

Library of Congress Cataloging-in-Publication Data has been applied for.

ISBN 978-0-06-300127-5

21 22 23 24 25   LSC   10 9 8 7 6 5 4 3 2 1

To Jordan, Taylor, and Nora

Contents

STEVE
KERR

Prologue

Steve Kerr and Bob Myers projected gratitude in the strangest place and at the strangest time, on the court as the opponent began celebrating a title at their expense and minutes after the 2018–2019 Warriors season had come to such a blunt-force conclusion that it was easy to imagine their 2020 playoff aspirations extinguished as well. Golden State had been that disfigured. The defending champions in one night were dethroned at home by the Raptors, and star shooting guard Klay Thompson tore a knee ligament that would sideline him for much if not all of the next season, one game after star small forward Kevin Durant ruptured an Achilles' tendon that would likely cost him all of 2019–2020, if he returned at all as a free agent. The franchise so came apart in the series that a minority owner had earlier shoved Raptors guard Kyle Lowry after Lowry crashed into the front row near him chasing a loose ball.

Late on June 13, 2019, Kerr was emotionally wrung out after five playoff marathons in as many seasons as a coach, more than by the loss that euthanized a cursed Finals. He would soon head to the home locker room, visit with Commissioner Adam Silver, and ask if the Warriors could skip next season and instead spend the months riding bikes and sipping wine in Italy. First, though, near the vacated Golden State bench, Kerr and General Manager Myers stopped to hug. Their embrace came across more as appreciating their good fortune than as consoling each other for the basketball agony flooding the operation. They may have been near tears in the brief conversation as Thompson headed to the hospital and the severity of the injury became evident, but the close friends also appeared to share a moment of appreciation as they conceded that the run as they knew it had come to an end.

For all his championship riches, Kerr through the years mostly revealed himself in adversity and defeat. There was the superhuman composure the first game back after the assassination of his father, the knee injury that could have ended his career in 1986, and his struggles to stick in the NBA. Even his greatest starring roles as a player—the Chicago '97 jumper, the unimaginable rescue mission with San Antonio in 2003—were responses to some of his lowest times on the court.

The earliest minutes after losing the championship to the Raptors would be no different. After months of urging the Warriors and their fans to treasure the magical five seasons before it was too late and only memories remained, Kerr gathered the assistant coaches and the video team in his office to practically insist they cherish a last moment together before scattering into the offseason and preparing for a 2019–2020 everyone knew would be different. Handing out his favorite beer, Modelo Especial, he went around the room "and connected with our staff, talking about his appreciation for each of us, which he'd never done like that before," Bruce Fraser, a close friend and assistant, noted. "Not trying to make us feel better. Just letting us know he cared." Carrying the same message to players, Kerr's postgame address skipped somber and, as he later related, was ruled by appreciation. "I can't tell you my gratitude in terms of just being put in this position to be with this group and to coach them and to help them," he said.

Kerr had always been genuine in valuing the positives, a trait established as early as his teen years. He was the first to say, accurately and not in false modesty, that he did not deserve the scholarship to the University of Arizona that fell from the sky, just as he had been realistic as the 1988 draft approached that he had little chance to last more than a season or two in the league. To then have a dream outcome in Tucson and spend fifteen seasons in the pros, with five titles and the chance to learn his future craft from greats Phil Jackson and Gregg Popovich, would not be taken for granted. Cracking open beers in his office with appreciation amid defeat was just Kerr's June 13, 2019, version of nearing the end of the Arizona years and deciding, "I've been one of the luckiest people in the world," because the '86 knee injury taught him perseverance and "my father's death has helped me put things in their true perspective."

The 2019–2020 that followed was even worse than expected. If it was, at the very least, a pause for the franchise that would regroup for 2020–2021, it was also the season that most mirrored Kerr's personal history as an unwanted college recruit who became a late draft pick and then spent several years as a replaceable journeyman making minimal contributions. He was practiced at being left behind—and responding. The Warriors in last place may have felt strange, but finding himself on a steep climb was familiar. Kerr was in exactly the right place again.

CHAPTER 1

Beirut

They were sure they spotted two Japanese submarines in position to attack Southern California on December 7, 1941, or at least spy on the mainland, and four more hulking pieces of enemy machinery treading water in the Pacific Ocean the second day of self-appointed reconnaissance work. Seven-year-old Ann Zwicker and other neighborhood kids went to the bluffs of Palisades Park in Santa Monica to do their part in the infant war effort. In the Zwicker household, that would come to include her father standing watch as an air raid warden, his heavy woolen sweater, cap, whistle on a long chain, and armband laid out on a bedroom shelf between shifts for quick access if needed. Ann and a few friends likewise considered it their patriotic duty to trample the Japanese lilacs that grew wild on the bluffs and in some backyards.

Mostly, though, she grew up in a bubble. Santa Monica was a tranquil world of tree-lined streets, two doting parents in John and Susan Zwicker, John's work for the same business firm for forty years, a warm relationship with her younger sister Jane, and nearby fields of undeveloped land for play. The days of potential submarine attacks were terrifying, but also entirely atypical. The girls' world mostly consisted of neighborhood friends, and their wandering imaginations came from listening to *Tom Mix* and *The Lone Ranger* on the radio, and from the fright of tuning in to *I Love a Mystery* and *This Is Your FBI*. Even trips into Los Angeles, the burgeoning city fifteen miles east, were rare. And when the possibility of emotional crisis arose with the family's eviction in 1944, after the landlord raised the rent to what John and Susan considered an unacceptable amount, Ann would spin it into the idyllic memory of little more than the inconvenience of needing to relocate a few blocks. The retelling came complete with the serenity of the beautiful curtains and slipcovers her mother sewed for the new home, the red wallpaper her father hung in the girls' shared room, and the long desk ordered for the two elementary school students.

Santa Monica High School was later so much fun that Ann practically hated to graduate in 1952. Choosing Occidental College, some twenty-five miles from home, all the way on the other side of Los Angeles, was adventurous by her standards. A conversation with a neighbor in Erdman Hall who had recently returned from a junior year in Greece with stories of living abroad, though, sparked a surge of wanderlust in Ann Zwicker as unexpected as it was life-changing. From then on, she worked toward a degree in Education and mentally scanned the globe for an opportunity.

India was the initial target, until her parents disapproved. Too adventurous. They steered intrepid Ann toward Europe, but that was not exotic enough for her in the search for someplace very different. When the minister at the family's church returned from the Middle East and raved about the beauty of the region and the high academic standards of a university on the coast of Lebanon, with the Mediterranean tides practically lapping at the campus grounds, it seemed the perfect compromise. The Presbyterian Church even had a program there, a junior year abroad at American University in Beirut.

In August 1954, twenty-year-old Ann boarded a propeller plane in Los Angeles for a bumpy ride to Boston and a visit with her maternal grandfather. She continued from there to New York to meet six other students making the same journey on the Dutch freighter bound for the Lebanese capital. Seventeen days later, on October 5, the MS *Bantam*, engulfed by heat and humidity even in the morning, pulled into port and was met by an AUB car that took the female travelers to their quarters among the three-story apartment buildings a few blocks from campus.

Ann unpacked in the room she would share with four others, a change from dividing space with only her younger sister, and went to the dining hall for lunch. A five-foot-seven California blonde with fair skin and green eyes, she instantly stood out in contrast to the many students from Cyprus, Iraq, Jordan, Lebanon, and other locales a world removed from Santa Monica. The warmth and hospitality of students from the region, though, instantly made the newcomer feel welcome, not out of place. Next, wanting to learn more about classes and activities as the journey began in earnest, Ann made the short walk to the school to meet the Adviser to Women Students. Elsa Kerr rose from behind a desk to greet her.

Ann Zwicker and Elsa Kerr had much in common, beyond the obvious of being American women far from home in an era of parents preaching domesticity to daughters. Like Ann, Elsa, at nearly six feet, stood out physically. Both also had a passion for education—Zwicker planned to make it a career, and Kerr was a university administrator married to a professor who would later rise to chairman of the AUB Biochemistry Department. And of course, the shared spirit of adventure.

Elsa Reckman left Ohio to study Turkish in Istanbul, where she met Stanley Kerr and married him in 1921. Together, they worked to rescue Armenian children by sending them to Lebanon, and they ran an orphanage for Armenian boys in Beirut in the 1920s, before Stanley began teaching at AUB and Elsa at Beirut College for Women.

Finding an ally in an important position so soon after arriving would have been fortuitous enough for Ann. Far more important to her future, as Zwicker would eventually learn, was Elsa telling her son Malcolm he should meet this young lady from California. Had Ann known at the time, she might have waved off matchmaking that involved an American. She hadn't left the United States to date someone from the United States, after all, as her dating life the first couple weeks in Beirut indicated: two Lebanese men, a Palestinian, and a Greek, people she had met either in class or through a widening circle of new international friends.

Malcolm was different in his own way, though, and American or not, unlike anyone Ann would have met at home. The first time she spotted him across the room at a bar in the city's popular nightclub district, Zwicker saw his features—tall, slim, clean-cut, light-brown hair, boyish—but also noted his blue corduroy summer jacket that to her represented Ivy League. That he was there at all was a fluke—Malcolm had been bound for graduate school at Oxford before a recurrence of debilitating early-onset arthritis, a lifelong problem, forced him to remain with his parents and three siblings in Lebanon. When they happened to be at the same Sunday afternoon social the next week, the young man cut in as she danced and introduced himself. The more Ann learned over the weeks the more captivated she became. Malcolm had graduated from Princeton—the jacket didn't lie: Ivy League—was pursuing his master's in Middle East studies at AUB, and was fluent in Arabic. He was smart, a man of integrity, but possessed an irreverent sense of humor as well. Most important, he was as taken with Ann as she was with him.

Malcolm proposed on March 17, 1955, barely four months after their initial meeting and with four months remaining before the end of the school year and Ann's return to California. They would be married the following summer, after she graduated from Occidental and he completed the master's program at AUB and began Ph.D. studies at Johns Hopkins's Washington, D.C., campus. They were still three time zones apart, but at least on the same continent.

They wed August 18, 1956, in a candlelight ceremony at Santa Monica Presbyterian Church, accompanied by selections from Bach and Mozart chosen by the groom, followed by a reception in the garden of the Zwicker home. The newlyweds moved to Massachusetts so Malcolm could work on his dissertation at Harvard, until he graduated in June 1958 and was hired to teach in the Political Science Department at American University in Beirut, a move that came when Ann was pregnant with the couple's first child. This time, she would be returning to Lebanon indefinitely, with a husband and a baby on the way but the same embrace of adventure as four years earlier. Ann and Malcolm both rated the three-year commitment to AUB the number-one preference for his employment.

The teenager from the Santa Monica bubble had become so

worldly that daughter Susan arrived November 13, 1958, in the same Beirut campus hospital where Malcolm had been born. "Never mind, next time you'll have a boy," his barber told the new father in Arabic on his first visit after Susan's birth. Further shaming from the men of Lebanon was avoided with the birth of John Malcolm Kerr on May 21, 1961. They were a family of four when the three years ended and the plane lifted off in August for the next adventure, a postdoctoral study for Malcolm at St. Antony's College in Oxford, England, and a contract to join the UCLA Political Science Department afterward. The time had come, the new parents agreed, to build a base in the United States.

It took only until the fall of 1964 for the next departure: Malcolm received a grant to spend a year in Cairo writing a book, an opening he promptly turned into a two-year leave from UCLA to also include twelve months in Beirut. It was in Egypt that Ann and Malcolm learned that they would have another child. Not only that, they would be in Lebanon by Ann's due date, which meant the third baby would be born in the same hospital as brother, sister, and father. Stephen Douglas Kerr arrived in the AUB Medical Center on September 27, 1965, with blond hair and a hearty cry.

Some of his first hours were spent in smoke, with dozens of guests bearing chocolates and flowers and puffing away on cigarettes while visiting the other new mother in the shared hospital room. Thankfully, the babies were usually in a separate nursery, but Ann and Malcolm, who would stay through the night, sought refuge anyway in a corner behind a curtain that could do little to filter the constant conversation or, worse, the maddening stench of tobacco. Relief finally arrived when the infants were brought in for a 10 P.M. feeding, amid what remained of the fumes, and all guests were asked to leave. In the coming months, when Ann took Steve for afternoon walks in the stroller, she would have to maneuver around piles of garbage on the corner near their home in the Ain Mreisseh quarter, and similar route adjustments were necessary even in neighborhoods with elegant shops. The smells were so bad at times that Ann plugged her nose as she pushed the buggy.

Mostly, though, Steve was born into a sophisticated city of international commerce, education, and colorful gardens that flowed down from balconies like waterfalls. AUB, with 3,246 students representing 59 nations and 24 religions, was the perfect symbol for the diversity of a land friendly to Americans, especially those who called Beirut home. They were emotionally invested in the seaside capital, not just visiting.

Ten years before civil war devastated Lebanon and changed it for generations to come, Beirut remained every bit as captivating to Ann as it had been during the magical junior year abroad in college that changed her life. She hadn't merely followed Malcolm back as a compliant wife, after all. She was excited to return, even with the challenges that could have been avoided by staying close to Santa Monica. Newspapers in English, Arabic, and French were available, as well as food from around the world, often prepared tableside in restaurants with white tablecloths.

A little less than a year after Steve's birth, the Kerrs returned to Southern California and Malcolm's role at UCLA. When Andrew arrived in July 1968 as the final addition to the family, he was delivered at the same hospital in Santa Monica where Ann was born. They were a family of six in need of more space. Ann found her dream home on a mountaintop in Pacific Palisades, with views of the Pacific to the west and the cityscape to the east, surrounded by canyons on three sides, and Will Rogers State Beach was a five-minute drive down the hill. Even in the moment of finding their forever home, the ultimate sign of putting down roots in the United States, or as much as could realistically be expected in the delightfully transient Kerr world, they were thinking of Lebanon. The stone patio with wooden gates that opened over the canyon reminded Malcolm of a second home his parents had in a mountain village fifteen miles south of Beirut, with a similar scenic vista toward the city and the Mediterranean coastline, and Ann was likewise struck by the similarity to their once-upon-a-time vantage point of cityscape and the sea.

Steve was three and a half when he moved into the only home he would know in the United States until college, providing stability as temporary international relocations continued. He would attend kindergarten in Aix-en-Provence in southern France in the 1970–1971 academic year. Even decades later, as Steve reached adulthood and then well into his fifties, Pacific Palisades and the rambling white home on the mountaintop, with adjacent guest quarters, remained a family constant. The delight was especially pronounced for Ann during the five years after they returned from France and the ensuing summer in Tunisia, a golden time of walks with the dog in the adjoining hills, barbecues on the big brick patio, outdoor play time, and parties for special occasions. The pine and eucalyptus trees she planted in the canyons as saplings aged into the sky.

The second Kerr son's delight at finally getting to stay in one place showed most of all in a growing love of sports, especially basketball and baseball. Steve, the vagabond youth, found important connections through the typical boys' activities that gave him a chance to be part of something with American peers as well as an outlet for his competitive side. Though he would later play tennis, established by his parents as the Kerr family game, and surf, he gravitated to team sports, an early reveal of the basketball player and coach who detested the individual, one-on-one approach. "Whenever we were in L.A., my dad would take me to Dodger games and UCLA basketball games all the time," Steve said. "He loved it almost as much as I did," even if the bookish father, as they'd add for decades to come when recounting the memory, read *The New Yorker* in the bleachers of Dodger Stadium as his boys chased batting-practice home runs.

By the time he was six years old, Steve was a regular evening presence on the flat driveway, with an early and obvious passion for hoops that endured despite, in the words of Andrew, "vicious" bullyball battles against older, bigger brother John in the typical sibling rite of passage. (Their father finally one day pinned John to the ground to show him how it felt.) Other times, Malcolm helped with dinner before going out front for civil competitions, in contrast to John's full-contact approach, as Steve created methods to muscle the ball to the rim.

"It was a remarkable sight," Ann recalled in her memoir, flush with motherly pride. "Standing with his back to the board he held the ball in his arms at knee height and with a big jump, hurled it up over his head in a backward motion. The ball, so large relative to the small boy throwing it, almost seemed to carry him with it."

If Steve's determination was obvious, so were the dark mood swings that too often began to rule his world. The delightful boy grew into a young man with a temper who lashed out when he lost or didn't play well, especially as a pitcher. The constant pauses in baseball gave him too much time to think on the mound, in contrast to the near-constant motion of basketball. Long before the image of Kerr as uncommonly grounded under heat lamps of pressure and scrutiny, there was the boy throwing so many tantrums into his preteens that Ann called learning to control his temper one of Steve's greatest accomplishments. His parents were relieved when hoops ultimately emerged as his sport of choice.

When the Kerrs moved in 1976 to Egypt, where Malcolm would be a distinguished visiting professor at American University in Cairo, Ann warned the kids that they were not going to like the country much. "The food is terrible, the weather is hot and sticky for months on end, everything is always dusty, and the TV is in Arabic," she told them. But, she added, "we'll learn a lot and it will be a great adventure." Steve responded to the news of the latest upheaval by stoically shooting away at the rim bolted to the roof above the garage in the driveway in Pacific Palisades. He was especially disappointed by the latest relocation because it meant being taken away from basketball.

The Cairo airport was a boiling cauldron of crowds and late-summer heat when the Kerrs stepped off the AUC charter flight from New York with two adults and four kids, ages eight to seventeen, carting boogie boards, tennis rackets, stuffed suitcases, and, of course, a basketball. A small bus arranged by college officials whisked them south from the chaos and down the Nile Corniche, the waterfront promenade, to an apartment near campus in the sleepy suburb of Maadi. The new residence was about one-fourth

the size of the Southern California forever home, and they would
be sharing a single bathroom. From time to time, a tribe of goats
would amble along the dusty streets, led by women in long black
garments.

Steve took to sixth grade with enthusiasm despite not wanting
to be in Cairo. He would never match the academic passion of his
paternal grandparents, both educators, or his parents, both educators, or his three siblings, all bound for postgraduate college degrees,
but neither would he ignore classwork. Much of what his mother
ominously predicted before the trip came true, inconveniences that
would have driven many eleven-year-olds to surrender, but Steve's
positive disposition and competitive nature nudged him forward,
just as they would countless other times through the years.

At the same time, Ann was energized by growing teaching opportunities, and Malcolm made such an immediate impact that
the AUC president confided he was planning to retire in a year and
hoped the distinguished visiting professor would consider leaving
UCLA for a permanent move to Egypt as his successor. Though he
couldn't have known, Steve's life was at a crossroads. Tempted by
the opportunity to stay in the region with a promotion to a critical
role while Ann relished the chance to be in the classroom, they debated the family's future before ultimately choosing to return to
Los Angeles as originally planned. If the Kerrs were to leave Pacific
Palisades for several years, the parents decided, it would take an
offer from what both considered the ultimate destination: the familiarity and personal connection with American University in Beirut.

Back in Southern California in the fall of 1977, they couldn't help
but wonder what might have been, especially Ann as she missed the
Arab world and the imagined life as a teacher and wife of a university president. The longing increased when they watched on TV as
Egyptian president Anwar Sadat made a historic visit to Jerusalem
and became the first Arab leader to visit Israel. At least there was
the professional satisfaction of Malcolm reaching new heights when
President Carter appointed him a consultant on the region, the latest indication of an influence that transcended traditional academic

lines. The professor was now also an adviser to the White House and the National Security Council.

But there were also unwanted signs of his growing stature. One night in September 1978, Malcolm's car blew up in the driveway, just outside John's bedroom. A caller phoned the Los Angeles Police Department to claim responsibility on behalf of the Jewish Armed Resistance. No arrests were made. "Why did they do it?" friends asked rhetorically after learning the news, some from far away via international media reports. "You've written as critically about the Arabs as you have about the Israelis." It was impossible to miss the sad irony that after traveling in troubled lands for months at a time, the Kerrs were attacked in quaint Pacific Palisades.

While Ann and Malcolm were missing Egypt and facing the frightening reality of becoming targets in their own country, the return to Los Angeles led to Steve landing work as a UCLA ball boy. An official role with any prominent basketball operation would have been a thrill for a thirteen-year-old, but being on the court with the Bruins in particular was a dream job. The Dodgers in baseball and UCLA in basketball were his teams and he was already emotionally invested enough that he cried when the Bruins' record eighty-eight-game winning streak ended in 1974. In 1978, Kerr had the jackpot role of rebounding for players during pregame and half-time warm-ups and sitting under the basket during the action to wipe sweat from the hardwood.

It was as if he was being paid back for the years of forced country hopping when he craved the simpler life of hoops, baseball, and riding the Pacific with a boogie board and body surfing. He briefly played football as well in middle school, but quit after breaking a hand and separating a shoulder. Sticking with basketball led him to Herb Furth, who organized youth leagues in Pacific Palisades. Furth ran the game clock at UCLA home games and was involved in the interview process for ball boys. Steve's required blue corduroys and white tennis shirt became the envy of countless boys watching from the stands.

While coach Gary Cunningham had little contact with the ball boys, and even less conversation beyond a basketball task on rare occasions, star forward Kiki VanDeWeghe paid attention. A student of the game who even as a college player appreciated young prospects, he would have noticed no matter what. More than that, though, the 1976 Palisades High School graduate also knew Furth had been given advance notice that Kerr and his common connections were arriving to chase rebounds and wipe sweat. Kerr unknowingly worked under a watchful eye that led to VanDeWeghe noting, "He hustled. Every now and then he'd sneak up a jumper. Maybe when people were done. Maybe when they weren't. I tend to notice the guys who can shoot, how it comes off their hand right and it goes in, and they just look like they know what they're doing. You can tell the guys who have a knack for scoring, and you can tell [the guys who] have been around the gym a lot—and you could tell he was that type of kid."

VanDeWeghe analyzed the same scene Ann Kerr lovingly observed years before as a mother, of Steve using his entire body to thrust the ball up from his hips. "He had kind of a different-looking jumper, but the thing went in almost every time he shot it," VanDeWeghe said. Kerr couldn't stop himself from risking trouble—"They were pretty strict"—and broke the rules to sneak in occasional shots.

His young life was becoming increasingly intertwined with UCLA. Beyond the obvious connection through Malcolm, he attended the Wooden basketball camp at Palisades around the same time he embraced the menial tasks of a ball boy with far less anonymity than he might have imagined. Furth was a John Wooden loyalist, and the coach at the high school, Jerry Marvin, was friends with Cunningham and likewise a Wooden disciple. The legend in retirement was everywhere in the Kerr world and would always be an influence as Kerr grew into an adult who despised one-on-one basketball and a player who believed everything came from staying ready. (He would never beat Wooden as a preparation freak, though. Wooden kept index cards of practice plans on specific days from years before and each year taught players how to put on socks, lest they do it wrong and get blisters.)

Malcolm accepted a post as director of the University of California Study Abroad Program in Egypt that left Ann particularly delighted. The latest relocation was made more for her sake than her
husband's career; it gave her a chance to teach again at AUC and
pursue a master's in applied linguistics. This time Malcolm was going along for the benefit of others, though getting him to the Middle
East was never a hard sell.

Steve reacted to the news with predictable gloom. Not only was
he being uprooted again a month before turning fourteen, but he
was being separated from his true love, basketball, at a time when
his improvements in the community recreation league were obvious. His desire was never in doubt, and now there were signs he
could one day be an impactful player at Palisades High, if only his
parents allowed it. In August 1979, though, he was heading for the
airport, not a sporting future, with his parents and Andrew. Susie
would stay behind for her junior year at Oberlin, while John began
freshman life at Swarthmore.

Cairo became the Kerrs' second home in the Arab world, after
the bond with Beirut that could never be broken, as the disappointment of the latest uprooting began to wear off, sometimes quickly
and on several fronts. For one thing, their apartment, in the same
suburb of Maadi, was bigger than the cramped housing of the previous stay, and they were a traveling party of four instead of six.
The entrance to the Maadi Sporting Club was across the street for
swimming and tennis. A nearby grocery store sold Frosted Flakes
from America, television sets from Japan, and electric fans from
Taiwan, at the same time the family saw the less fortunate in line
at government stores to purchase bread, chicken, cheese, and milk.
Dinner-table conversation included noting with some humor how
the son of the deposed Shah of Iran enrolled in Malcolm's AUC class
on introduction to Middle East politics.

Besides, there was basketball. Games often took place on outdoor
courts littered with rocks, and his team of fellow ninth-graders at
Cairo American College, a school filled with dependents of U.S. citizens in the capital city, played adult clubs in a country that had little

tradition with the sport. He came to cherish this period in his life, even in a setting that most in California couldn't grasp, as it was just as difficult to relate the joy of riding horses in the desert and climbing pyramids. When he scored forty points in a game against a roster of Egyptian men in their twenties, the opponent the next day offered him a monthly salary, a car, and an apartment, before the family declined rather than lose Steve's amateur status for college.

"People don't understand what Cairo is like," he said years later. "They think of Egypt and they think of pyramids and camels. Actually, for an American teenager Cairo is a great place. There are Americans all over and there aren't very many rules you have to follow. I had a great time over there."

He wanted to leave anyway, to return to America and a more structured system where he could grow in baseball and basketball against better competition and without having to maneuver around rocks. The eagerness to challenge himself in the Southern California high school scene, one of the most competitive in the country in both sports, with basketball indoors and on wood courts and everything, convinced Malcolm and Ann to let Steve move back and stay with friends. "He's always been single-minded about basketball," she said. Entering Palisades, known colloquially as Pali, in the fall of 1980 as a sophomore was also particularly good timing. VanDeWeghe had been drafted by the NBA in the first round, number eleven overall, months before, and another standout, Chip Engelland, was playing at college powerhouse Duke. Jeanie Buss, daughter of new Lakers owner Jerry Buss, was one of the team's scorekeepers before graduating in 1979.

Malcolm was building an extraordinary profile in the Middle East just as Steve was removing himself from that world. While Susan and John jetted to Cairo to spend the summer of 1980 with the family and Andrew was already there, Steve headed for California and the start of his sophomore year at Palisades. Yasser Arafat sent for Malcolm about the same time.

The Palestine Liberation Organization (PLO) leader heard through an adviser, a former Kerr student, that the leading U.S. expert on the region was in Beirut on a side trip from his Cairo post with his oldest son. Arafat wanted a meeting. Malcolm was taken to a house, only to learn that Arafat, long famous for staying in constant motion as a security precaution, was not there. Getting to know Arafat, it turned out, would not be as difficult as finding him.

After moments of tension and screwball comedy as they looked for the famous man somewhere amid the darkness of Beirut, Malcolm and the adviser pulled up to a drab apartment building in a crowded Muslim quarter on the west side of the city. Kerr entered to find Arafat sitting on a big couch with two children on his lap and an AK-47 within reach. The host leaned over to push the assault rifle aside to clear a spot for Malcolm to sit close.

Arafat told both Kerrs of his respect for American University in Beirut and said the PLO would continue to provide protection for the school as the Lebanese civil war reached its fifth year. They took it as good news at a time when PLO militias controlled the campus area in west Beirut. At the same time, they were concerned about the university losing support in Washington from legislators who could imagine the optics of voting to contribute U.S. funding to a school publicly backed by terrorists.

AUB board members approached Malcolm during the same trip to gauge his interest in becoming the next school president, probably in a year or two, as a leadership change came into focus. Informal inquiry or not, absent a firm time line or certainty it would happen at all, Ann and Malcolm were thrilled by what felt like a natural next step. More than that, they were sure that a return to Beirut would be an ideal outcome.

CHAPTER 2

Shelly Weather

In early November 1980, a couple of months into the Palisades High academic calendar, one area resident was home in his midcentury modern at 1669 San Onofre Drive, four miles from campus, when word came to Ronald Reagan that he had been elected president. Tenth-grader Steve Kerr may have wanted life as a typical American student, but this was hardly it.

Though Pacific Palisades still had pockets of middle-class and affordable homes, unlike the wide swath of affluence that came later, it was also home to movie stars, corporate CEOs, emerging sports magnates, and now the head of the free world. Parts of several movies and TV shows had been shot at Pali, and the 1970s NBC series *What Really Happened to the Class of '65?* was based on a *Time* magazine story from the previous decade. Forest Whitaker graduated the year before Kerr arrived, along with Buss and Duke-bound Engelland, and future NFL quarterback Jay Schroeder; other alumni of the era included future entertainers, volleyball stars, and an upcoming foreign minister of Armenia. The location, about a mile from the beach, across Pacific Coast Highway, was close enough to the sand that the football field was tagged the Stadium by the Sea.

Kerr had already seen enough poverty in other lands to be grateful for his Pacific Palisades existence and never forgot kids in the Middle East bundling rags into a soccer ball to be aimed at invisible goals marked by rocks. His parents, even more worldly, seemed similarly unfazed by students from low-income areas being bused to Pali, in contrast to many local families who broke out in a white-flight sprint to enroll their children in private schools. "It made me

more compassionate, and it also made me appreciate our own country, for not only the comforts and freedom we live in but also just
for the joy that we were allowed every day," Steve recalled. "Most
people don't grow up with great joy in their lives; they're struggling
to survive. That struck me pretty hard at a young age."

The closest Kerr got to the diverse world he had just left were
the less-affluent students who were bused in, before they left at the
end of the day and former Pali students returned home from their
escapist private schools. "That's when I saw the so-called ugly American side to people," he remembered. "It was emphasized even more
when you come back to it. Over there, we were doing all these things
and having all these friends from different backgrounds, and then I
got back to Los Angeles and all of a sudden it was a big competition
over who could out-dress each other and who had the cooler car,
and I had a hard time. I was not cool in high school. The only thing
I had going for me was sports."

Even that was temporary. He spent the first semester and one basketball season at Palisades and rejoined the family in Egypt during
Christmas break, accompanied by his maternal grandparents as
the Zwickers celebrated their fiftieth anniversary with a family reunion. Driving trips into the desert to camp and the Red Sea for
snorkeling expedited Steve's transition back to the Middle East life,
excursions eventually followed by touring the Nile for hours on
rented sailboats, sometimes while drunk. If it was his most uneven
school year, split across two drastically different continents, part of
the time without immediate parental oversight, it was also a year
when he could appreciate his good fortune. To have an American
high school life one week and the next be back in the Kerr fold, enjoying the many pleasures of the Arab world, was having the best
of everything, with Pali wardrobe competitions thankfully far behind him.

In his nearly sixteen years, Kerr had lived in the United States, the
Middle East, Europe, and, counting months-long vacations, northern Africa. He had seen additional lands from car windows, played
basketball on dirt courts against men, and been uprooted enough

times to either build resilience or lose the stability kids cherish, or both. He met John Wooden, got to be a UCLA ball boy, and had a bomb explode in his driveway. As he boarded a plane in the summer of 1981 to begin the trek back to California and his junior year of high school, this time in his own house with his parents and Andrew, it would be the last time the boy from a passport world would live abroad.

His father, though, was already eyeing not merely the next move but also what was for him the ultimate career accomplishment: becoming the ninth president of the campus where he was born and felt a deep connection. Creating a home in Lebanon as the civil war reached into a sixth year would be no more dangerous than living in New York City, he often told friends, and Ann, likewise worked so hard to convince herself of Malcolm's safety that she rationalized Pacific Palisades had violence and crime as well. Except that no families in Pacific Palisades split up and walked home by separate routes to make sure the entire group wasn't wiped out in the event of trouble, as they did in Beirut. Ann manufactured a false reality to fit the answer they wanted in a time when Beirut residents flipped coins to determine who would walk the dog and risk becoming a sniper target. Chaos remained so commonplace in the era that an AUB administrator and his sixteen-year-old son had their Royal Jordanian Airways plane hijacked at the Beirut airport, were released the next day, boarded a Middle East Airlines flight and had that hijacked as well, minutes before landing in Cyprus. All aboard, including the administrator traveling under a dark cloud, were freed unharmed.

Privately, Kerrs of all ages were scared as Malcolm was nominated by the board of trustees for AUB president in November 1981, weeks after the assassination of Egyptian president Anwar Sadat. Hearing the news "made me nervous about Dad going to Beirut," John wrote his sister. "It's sort of reminded me that if someone doesn't like you they might just shoot you." Months of debate followed on whether he should take the job, including a family meeting in the living room in Pacific Palisades with Malcolm wanting everybody to express their concerns. Seventeen-year-old Steve chose not to weigh in. In retrospect, he would wonder if he was too young and naive to believe that his family could be harmed, or too nervous, but he did not speak up. "I regret to this day that I never said anything. I never said a word." Looking back as an adult, he never stopped asking, "Why did he go over there? How did he take that job? And I wish I had spoken up then."

Malcolm was still searching for the right answer as he returned to New York in March for the board vote, unable to turn his back on the dream job but also wrestling with obvious doubts. "Do you think I should go?" he asked Susie after she took the train from Boston and grad school at Harvard to join him when Ann was unable to accompany her husband. In the room they shared at the Roosevelt Hotel the night before the trustees would decide between two finalists, father and daughter checked off the pros and cons of accepting the post if offered, a list that among other items attempted to weigh the impact on Steve if he was again forced to leave Pacific Palisades and finish high school in Beirut. Understanding that it was her father's chance to achieve the last major goal of his career, aware he expected to be appointed, and certain he would make an invaluable impact, the oldest Kerr child said from her bed in the darkness as they prepared to sleep that, yes, he should go.

With the lights still out, she asked what he thought about the dangers. Malcolm responded from his side of the room in a clear and sober voice.

"I bet there's a 50-50 percent chance that I'll get bumped off early on."

Then he went quiet in the darkness of the room.

"Dad is really president of AUB now," Susie recorded in her diary the next day, March 21. "For such a long time it was a possibility and now that it's really true it hits home with quite a thud. Of course, it's very meaningful for my parents to be able to return to Lebanon. As Dad said, 'Granny and Grandpa lived there, Mom and I met there, and my children were born there! That's where everything happened! How can I not go?' Well, it's terrifying as well." Malcolm, she admitted in terms that would remain haunting, was "an especially visible target." "John and I talked to each other about how scary it is, but whenever I've approached Mom and Dad about it they say, 'Yes it's very dangerous, but we could never turn it down.'"

It was so dangerous that Malcolm was based in New York, not Beirut, yet still rated the appointment the highest honor he could receive. "The only thing I'd rather do than watch Steve play basketball is be president of AUB," he told Ann. It soon came with the reality check the Kerrs didn't need but got anyway when the interim president Malcolm was replacing was clubbed in the back of his head while walking on campus, hustled into a red Renault and kidnapped. David Dodge was released one year later to the day after being held in Lebanon and Iran.

Steve, meanwhile, immersed himself in Pali activities, especially basketball, baseball, and the school newspaper. While he would eventually portray joining the *Tideline* as a fun time in the distant past, covering Dolphin sports was actually the official start of his lifetime appreciation of journalism.

His early published work was a mix of the typical high school fare—features on players and teams, straightforward and clean, peppered with inside jokes in a regular attempt to include humor. Most of the "Riptide" columns doused in sarcasm were coauthored with Michael Silver, making it impossible to know who deserved the credit or blame for a skewering, but clear that attempts at humor were everywhere and the *Tideline* had a forgiving adult adviser. Chronicling senior awards for the Class of '83, the "Riptide" declined to hand out "Most Authentic Mod" because "there's no such thing. That's like a sober Pali soccer player." Kerr and Silver also proposed Uranians as an appropriate class name because "we truly are the class that comes from Uranus." Another item that school year referenced talk about forming a surfing team to "challenge Ridgemont High, led by you-know-who, for the mythical national surfing championship and the prestigious Golden Bong Trophy." That was followed by a reminder. "Warning: Taking the *Riptide* seriously may be hazardous to your health. C'mon Pali, we don't want to hurt anyone's feelings, but try to lighten up a little."

Other times, Kerr's writing was direct and conversational, hinting at his future signature style. Discussing a proposed realignment
of the City Section of the California Interscholastic Federation that
would move Palisades into a league with teams farther away, Kerr
argued, "Now, with schools being divided according to quality of
play, the whole concept of geographic location is destroyed. Schools
like Pali and Banning may be placed in the same league, yet the two
are an hour bus ride away from each other. This not only discour-
ages fans and parents from attending away games, but it also poses
the problem of players arriving home very late at night." Showing
a willingness to deliver pointed commentary, bordering on too
pointed, a "Riptide" column noted the new academic requirements
to be eligible for sports and folded in mention of the school's success
at the Academic Decathlon, led by longtime English teacher Rose
Gilbert. "Speaking of the city champion Academic Decathlon team,
there have been rumors [that] Coach Rose Gilbert offered the team
members some extra incentives," Kerr/Silver wrote. "So now the
CIF is investigating her husband Sam, who allegedly bought new
cars" for a couple of students on the squad. It was less than two
years after UCLA had been ordered to break ties with prominent
booster Sam Gilbert as part of an NCAA investigation that included
the purchase of cars for several players.

"In class, he seemed pretty confident," said Ruth Wechsler Mills,
one of his English teachers. "Maybe that was a place where he was
confident, where he did have confidence in his ability to write. I'm
speculating now. But I never saw him as a kid who was quiet or
taciturn or down on himself or depressed or anything like that.
He was always cheerful and participated. He didn't overdo it. He
knew where to draw the line in terms of how much to talk and how
much to contribute and when to keep quiet. I had no recollection of
thinking, *Huh, I wonder if everything's okay with this guy*, or, *I wonder
why he doesn't seem to have the confidence that clearly he deserves.* He
just seemed in all aspects to be as confident as he should have been
because he did have such high ability." Another instructor familiar
with Kerr's writing remembered a student who "didn't need any-

thing from a teacher except where to go and how to improve. It was good stuff to start with."

His junior season on the basketball team went by with little outside notice. All some opponents knew ahead of time was that Pali had a player from Lebanon, so they expected someone to emerge from the locker room who looked and sounded Middle Eastern, perhaps with a name difficult to pronounce. Instead, they got a Steve with blond hair and blue eyes, the stereotype of a Southern California beach community. An explanation occasionally followed.

Kerr as a junior made more of an impression in baseball, as an infielder and pitcher, and also enjoyed his greatest team success. "If he thought you were trying to steal his signs, he'd hit you," said Sean Waters, a sportswriter with the *South Bay Daily Breeze*, one of the outlets that often covered Pali. "Or if you crowded the plate, he'd throw inside. He was a thinking man's pitcher. His stuff was good, but not great. Steve was more of a strategist. Anytime you'd see he was pitching, you were thinking about hitting the ball onto Sunset Boulevard in right-center. Then you'd walk up to the plate and he'd throw you a pitch and you'd be completely fooled. He would make you look stupid."

The Dolphins beat the top-seeded team in the semifinals to reach the City title game with a 17-4 record. Even better, the championship game against Cleveland and its undefeated starter, senior righthander Bret Saberhagen, would be played at Dodger Stadium, on the field that Kerr's favorite team called home. Kerr batted seventh and started at shortstop. It was the only part of his sporting youth that could compare with watching UCLA games from under the basket, except this was playing, even if for just one night. It ended, though, with Saberhagen throwing a no-hitter, Palisades losing 13–0, and Kerr going 0-for-2 while allowing six runs, three earned runs, nine hits, and one walk, with one strikeout and two wild pitches in four and 1/3 innings of relief. A year later, he was at third base and batting fifth, with a 1-2 record and a 2.80 ERA if needed on the mound, as the Dolphins returned to Dodger Stadium for the 1983 championship game. They lost 7–4 despite Kerr driving in two runs with a hit in three at-bats and pitching 2/3 innings of scoreless relief with one walk.

Though he lacked standout talent in any one area in baseball, Kerr displayed enough shooting range as a senior, along with maturity and smart decisions at point guard, to separate himself from the typical high school basketball player. That sport was his best chance for a college scholarship, a possibility that thrilled him as his love for the game grew. The only drawback was that Malcolm had moved to Beirut in August, just before the 1982–1983 school year began, prompting concern from the family as his wife remained in Pacific Palisades with Steve and Andrew.

"You wouldn't believe Steve's game last night," Ann wrote her husband in late January. "Palisades High won in the last four seconds of overtime against Hamilton in a series of plays that I couldn't begin to recount. Steve was the pivot of it all, of course, in an unending number of tight situations. He was 8 for 8 in free throws, the last two of which won the game, but not until Hamilton got the ball away again twice and Pali recovered it twice, all in the last few seconds. . . . Steve will explain it all in more detail—if he can get away from the TV this weekend. It's Super Bowl Sunday."

"Forget to tell you a nice story," she interjected later in the note. "Steve and I were talking after dinner the other night as we were washing the dishes about how lucky he was to have such a privileged life. A few minutes later he murmured pensively, 'No—I don't have my Dad.' But then we rationalized that he had been pretty lucky to be under the same roof with you for as long as he had. (And I wanted to add, now to have me staying home with him while he finished high school.)"

Once a game started, Kerr would dice up teams with an efficiency that set him apart. "Almost a mistake-free player," Engelland recalled, special praise for someone that age and the kind of glowing review of Kerr's performance that would continue through college. By his senior season, he could trash a scouting report so fast that coaches who thought they properly prepared for the guard with the long-distance accuracy would watch in instant frustration as Kerr found every opening. Tipoff would quickly give way to several jumpers raining through the net or smart passes that set up teammates, until the opponent had to stop play for a defensive adjustment when the game had barely started. A "Steve Kerr Timeout," some called it.

None of it was enough to earn him even one of the twenty spots on first- or second-team All-City, not at 13.6 points a game, while settling for second-team All-Central League and All-Westside region by the *Los Angeles Times*. It certainly was not enough to generate college interest. Even with Palisades known for producing talent—VanDeWeghe to UCLA in 1976, Engelland to Duke in 1979, Kevin Steward to USC, and Leroy Smith to California in 1982—Kerr's chances were reduced to Jerry Marvin calling universities in hopes of manufacturing a scholarship. Rose Gilbert's husband no longer had influence with UCLA, Kerr's dream school, and family history inside the Political Science Department did not matter when it came to a basketball scholarship.

Marvin privately shared his concern with VanDeWeghe, among others, that Kerr would get overlooked for a scholarship, despite his best efforts to alert colleges to the availability of a smart, team-oriented, mature guard who could beat most anyone in a shooting contest. Whether Kerr knew it or not, his coach who worked to keep players from growing big heads was operating behind the scenes as the best salesman his star player could have picked. Marvin was gruff and a pessimist—his worry over Kerr's future was partly fact-based and partly a reflection of his personality—but he cared deeply about his players and dreamed basketball.

It did no good. Marvin told VanDeWeghe, a rising NBA start in his third season, that high school senior Kerr would be a better shooter than VanDeWeghe and tried to project the same gaudy future to colleges, yet coaches still looked away. "He could play," Arizona State coach Bob Weinhauer said years later. "Don't get me wrong. He could definitely play. But if you were out there on the recruiting trails and you were looking at high school players, he would not be on the top of your list." Or anywhere on the list—

Weinhauer didn't pursue Kerr either. Colorado assistant coach Alvin Gentry concurred with the assessment of Kerr as a perimeter threat, but also that "you worried about what kind of athlete he was going to be and playing in a major-college situation." The message was clear from everyone: Kerr would not be able to keep up athletically, had unimpressive scoring numbers, wouldn't be able to defend, and, although a good shooter, was not good enough to make up for his many shortcomings.

He got as far as the tease of a campus visit to Gonzaga, only to be told, when he showed up, to jump into a pickup game with some of the team (an NCAA violation) and get taken apart by the Bulldogs' relatively unknown point guard, John Stockton. "I thought to myself, 'This guy is pretty good, and I'm terrible,'" Kerr said. "It was pretty depressing. Nobody else called. I had no other offers." While Kerr spent the rest of his life joking about the demoralizing trip—it's one thing to be a step slow, he said he was told, but you're two steps slow—he also felt double-crossed at being expected to audition on the spot and warned future Gonzaga candidates about his bad experience.

Lute Olson began recruiting Kerr without realizing it. Arizona's coach, hired away from Iowa, had been on the job three days when he drove from Tucson to Phoenix to scout a high school tournament, with Sacramento point guard Kevin Johnson his primary target. Next, Olson would fly to Los Angeles to watch more prospects and speak at the *Los Angeles Times* high school basketball banquet at the paper's downtown headquarters. Being asked to deliver boilerplate comments to the best players in a recruiting hotbed, a few words of congratulations on their recent success, and encouragement for the road ahead was an attractive invitation for the head of any college program. It was especially appealing to Olson. He knew the region and its hundreds of high schools well from his years with three area high schools, Long Beach City College, and Long Beach State. Handing out awards and speaking to players, parents, and coaches would provide the ideal casual setting to promote his new program.

The ability to mine Southern California would be critical to Olson's success, far more than at Iowa. Many players in the auditorium probably recognized the ghost-white hair and the unique name from the nine years at Iowa that turned a losing program into five consecutive trips to the NCAA tournament. But little of that success had hinged on luring teenagers from Los Angeles to the farm belt as friends bombarded them with wiseass comments about winter weather and driving tractors. While Arizona was anything but a glamour destination in college basketball after 4-24 and 9-18 records the previous two seasons, at least the location, in the West and the Pacific 10 Conference, was appealing. There was also the reality that the Wildcats were on their third coach in as many seasons and trying to pull talent to a town where the team was an afterthought.

Ann Kerr, in the audience with her son the All-Westside selection, was drawn to Olson's speech that emphasized academics. Olson didn't say anything particularly compelling, or anything that dozens of others wouldn't have said in the same setting, yet the educator in Ann loved his approach nonetheless. It wouldn't matter anyway because Arizona had no interest in her son, to the point that Steve was unrecognizable to Olson, but she was still impressed. "That's the kind of man I'd like you to play for," she told Steve on the drive from Los Angeles back to Pacific Palisades.

Months passed without any reason to think Ann's comment was anything other than a simple compliment. Trying to find a landing spot after graduating from Palisades, Kerr planned to play for Colorado and assistant coach Gentry as a walk-on in hopes of earning a scholarship, a realistic plan on a team that had just gone 13-15. Then he changed his mind. He would go to Cal State Fullerton, which had better players than Colorado but was also just fifty miles from home. While Kerr for decades would change his story about whether Fullerton offered him a scholarship or he was going without one, he committed to the Titans.

Quickly realizing the new staff had to slam years of work together in months, Olson and Arizona were having their own problems. Johnson said he would come for a campus visit, then backed out and chose the University of California. Reggie Miller, a shooting guard from Riverside, seventy miles east of Los Angeles, did visit, raising Olson's hopes, only to sign with UCLA. (Getting turned down was bad enough, but the Wildcats would also have to contend with both as conference opponents.) Knowing it needed some forward progress to resuscitate interest in Tucson and send a signal to future recruiting classes, Arizona signed junior college players who were at least older and more experienced than the high school prospects the coach wanted most.

It was not until July 29, more than a month after graduation and near the end of the summer signing period, that Kerr appeared on Arizona's radar. Even then it was accidental. Thinking more about the recruits of 1984 than how to spend the final scholarship of '83, Olson went to summer league at Cal State Long Beach, his home before Iowa, to watch prospects still in high school. He arrived with plans to focus on one player, "but it was a thin, 6'2" towheaded guard on the opposing team who caught my attention. That kid's interesting, I thought; he plays very well. He's intelligent, shoots the ball well, and is a real leader on the floor."

Olson found the towheaded guard's summer league coach after the game.

"Tell me about number twenty-five," he said.

"He's a great kid," the coach replied. "His name is Steve Kerr. He graduated from Palisades, but he's got nowhere to go."

Everything Olson had just unexpectedly seen was confirmed in the conversation, that it wasn't just a good showing that day. Kerr had enticing shooting range, he was smart, and he was a leader.

"There was just something about him that intrigued me," Olson later wrote. "He wasn't quick; he wasn't a great athlete. He looked like he would have a difficult time playing at a top college level. But for some reason I was intrigued by him. He played like a winner."

Olson came back to watch Kerr the next day, was again impressed by what he saw, and called Steve at home that night to introduce himself. Kerr knew him and said he was in the audience at the *Los Angeles Times* banquet. When asked if he was interested in learning more about the Arizona program, Kerr quickly answered yes. Wanting a final look, Olson asked Marvin, a longtime acquaintance, to arrange a game that included Kerr and some Pali alums, maybe a few current college players in the area.

Olson, accompanied by his wife Bobbi, who often came along on his scouting runs, watched Kerr for two more savvy hours of directing the offense with sound decisions and maturity that would entice any coach. The Olsons didn't learn until years later they had been set up—Kerr's friends in the game, opponents as well as teammates, made sure he got open shots, didn't defend him as hard as possible, and rigged the night to the point of placing Steve on the better side to elevate his game. The plan worked to perfection.

Arizona was interested in Steve, Olson told Malcolm, but had already used its allotted campus visits. The Kerrs would have to pay their own way if they or their son wanted to see Tucson before deciding whether he would move there. Olson returned to the many other aspects of laying a foundation for a program in search of stability, waited for a response and heard nothing. Steve, in turn, called the Athletic Department, did not get a reply, and took it to mean that Olson had lost interest. The seventeen-year-old who later in life would become a master communicator, one of the best in professional sports through training and natural ability, almost tripped over a major opportunity because of a misunderstanding.

For anyone who knew him later in life, in the second half of his playing career and as a general manager, broadcaster, and coach, it would be difficult to imagine Steve Kerr being unable to speak up for himself. Yet there he was, frozen in place, with his future in the balance as the greatest sign of the lack of confidence that would plague him well into his twenties. Despite the public persona as a scrapper who backed down from nothing and overcame the harshest of setbacks, depth of his self-doubt was rarely more obvious than during the summer of 1983.

Finally, Malcolm asked his son for a bottom line on a college preference. Arizona, Steve replied. It was Malcolm, not Steve, who called Olson to ask if the scholarship was still available and to report Steve's desire to go there.

"If he wants to come, we'll take him," Olson said, hardly the flowery recruiting push that Kevin Johnson or Reggie Miller received, but a red-carpet invitation compared to the deafening silence Kerr was getting from everyone else. So what that Arizona had a bad history and a new coach who had never watched Steve in a real game, or that he hadn't visited campus. Kerr had a destination at last, with a scholarship and everything.

His immediate future resolved, Steve returned to his birthplace for an eight-day stay with his parents and Andrew as the civil war reached into a seventh year and Beirut seemed to be deteriorating by the week. Writing to John and the newlyweds Susie and Hans van de Ven soon after arriving, Ann reported "life has been predictably tranquil and pleasant" and that "we only hear occasional booms off in the distance." The Kerrs had become accustomed, even alarmingly numb, to sounds of battle as the country, and especially the capital city, cast its spell over much of the family, including Steve. He hiked nearby mountains, swam in the Mediterranean, and enjoyed dinners followed by outdoor card games at Marquand House, the campus residence of AUB presidents that came complete with a butler.

The plan was for Steve to end the trip with a flight out of Lebanon on August 12, while Ann and Andrew stayed in Beirut with Malcolm. But in the airport terminal with his mother, bombs began to sail through the sky, an occurrence so common by the summer of 1983 that locals had a quip name for it: "Shelly weather." "You can never know what death sounds like until you hear one of those shells hit near you," Steve said. "It was the sound of death. I'll never forget it."

With the airport instantly shut down, for weeks it would turn out, the family scrambled to get Steve to America. They tried hitching a ride on a military plane to Cairo, but the flight was scrubbed. They considered but then dismissed several ideas: taking a helicopter ride to Tel Aviv; taking a cruise ship to the Syrian port city of Lattika and traveling on from there to Cyprus in the eastern Mediterranean; or even making the 275-mile journey to Tel Aviv by bus. Steve finally ended up in a car with a university driver who had a reputation for taking risky assignments others would not. Heading east through Lebanon and into Syria, then passing over the mountains, they reached Damascus and made a right-angle turn south into Jordan before arriving in Amman for an Alia Airlines flight that took him out of the Middle East. Kerr eventually landed in Los Angeles to a welcoming party of John, Susan, and Hans that found him, in his sister's words, in "high spirits," she would later recognize as "giddy relief" at reaching the end of the harrowing journey. A short drive later, the four were in Pacific Palisades for a home-cooked midnight feast of French toast.

"Poor Steve!" Malcolm wrote John, Susie, and Hans. "I'm fearful that all this uncertainty and inconvenience, not to mention even a sense of physical danger, has not done Steve's image of Beirut much good, and in his present mood he wonders what any of us are doing here," his father added. "It's too bad, because until yesterday we were having a really good time and I think he was coming to appreciate the value of our being here."

Beyond the usual optimistic front, though, Malcolm was growing increasingly worried about the safety of his family in Beirut and sent his wife and youngest son to Cairo for six weeks soon after Steve got out. Malcolm went from concern over the safety of close friend David Dodge during the first year as AUB president to needing to send loved ones away for their protection. The danger in Lebanon was becoming that pronounced.

CHAPTER 3

It All Came to an End

He couldn't have known it at the time, but fleeing Beirut was not the biggest challenge Steve Kerr would encounter in 1983. While days of deadly blasts and plotting escape routes were frightening, they were also temporary. College, on the other hand, would be years of his life. And although Arizona was obviously not the bloody world he had just left and his parents and younger brother would still endure, Kerr was blindly walking into a different kind of personal crisis: Olson was already planning to replace him. "To be honest," the coach said, "I brought him on the team assuming we'd recruit over him the following season."

Lacking athleticism and showing more of a pleasant boyish disposition than the killer instinct required to excel in a major conference, Kerr was of course easy to dismiss. Practically every Division I coach in America had done it months earlier in an overwhelming referendum on his future at the top level, and his new teammates quickly saw why for themselves. Whether or not they knew he was there thanks mostly to Malcolm's persistence, they surely, and rightly, assumed that Kerr's scholarship was the act of a desperate coach trying to fill the roster of a gasping program. Olson didn't try to talk himself into believing Kerr was anything more.

As if immediately setting out to prove Olson right, Kerr's showings in early pickup games with Arizona players that fall left other Wildcats so underwhelmed that junior Brock Brunkhorst went back to his dorm and told his roommate "that I couldn't understand why this new coach would ever sign this guy." Kerr got exposed on defense and couldn't do much on offense other than shoot. He was six-three, decent size, but lacked confidence and was not strong enough, not quick enough, and not experienced enough to make a meaningful contribution—not even on a team almost certain to be bad.

Not skilled enough to win over teammates but at least smart enough to realize it, Kerr confronted the uncomfortable reality with the candor that would make him popular with fans and television audiences for decades. "Honestly, I wasn't that good," he admitted. "Every day I'd go out to practice and I was like overmatched physically." Not only that, "I had an edge and an insecurity about my place in the basketball world. So I would snap every once in a while. I mean, it definitely drove me to work really hard. But I had a temper, for sure." Turning the doubters in pickup games into friends was easy with his mix of self-deprecating humor and a buoyant personality that masked the flip side of the worrier who would overthink situations. Earning their confidence on the court, as teammates, was a different matter.

If few outside the locker room noticed the shortcomings of a slow, weak reserve who lacked confidence and was a place-holder at point guard until the next recruiting class, it was for all the wrong reasons. As Olson got into the coaching portion of the renovation, Kerr was the least of his worries. That much was obvious from the first practice, on October 15, as Olson devoted three and a half hours to defensive drills and sprints, telling the Wildcats, often loudly, how bad they were, before closing with a twelve-minute scrimmage. Kerr would later term the inaugural session "basic hell."

"What surprised me that first day was how much work needed to be done," Olson said. "I was astonished at the lack of knowledge of the basic fundamentals. There was absolutely no concept of team defense." Also, "it wasn't just the lack of knowledge that surprised me, it was also the lack of physical skills. . . . We had a rule that you have to make 10 consecutive free throws before you can get a drink of water. Usually that takes a few minutes. At that practice we sat and watched and waited and waited. It took about a half hour. I remember [assistant coach] Scott Thompson and I looked at each other and sort of shook our heads. I don't think either one of us realized until that first practice how much work needed to be done just to be competitive."

Eight days later, shortly after dawn in Lebanon, a yellow Mercedes-Benz stake-bed truck headed toward the Beirut airport, detoured down an access road, and aimed for barracks housing U.S. Marines sent by President Reagan as peacekeepers in the civil war. The vehicle, carrying 2,500 pounds of explosives, crashed through concertina wire and a guard shack in front of the building with an estimated 300 Americans asleep inside on a Sunday morning, before coming to rest in the lobby. "All I can remember," one Marine would later say of the driver, "was that the guy was smiling."

The blast struck with so much ferocity that concrete support columns fifteen feet in circumference were sheared away and the four-story building was lifted off the ground. The structure landed and collapsed onto itself from a blast so concussive that it shook people awake ten miles away. About two minutes later, a truck loaded with another round of violence on its back charged into the headquarters for French peacekeepers a couple of miles north, in Jnah. The explosion from the second half of coordinated mayhem turned eight floors to debris.

Two hundred and forty-one members of the U.S. force—220 Marines, 18 sailors, and 3 soldiers—died in the biggest single-day loss of life for the Marine Corps since the Battle of Iwo Jima in 1945, and the deadliest day for the U.S. military since the initial hours of the Tet Offensive in Vietnam in 1968. Rescue workers toiled furiously the rest of the day and late into the night under floodlights, using blowtorches, drills, and cranes to pry the dead and wounded from smoldering rubble, occasionally while under fire from snipers in the nearby southern suburbs. The death toll from Jnah would reach sixty-three.

Unlike the crackling of gunfire and the thunder of bombs Andrew was used to, the attack on the American base struck him as a thud, a deep rumble that shook the windows of the residence of the AUB president. Ann heard the explosion inside Marquand House as well, and she couldn't help being struck not only by the amount of human loss, but by how personal the tragedy felt despite not knowing any victims. She grew numb listening to radio reports with Malcolm and Andrew and ached as the casualty list grew by the hour. It was impossible for her to fathom that some of the same clean-cut troops she saw jogging on the AUB grounds and constantly ended sentences with "Yes, ma'am," were likely among the lost. Some, she imagined, had also been among the players in pickup basketball games with her youngest son. As a mother, she was painfully aware that many of the casualties were similar in age to her first three kids and only slightly older than Andrew.

Ann and Malcolm spent part of the afternoon unpacking cartons of books that had been stacked in the study for weeks, oddly but defiantly settling in at the very moment that seemed to demand a retreat. Ann and Andrew later went to the AUB hospital to visit service members and deliver homemade chocolate chip cookies, even as she understood that the visit was more for their sake than for the wounded, the unconscious men they saw with heads bulging and eyes popping from the blast waves. They wanted to help in some way, as did the young women from AUB and the American Community School who arrived to sit at the bedside of injured Marines and hold hands with them while talking softly. Thinking he was prepared to see their wounds, Andrew instead walked into sights so grotesque that they became permanently imprinted in his memory. Inspecting new shrapnel marks around the neighborhood and picking up spent bullets became a favorite pastime anyway.

From the safety of southern Arizona, Steve saw pictures of the destruction in *Time* magazine and recognized some of the victims from his visit to the grounds when he was trying to leave in August. They were "the nicest people, who I met and they were showing us around the base and just trying to do their jobs and keep the peace. And a truck bomb?" Thirty-three years later, during an interview with the *New York Times,* he would still cry at the memory of the images of hate. "There is a chaplain who had come over and kind of taken us under his wing. The nicest guy. And I saw his face. . . ." In 2016, he needed to take a deep breath and wipe his eyes.

Malcolm built a Tucson stop into a U.S. swing in November as part of the AUB board of trustees meeting in New York, an especially welcome visit in an uneasy time. Father and son, always close, stayed in Steve's room in Babcock dorm, Steve on the floor and Malcolm in the bed, and attended the UCLA-Arizona football game, laughing about setting aside the new loyalty to the Wildcats and secretly siding with their longtime favorite. Malcolm toured the campus with his son, watched basketball practice as the first game approached at the end of the month, got better acquainted with Olson, and met the players. His early-morning departure for Texas and the next leg of AUB business was so rushed that it required a return about fifteen minutes later to reclaim the suits he had left behind in Steve's closet. Phoning Ann after leaving, Malcolm reported a fun reunion, but also that Steve was concerned about the deteriorating conditions in Lebanon and the safety of his family a world away.

Their son had good reason to be troubled, and not just because of the recent attack on U.S. and French forces. While Steve fretted about keeping up in basketball as the 1983–1984 season drew near, AUB students were often studying without electricity and in fear of when the inevitable shelling would resume. Ann, teaching English, learned that some of her students had been pressured to move out of neighborhoods where Christians and Muslims lived side by side and relocate to areas where their own religion dominated. Important cable traffic bounced between Washington and the U.S. embassy in Beirut nearly every other day.

The AUB grounds may have been considered an oasis from violence, and its views of the Mediterranean a serene distraction, but working there in the early 1980s meant potentially ducking to dodge stray bullets that could whiz by while crossing the street at the hospital. The injured from rival militias packed the Medical Center such that each band of marauders had its own health representatives in the hospital, to monitor the care of their fighters.

They also kept an ear out for details on the health and location of opponents receiving care in the building, to find them and finish the job. One combatant threatened an intern with a hand grenade to secure a lab coat and disguise himself as a doctor, the better to search the hospital without raising suspicion. Armed men who were not security roamed the hallways. One night twenty-three emergency surgeries were performed within eight hours, and in one thirty-six-hour stretch a single surgeon performed thirteen brain surgeries that involved removing part of the skull.

Malcolm, Ann, and Andrew were immersed in a time and place where some locals stopped bothering to replace windows that had again been blasted out at home or work. They chose to cover openings with plastic wrap, which was more suited for packaging a sandwich, but was also a cheaper option and simpler fix when the next hellstorm passed through. The *New York Times* man in Beirut, Thomas L. Friedman, came to regard a window-glass salesman as a political analyst and practically a one-man poll. When business was good and customers replaced windows, it signaled residents were optimistic about the direction of the country. When business fell because few people were bothering to spend for what soon would surely be destroyed, it meant that pessimism reigned. The disorder hit particularly close to home for the Kerrs the day a Marine shot at Andrew, and fortunately missed, in a case of mistaken identity.

Malcolm stepped back into the anarchy after his U.S. trip, with plans to return stateside in March to combine an AUB board of trustees meeting in San Francisco with a side trip to Los Angeles to watch Arizona play UCLA. The Wildcats, in the meantime, started the season with a victory over Northern Arizona before an estimated 3,000 people in 13,658-seat McKale Center. As if the dreary atmosphere had not been harsh reality check enough, the win was followed by six consecutive defeats, including a setback to lowly Texas–Rio Grande Valley that drove Olson to tell his team in the locker room, "I see why you were a bunch of losers last year." Then he walked out.

In an early example of the timing that would grace his playing career in later years, Kerr benefited from the bad days in Tucson. With the Bulls, most notably, he would arrive just as championship hopes had disappeared and coach Phil Jackson had a sudden need for scoring in general and guards in particular; Kerr turned this unexpectedly large opening into his best years as a pro. The Magic traded for him months into the Shaquille O'Neal era, a prime platform for a shooter. Kerr could not capitalize, but at least he had been given the ideal circumstance. Going to San Antonio was joining a franchise that had never won a title, and five months later celebrating a championship. Falling forward into the Arizona scholarship was a program desperate enough to sign Steve Kerr and then immediately being bad enough to have to play Steve Kerr.

He was, in what at the time constituted a glowing review, not as bad as expected in the early weeks of 1983–1984 as he got minutes as the third point guard and even pushed for the backup job as Olson grasped for answers. His family finally got to see for themselves when the videotape of the Northern Arizona game reached Beirut at Christmastime. With John visiting from Cairo, most of the Kerrs gathered to squint at Steve's college debut with glee, undeterred by the grainy and soundless footage captured from such a distance and with such poor quality that his parents and brothers couldn't be sure at first which of the three blond Wildcats was Steve. They studied the view from a lone camera that seemed to be stationed at midcourt but on a concourse far from the action. "We had the time of our lives," John said. "It was just so much fun."

Eventually determining the player they should be rooting for, the family delighted in every detail mined from the fuzzy motion of a November 25 game that was either mostly ignored or quickly forgotten in the southern Arizona desert. Just off the Mediterranean Sea, inside Marquand House, they dissected Kerr's three baskets in five tries over and over, rewinding and replaying each launch what must have been ten times. Watching Steve in a college game, John observed, was the highlight of their father's life.

More than a special family moment, catching up with his son's debut was a particularly welcome diversion amid the peril of Ann and

Malcolm realizing his life was in danger and considering a return to California. They were concerned enough about raising Andrew in a setting where he was collecting bullet casings and souvenir shrapnel after the latest battle. Malcolm's security as a high-profile American in a land now hunting Americans, had been a topic of conversation with his wife since he arrived, but the president who took pride in being accessible to students and staff felt constrained with a body-guard. Besides, Malcolm reasoned with his typical dry wit joined with blunt judgment, there was no point in being assigned a jogging partner if the protection ran out of breath and quit after the first lap. Malcolm ultimately rationalized in a letter to Susie and John that his primary detail, the deputy director of campus security, is "ba-sically nice as thugs go and I do feel a little safer having him follow me around wherever I go." Still, he used the escort less frequently, partly from a growing concern at the overtime pay the protector was earning, then stopped using the detail at all.

Malcolm was "marked," one of the top U.S. diplomatic experts on the Arab world later concluded. "The institution was marked for de-struction." Likewise realizing the growing risk as 1984 approached and with the synchronized barracks attacks still an exposed nerve, university trustees voted in December to employ military guards for round-the-clock protection, even though Ann and Malcolm bris-tled at the loss of privacy. The school would just need time to put the plan in motion.

On the gloomy morning of January 18, with a chauffeur but no bodyguard, Malcolm Kerr was driven to the bank before return-ing to campus around 9:00 A.M. He briefly stopped to speak with a staff member before continuing unaccompanied to College Hall, the main administration building. He worked his way through the bustling courtyard in front, filled with students registering for the spring term set to begin in February, before entering the elevator that would take him to his office on the second floor. Two males followed.

With his briefcase in one hand and an umbrella in the other, Malcolm stepped off the elevator, passed a staircase, and walked down the corridor. A dean was waiting for him in the office.

"Oh, here he comes now," Kerr's secretary told the dean before looking down.

Malcolm may never have seen the two attackers, who could have been the pair from the elevator or maybe came from inside the stairwell, as Ann believed. Perhaps they were lying in wait in another part of the hallway. In any event, one of the men, armed with a 7.65mm pistol fitted with a silencer, put two bullets in Kerr's head. All the secretary saw upon looking up again were the backs of the killers running away; the best anyone else could offer was that one rushed from the hall in blue jeans and a leather jacket and carried a zippered briefcase. Otherwise, the assailants blended in easily with the crowd of students gathered for registration. From there, they were apparently able to get beyond one of the four gates to the city before police and soldiers from the Lebanese Army, armed with M-16 automatic rifles, could close the escape routes and conduct a building-by-building campus search.

Ann, after teaching one of the final sophomore English classes of the semester, was waiting in a light drizzle at the main gate for a friend to pick her up to shop for fabric to redecorate Marquand House. A gateman encouraged her to take shelter in the guardhouse to avoid the rain, but she politely declined and said she preferred to wait outside. About five minutes later, the same gateman returned, this time with the urgency of nearly pulling her with an insistent arm tug. Something has happened in the president's office, he told her in Arabic.

Rushing there, she went up the stairs and into the hallway to see her husband facedown on the floor a few steps from the elevator, the briefcase and umbrella just in front of him, blood coming from his head. Ann knew instantly that Malcolm was gone and that he was being taken to the hospital in vain.

The team worked desperately on the long, lean body lying flat on the stretcher as his blood continued to spill. The dean of the medical school finally came out to deliver the official word Ann had already surmised: Malcolm Kerr had died at age fifty-two on the campus where his parents taught for forty years, where he was born and practically raised, where he fell in love with visiting junior Ann Zwicker, and where three of his four children were born. In the dreadful moment, she had the involuntary reaction of biting down on the umbrella handle.

Playing a video game at a café during recess from his school adjacent to AUB, Andrew heard a worker relay the news just delivered on the radio, that the president had been shot. Andrew ran out, found a gate to campus sealed in the lockdown to catch the killers, and instead scaled a fence as a guard called for him to stop. When someone who recognized him on the dash to Marquand House asked the fifteen-year-old if he heard the news, all Andrew could do was ask where Malcolm had been hit, thinking and hoping his father was wounded in an arm or leg. No, he was told. The head. Clinging to hope, he immediately thought of James Brady, Reagan's press secretary who survived a bullet to the head in a 1981 assassination attempt on the president in Washington. If Malcolm ended up requiring a wheelchair, like Brady, *that's good enough, I'll take it*, thought Andrew.

Ann was either at the hospital or in transit, so disoriented that she wasn't sure who was in the car with her, as Andrew reached Marquand House among the trees of the campus. Their housekeeper, practically a member of the family, took the boy to the medical center. The youngest Kerr child was led to a room and informed by a doctor that Malcolm was dead. Andrew dissolved in tears before the doctor demanded he stop crying, with the additional admonishment that it was time to be a man.

Needing to escape that environment, needing to find his mother, Andrew returned home. Ann spotted him walking him up the circular driveway, ran to meet him at the door, and shared a tearful embrace in the entry hall. There were no words until Andrew spoke.

"I want to get those guys who killed Dad."

Moving the conversation to Andrew's bedroom upstairs, Ann, still in her raincoat and boots, encouraged forgiveness as mother and son lay on the bed and talked about how Malcolm had been doing valuable work in a role he wanted. Andrew agreed and moved toward the compassion Ann encouraged. "And that lasted for about an hour," he said. "And I didn't really feel like forgiving anybody after that." When Malcolm's briefcase was brought to Marquand House, Andrew accepted the delivery, then cleaned off the blood to protect his mother from that anguishing sight as well. A few days later, with other family members in town, his father's glasses were dropped off, with a residue of dried blood in the broken frames barely visible.

Attempts were made to call the other kids—John in daytime in Cairo, Susie and Hans in the evening in Taiwan, and Steve around midnight in Tucson—with some difficulty in long-distance connections and time differences. They also needed to inform Ann's parents, along with Malcolm's brother and two sisters in the United States, and someone had to get word to Malcolm's mother Elsa Kerr in New Jersey two days after she had suffered a stroke. Susie had returned home to the suburbs after work teaching English to students and businessmen in downtown Taipei. She had routinely and purposely avoided turning on the radio since the Marine barracks were attacked in October and "Dad's fate had seemed to be flaunted before our faces." When the call she had been expecting for months did arrive, Susie knew as soon as she heard her mother's voice on the other end. John was at work when Ann phoned and delivered the news through a fuzzy connection.

Ann somehow managed a diary entry within hours. "It all came to an end today—all the goals achieved and the dreams and goals still hoped for." Agony and despair dripped from the words. "I can't imagine how I can live without Malcolm. Somehow we never really thought this would happen—lots of troubles and problems maybe, but never really this. We were so happy to be here doing what we were doing.

"Right now I think I hear Malcolm coming up the stairs. People are swarming into the house. Have been all day—so many interruptions. Can't write anymore."

Up to that moment, Steve's life was, in his own words, "impenetrable. Bad things happened to other people. I thought I was immune from anything like that, and so was my family." Everything changed when AUB vice president Vahe Simonian, helping Ann amid problems getting a connection from Beirut to Tucson, called from New York at approximately 3:00 A.M. on January 18 in Arizona. The family friend, wanting to make sure Steve heard the news from a sympathetic voice and not the media, tried to speak with tenderness.

I hate to tell you this, Simonian said, but your father has been shot.

Arm? Steve immediately asked, echoing Andrew's reaction in Beirut. Leg? Is he okay?

There was a long pause.

Your father was a great man, Simonian replied.

Kerr bolted from his dorm in shock, out of Babcock entirely and into the street "sort of hysterical." Stunned, raw, and lost, desperate for comfort as the ground opened below him in a place where he'd barely had time to make friends, he ran to the room of a teammate, banged on the door, and, still hysterical, screamed through his mental cyclone as the player answered his knocking half asleep. They walked across the street to sit on the curb in the middle of the night, amid the new darkness of his world.

Not merely slammed by the worst news of his life, Kerr was having to endure the emotional free fall without a support system in sight. He was eighteen years old and, as far as he knew, alone. He had connected with people on campus, especially within the basketball program, and there was no indication he was homesick, not when he understood being at Arizona was a gift he did not deserve, but he still had been there only a few months. Now his father was gone, suddenly and violently, his mother and younger brother were in Beirut, his older brother was in Cairo, and his sister and brother-in-law were in a Taipei suburb. "I was running up and down the road in Taiwan," Susan said. "But Steve was the one who was alone, and he was still just a boy, really. We just couldn't imagine him getting that news in the middle of the night alone in his room."

Olson had the same regret, wishing someone had told the coaches first so that one of them could have been with Steve when he got the news. Instead, assistant Scott Thompson, alerted by an Arizona booster who heard the news on the radio, raced to Babcock to find Kerr sitting alone and motionless on the bed. Ann finally reached Steve in the room and right away knew from her son's voice that he had been told. Around 5:00 A.M., Thompson took him to an all-night diner, where they talked for a couple of hours. Nearly a quarter-century later, Steve would reflect, "To this day, my teammates are still my best friends. Coach and Bobbi and everyone else down there, I never will forget any of them for what they did and who they are."

Olson, finding Kerr in a state of shock when they spoke, held the door open for him to step away, emphasizing that basketball was unimportant at the time, that Kerr would decide when he was ready to rejoin the Wildcats, and that "You tell us what you need." The coach thought Kerr would escape for a couple of weeks. "You just need to take your time, and you can stay away from the game or whatever you want to do," Olson told him.

"Coach," Kerr responded, "the only time I can keep from thinking about my dad is when I'm playing basketball."

President Reagan put out a statement within hours: "It was with the greatest shock and sadness that we learned early this morning of the death of Dr. Malcolm Kerr, the president of the American University of Beirut. He was a highly respected member of the academic world who, as president of the American institution in Lebanon, worked tirelessly and courageously to maintain the principles of academic freedom and excellence in education. His work strengthened the historical, cultural, and academic ties between the United States and Lebanon and other countries of the Middle East. Dr. Kerr carried on a family tradition—he himself was born in Beirut to parents also dedicated to the service of mankind.

"Dr. Kerr's untimely and tragic death at the hands of these despi-
cable assassins must strengthen our resolve not to give in to the acts
of terrorists. Terrorism must not be allowed to take control of the
lives, actions, or future of ourselves and our friends."

Steve spent most of the day in Olson's office, sleeping some, as the
staff turned away interview requests from national morning shows
and teammates did their best to console him, before spending the
night at Olson's house. In Beirut, a man had telephoned the Agence
France-Presse news service to say the pro-Iranian group Islamic
Jihad claimed responsibility for the murder, just as it had carried
out the bombing of U.S. and French peacekeepers in their barracks
three months earlier. Malcolm Kerr, the caller said, was a victim of
the American military presence in Lebanon.

The United States added Iran to the state sponsors of terrorism
list the next day, an immediate assessment of blame against the entire government, not just a group acting in support of the country,
as the caller to Agence France-Presse had indicated. The murder
"added conviction on our part, but their position on that list was
earned well before that," one State Department official said.

"I watched him move through those days," Olson later wrote
about Steve in his autobiography. "He was only a freshman then,
eighteen years old, but he handled the situation with such maturity. He spent the next night at our house. Bobbi had been close to
him, but during this period they became much closer. Steve and
our son, also named Steve, went into the hot tub. Very quietly, so
quietly I didn't know about it, Bobbi brought them out beers."

Kerr was again encouraged to take a temporary leave from basketball, this time by Thompson just before practice. "This is my
family," Kerr responded. "I want to be here."

The coach had gone from initially expecting Kerr to miss the
Arizona State game on January 20 to realizing he would be ready
for tipoff in McKale Center no matter what, even as Susan and Hans
traveled from Taiwan to Lebanon and John from Cairo to mourn
with Ann and Andrew. "It was the only thing to do," Kerr said. "My
dad would have been very disappointed in me if I hadn't played.

What's more, there was nothing I could do at that point. I knew my family was safe. I was going to the memorial service the next day. It just wouldn't have made sense not to play." Basketball went from a passion to nothing less than a survival tool.

Arizona State coaches were not overly concerned whether a freshman reserve averaging 5.9 points might be on the court, but they also knew Kerr could cause problems from the perimeter. "When he first got there, nobody had a lot of concern about what he was going to be capable of doing," coach Bob Weinhauer said. "That would include myself. I had seen him in some nonconference games. There was nothing special. You could tell he could shoot the ball. But—and there is a big damn 'but' there—he could really shoot the ball." It was a scouting report that came not only from watching Kerr in high school, with Southern California an obvious target for Pac-10 programs, but with the unique insight of a team manager who attended Palisades and knew the newcomer in Tucson had a veteran's composure. Plus, there was the natural curiosity and concern in the wake of a tragedy that garnered international attention and official White House sympathy.

On January 20, the Sun Devils wanted to know whether they should prepare additional waves of zone defense to slow an outside game or stick with man-to-man and dare Arizona to try to get past the defense. Olson offered minimal insight when he picked Weinhauer up at the hotel around lunchtime and drove the ASU coach to an Arizona booster club event for a five-minute boilerplate speech to generate fan interest, a common move for Olson as program promoter and chauffeur in a season when the Wildcats were mostly invisible in their own town. He carted the team around the state for preseason scrimmages to generate interest: 250 miles west to Yuma, 70 miles south to Nogales on the U.S.-Mexico border, and 70 miles north to Casa Grande. Previous staffs had taken recruits to minor league hockey contests to showcase the city's enthusiasm for sports, and athletic department officials trolled campus libraries to offer students tickets to study inside McKale, just to import bodies for scenery. An unknown player at a nearby high school, Sean Elliott, was struck that the atmosphere at the Oregon-UA game the season before felt like a community college contest. It was no different for the rivalry game against Arizona State. Olson delivered Weinhauer to the luncheon and on the way back to the hotel said that Arizona coaches were giving Kerr every opportunity for private time, away from basketball, but that Kerr wanted to play.

Kerr even declined the offer hours later to stay in the locker room for the pregame moment of silence in tribute to his father, instead standing among teammates with his head bowed, moving only to wipe away the tears with his warmup jacket. Others in McKale similarly grieved. Olson's speech to the team before taking the court had kept to the basketball strategy and away from the delicate mood in hopes that players would not get overly emotional, but the approach was outdated within minutes as sorrow filled the building. The unknown recruit five months before had become a young man known far beyond the arena walls, throughout the city of 500,000 that embraced him in mourning and supported him as one of their own. He had also gone from the guy who couldn't handle pickup games to the first Wildcat off the bench, an accomplishment even on a 2-11 club.

Olson wasn't sure what to expect when he sent Kerr in with 12:58 remaining in the first half. If anything, on a night of raw emotions, "I was worried for him." But when Kerr got the ball for the first time, eighteen seconds after entering the game, and only a few minutes after crying through the memorial for the wonderful man he would miss forever, he moved on instinct. The twenty-five-footer swished. The crowd erupted in a frenzy—"an explosion of sound," Olson called it. The next shot, from fifteen feet, splashed the net the same way. Sitting courtside, assistant sports information director Tom Duddleston said, "It's like a chill going up your spine."

The longer the indescribable lasted, the more Weinhauer thought one of his defenders should knock Kerr down. Arizona State tried zone and Arizona State tried man, yet the Sun Devils kept losing track of the one player everyone else in the arena couldn't stop watching. Weinhauer invoked a mantra from Doug Collins, one of his former assistants, that a player who makes two or three jumpers in a row shouldn't be able to see the rim the next time. But Weinhauer couldn't get the message across. Make Kerr literally feel the defense, he implored, put a body on him, foul on purpose if necessary, but just don't let Kerr feel so comfortable. Nothing worked.

When Kerr made three in a row, Roger Sedlmayer spontaneously began to elongate both names over the public-address system, until *Steve Kerr* became *Steeeeeve Kerrrrr,* and the band jumped in a few games later with a copycat chorus. When fans followed, it became a constant McKale echo by his sophomore season, and practically an official name change as the Wildcats rose in national prominence in later years. Kerr would still hear it on returns to Tucson decades later.

The performance that in time would be shown to have changed everything—his career, his life as one of the most popular people in Tucson history, the trajectory of the entire Arizona program—didn't end until Olson removed Kerr to a standing ovation with 1:39 remaining, an acknowledgment from fans that they had witnessed something beyond twenty-five minutes of five baskets in seven tries and twelve points. "It might have looked like I wasn't thinking of my dad," Kerr said years later, "but I thought of him the whole time." Playing that night seemed "very natural. It was a nice outlet for me to play. If I hadn't played, I would have dwelled on it even more. I played well and we won. It was a crazy atmosphere. I remember going through 1,000 different emotions."

No longer an opponent as soon as the game ended in a 71–49 upset win for the Wildcats, Weinhauer made the unusual request to visit the Arizona locker room and speak with Kerr. "This was a special situation that required something, I felt, to be said by me to the young man directly." The conversation would be lost to time, forgotten in the decades that followed except for the basic message: that "You care for a young man who just lost a parent, and you go over and you express your condolences to that person." If Kerr was emotionally drained by willing himself through the previous forty-three hours, though, he hid it well and seemed to appreciate the gesture. When the media came in as well, he projected only composure.

The newcomer with four months in town was so overwhelmingly adopted on the spot that it became "an outpouring of affection and caring about him directly, but the rest of the team as well," said Thomas Volgy, a city councilman and later the mayor. "It had an impact on the community in addition to the enormous impact it had on Steve himself." Kerr was supported by strangers who wanted to protect him from further agony and cheered him as a symbol of the determination required to build the basketball program. As fellow point guard Matt Muehlebach later accurately captured, despite not arriving until Kerr's senior season, "He epitomized the program; he epitomized Lute. He was this underdog who had a great work ethic. He suffered through a lot of personal tragedy, and a lot of people embraced him. They rallied around him."

At the same moment Kerr received a visit from the opposing coach and handled the media with grace on Friday night in Tucson, his mother and three siblings were entering a third full day of mourning around breakfast time on Saturday in Beirut. Telexes from around the world, expressions of sorrow from presidents and kings, had been arriving all along, in addition to a series of reception lines in the living room of Marquand House, in accordance with Middle East grieving rituals. When the U.S. ambassador to Lebanon came to pay his respects, Andrew's only thought, in his rage, was that Reginald Bartholomew should have been the one killed.

The days came with an additional heart slash of guilt and a gnawing unknown grew in the empty spot where Malcolm belonged. Why was he killed when other targets in Lebanon had been kidnapped? At least there would have been a chance the family could get him back. For the rest of the decade and into the early 1990s, what Susie called the hostage years in the city, news footage of victims being released dragged out the pain and reminded the Kerrs of what their happy ending could have looked like. "I know he would have survived," Susie said of the alternative ending if her father had been kidnapped. Watching others have that reunion, it

was impossible not to think Malcolm should have also been stepping off the plane to a hero's welcome and a family waiting with endless hugs. Ann's torment also included the possibility that the killers
passed her in the escape through the gate closest to College Hall.
Once the gunmen went through and into the arteries of the lawless
city, capture was essentially impossible.

The family held an intimate service in the smaller Anglican
church on Sunday, ahead of the public ceremony being planned for
Wednesday at the AUB chapel. Arrangements continued as word
reached the family that the memorial could be targeted for another
attack, with the specific threat of bombing the historic chapel where
Malcolm had been inaugurated seventeen months earlier. The Kerrs
showed little concern and proceeded with the ceremony with representatives from warring factions in attendance and Ann and the
children holding hands in the front row, not far from the assigned
seats where the couple sat as students. Bouquets of white flowers in
vases were up front as Lebanon awarded Malcolm its highest award,
the Order of the Cedars. It was almost time to leave Beirut for good.

CHAPTER 4

The Banyan Tree

Ann, John, Andrew, Susie, and Hans walked the AUB grounds to find a resting place for the box with half of Malcolm's ashes, before the remainder went home to Pacific Palisades. They chose land near the banyan tree between College Hall and the chapel, a spot that provided both the tactile and the symbolic—under branches that would continue to sprout tangled tubes in a reminder that life goes on, a connection to the city and school he cherished, a spot where boyhood met adulthood, and even as a direct link to the family he loved. It was, after all, the very tree that Malcolm had delighted in climbing as a child and had once, as he would brag for decades, scaled to the upper limbs where he carved his initials to mark the conquest. Many years later, he and his girlfriend Ann Zwicker passed the big banyan while strolling the campus.

The Kerrs and van de Vens picked out a Corinthian capital from the campus museum and had it set near a wall in the oval-shaped garden with a view of the Mediterranean. Even in the anguish of losing her college sweetheart, her partner in international adventure, and her husband of twenty-seven and a half years, Ann couldn't help but laugh to herself at using a hunk of stone to memorialize the man who responded to attempts to get him to visit ancient monuments in Egypt with: "The pyramids are nothing but a pile of rocks." Malcolm may have had unending affection for the Middle East, but he drew a line at traveling to visit stone.

Burying one of the two boxes of ashes was the final task before leaving the next morning for memorial services at Princeton and UCLA, followed by Ann and Andrew making the break complete by moving to Cairo. The mother in her feared Andrew would be the new target if they remained in Beirut. The procession of family and close friends waited until late in the afternoon to make the short walk from Marquand House to the banyan, hoping fewer people would be passing the tree that time of day and that there would be less light. The unofficial ceremony was so discreet that the family brought a shovel from their garden to avoid involving outsiders.

The housekeeper who took Andrew to the medical center to find his mother on the awful day dug a hole in the oval garden as the group tried to remain inconspicuous. Once Malcolm's wife and three of his four children placed the box in the ground, some used their hands to cover the opening with loose dirt. Susie pulled out a recorder to play several of her father's favorite Renaissance tunes. They made a final visit the next morning to leave flowers and found that others had already done the same with single stems and small bouquets, before the drive to the airport and the flight to America. A group of Ann's students waited at the front gate of Marquand House to deliver an envelope of condolence letters, then waved goodbye as the car pulled away in bright sunshine.

The family pulled together in "almost an instinctive clinging together," in Ann's analysis. "I see each of us grieving in different ways, some more than others. All of us, I think, have a kind of permanent limp of the spirit. The loss is so great, but you eventually go on with your lives." For Steve, some 7,400 miles away, moving forward required tapping into the healing powers of basketball, what would become a lifelong security blanket but never as in the early weeks of 1984. When his mother and siblings fell into each other's arms in Beirut, he remained in Tucson—"the logistics were really tricky. And it was cathartic for me to just play."

He met the family in New Jersey for the Princeton memorial in the Ivy League town where Malcolm earned an undergraduate degree in 1953 and his paternal grandparents Stanley and Elsa moved after retiring from AUB in 1964. As family and close friends gathered in the guesthouse at Meadow Lakes, the retirement community where Elsa had lived for seven years after her husband's passing, the reunion came complete with a replay, via VHS tape, of Steve's superhuman performance against Arizona State. The next day, January 29, with snow on the ground, five hundred people crowded into Nassau Presbyterian Church for a remembrance with music by Bach and Brahms and readings from the Old and New Testaments. Ann, all four of her children, and Elsa listened from the front row, with Malcolm's brother and two sisters also among the mourners.

A third memorial followed, with four hundred people at UCLA, before Steve returned to his basketball security blanket in Tucson and "immersed myself in what I was doing and just kind of buried my head in the sand, really, and I didn't speak with anybody about it." Junior college transfer Bruce Fraser noticed a season later that his new teammate began showing a preference for comedies over action flicks when they went to the movies. Decades later, after they had remained lifelong friends, Fraser could not recall ever discussing Malcolm's death. The only time he "really dealt with it," Kerr said, was in conversations with family, and even those interactions, usually during summer gatherings in Pacific Palisades, were rare. "But we spoke about it a lot, and they'd go back to Egypt and I'd go back to school, and I'd bury my head in the sand again for another nine or 10 months. And that's kind of the way it went."

Whether by coincidence, the natural progression of a new group finding its rhythm, or the effects of a team forced by tragedy to bond, Arizona went from losing ten of its first fourteen before Malcolm's death to winning eight of the final fourteen, finishing 11-17, a seven-game improvement from 1982–1983. The Wildcats even won five in a row in conference play, an unimaginable achievement in the early days of practices that had left Olson exasperated. In almost every way, 1983–1984 turned out to be the foundation Olson had hoped for, especially the closing six weeks that allowed him to recruit with the honest declaration, not a hollow sales pitch, of a program on the rise.

Finding a replacement for Kerr on the depth chart was no longer the need it had once seemed either: the slow, weak reserve point guard lacking confidence followed the star turn against Arizona

State with fifteen points at Oregon, enough for Olson to say Kerr was playing better than any Wildcats guard. More impressively, the personal surge came while Kerr mourned and amid complicated travel logistics that included playing a home game on a Thursday, flying to the UCLA service on Friday and returning for a home game on Saturday. By the end of the season, the same freshman who disgusted teammates in pickup games months before had averaged 22.6 minutes per contest, fifth on the roster.

Reagan's invitation to visit the White House on May 24 gave Steve the reality check that his popularity was confined to college basketball and Tucson. While his emotional story line from January had drawn some mainstream attention, his presence alongside his mother, family friend and Washington businessman Najeeb Halaby, Reagan, Vice President George H. W. Bush, and Deputy National Security Adviser John Poindexter was not noted in the president's daily diary. Kerr, dressed in tan slacks and a white shirt, maroon tie, and navy-blue jacket, was, however, in sixteen official pictures in the Oval Office for the afternoon visit to thank the family for Malcolm's commitment to sharing American values in the Middle East and promoting peace in the region. (Although Steve recalled the session lasting about thirty minutes, the Reagan diary logged the gathering from 4:14 to 4:19 and accompanying handwritten notes clocked it at 4:13 to 4:17.)

The one certainty as practice began for the 1984–1985 season was that the roster would be ready for the Olson practices, unlike the group that gasped through opening workouts a year before. The Wildcats were also more experienced and deeper after adding the rarity of a top prospect, Craig McMillan, as well as Fraser, an Olson family friend whose father replaced Olson at Long Beach City College in 1973. Kerr, for his part, continued to develop at a shocking rate through the hardest summer of his life, all the way into a starting guard as a sophomore.

When the momentum from the end of the previous season carried into eight wins in their first eleven games, the local interest Olson hoped to build became real. Around town, players were approached with trade offers—food at restaurants or entrance to movies for UA hoops tickets—and Olson said he learned long after the fact that Brock Brunkhorst had attached two comp seats when he turned in a test. Even more behind the scenes, but most important of all, a prospect at Cholla High School five miles from campus was noticing that the McKale ghost town he previously visited had been transformed into an energy dome. It likewise helped his college decision that one way Arizona players were building team chemistry was by going to Cholla games to watch senior Sean Elliott as he continued the transformation from middling prospect to star recruit.

It took Olson two seasons to turn a 4-24 program into 21-10, with a brief appearance in the top twenty late in the regular season, a pair of winning streaks of at least six games, and the school's first NCAA invitation since 1976. Kerr's contribution had jumped from 22.6 minutes as a freshman to 33.4 minutes, and from making 51.6 percent of his shots to 56.8 percent. Arizona's progress was so obvious, even after a first-round defeat to Alabama, that Kentucky, college basketball royalty, targeted Olson to replace the retiring Joe B. Hall.

A growing program in Tucson starting to capture national attention versus a leviathan turning fans away, not scrounging them up at the library, was a mismatch that made the Olson move seem like destiny. He was even already going to Lexington, for the Final Four and could interview hassle-free, without adjusting a line on the itinerary. By the time he met with the hiring committee as word of the courtship spread, the job seemed to be his. So many hopefuls angling to be a new Kentucky assistant coach were trying to reach him at the hotel and so many telegrams and phone calls from other interested parties were arriving that Lute and Bobbi checked out and relocated to a friend's horse farm.

After hours of conversation with Bobbi and deliberation with yellow pads, the couple declined the chance to live in the kingdom. They didn't want to leave Tucson and the program on the move, with Elliott set to arrive as a star recruit, Kerr among three projected starters returning, and fan interest blooming. Olson and his

Wildcats had the convenient timing of being able to celebrate the coach's decision, illogical to many, with a fifteen-game exhibition tour of Italy, the Netherlands, Spain, France, and Yugoslavia. Their host in Challans, France, was an American playing in Europe who kept his three-year-old son, Tony Parker, close by the visiting college team and guard Steve Kerr.

Back home for the start of 1985–1986, Olson could barely contain the anticipation, noting it would be his thirtieth season as a coach, "yet I was looking forward to the beginning of the season as if it were the first one. It was just as much fun, just as exciting. Maybe even a little more exciting this year because I was confident we were going to be a very good team. This time, when I looked through the schedule, there wasn't a single game in which I thought we would be overmatched." The 2-3 start that followed did nothing to extinguish his spirit or the growing list of believers that included newly installed co-captain Steve Kerr. The early stumble was followed by a five-game winning streak and then a 12-5 record in January, with excitement spiking. And when they closed the regular season with nine wins in eleven games, the Wildcats were Pac-10 champions for the first time, with the bonus of clinching at UCLA. Bobbi Olson commemorated the occasion by having the retired John Wooden, a favorite of her husband as well as Kerr, autograph her program while watching from the stands, a memento that Lute framed and hung on a wall at home.

A second consecutive first-round tournament loss—by ten points to Chuck Person, Chris Morris, and Auburn—could not dim the enthusiasm while looking ahead to 1986–1987 with Elliott off the freshman learning curve and several other key Wildcats returning, including Kerr as a senior. Not only that, Elliott and Kerr would have the added experience of playing in the world championships in Spain in the summer of '86, even if Kerr representing the United States after averaging just 14.4 points and 4.2 assists drew snide comments as the payment to Olson for coaching the Americans. Maybe Kerr could contribute an occasional three-point shot, a weapon in international play yet to be adopted by the NCAA or NBA, but making the roster was accomplishment enough before the expected fade into the scenery in a backcourt crowded with Tommy Amaker of Duke, Muggsy Bogues of Wake Forest, and Kenny Smith of North Carolina. Amaker and Bogues had never heard of Kerr before forty-eight invitees arrived in Colorado Springs for tryouts.

Team USA followed with three weeks of training at UA, then flew from Tucson to Los Angeles to Paris in late June for workouts and three exhibition games in France, before shifting to Spain. By the time the tournament started July 5, Kerr had morphed from roster leftover into a key part of the rotation as the first guard off the bench. It was the start of his college career all over. "I really didn't know anything about Kerr until camp started, but he's as good a guard as there'll be in the country next year," said Bobby Cremins, an assistant coach for the American squad, with the additional high praise that Kerr reminded him of a former Cremins star at Georgia Tech, Mark Price.

With Olson understandably showing more trust than other coaches would, Kerr had a team-best thirteen points in the opener against Ivory Coast, fifteen the next night against China, and seven points as a solid contribution versus Germany while playing for the third day in a row. Just as understandably, he seemed to delight in the surroundings and the adventure of it all.

When an off-day excursion was arranged for the American traveling party from their temporary base in the southern port city of Malaga, a visit to the Rock of Gibraltar two hours away by bus, Kerr spent about half the ride in conversation with *Arizona Daily Star* columnist Greg Hansen. Hansen had been personally dispatched by the publisher to Europe to file for readers mad for anything Wildcats, even Wildcats not playing for Arizona at the moment. Olson, Kerr, Elliott, and UA assistant coach Scott Thompson, in the same role with Team USA, were carrying the Tucson name around the world, and that in itself was news. That Kerr spent a portion of that hour asking numerous questions across the middle aisle about Hansen's life was so startling that the reporter was caught off guard. Are you married? Do you have kids? What do the kids like to do? And how about your parents—how do they spend their time? Hansen never had a conversation like it with a college athlete. Kerr seemed genuinely interested in the answers, not just killing time.

As the bus continued on a southwestern course to the landmark on a tip of the Iberian Peninsula, Kerr also wanted to make a few things clear. He did not like anyone, not just sportswriters, calling him Opie, even if the term was intended to be endearing praise for a fine young gentleman who would do a small-town Southern sheriff proud as a son. On another occasion, Kerr gently but pointedly asked Corky Simpson of the *Tucson Citizen* not to call him Opie after Simpson wrote a positive story loaded with gushy references to his wholesome image. Kerr was sick of overdosing on sugar. Moreover, he didn't like being referred to as an overachiever, despite usually being the one to point out he shouldn't have been at Arizona in the first place and had no place to dream of starting for a conference champion and representing his country in a major international tournament. "I'm not an overachiever," Kerr said. "I'm an achiever." He hoped to be an athletic director one day, he added, because there was no point thinking about the NBA.

Kerr in T-shirt and shorts, his hair contorted by a strong wind, had barely disembarked from the bus and started the walk toward the Rock's tourist entrance when he noticed that about six teammates were choosing to stay on board and sleep rather than explore. His mood changing on the spot, he wheeled around, stepped up the first few stairs at the bus entrance, and scolded them in an unpleasant fatherly tone, telling them to get their asses outside. You'll always remember today, he insisted, so get off the damn bus. The twenty-year-old who was supposed to consider himself lucky to be on the trip at all, and who was younger than six of the eleven other players, wasn't going for polite encouragement. Bogues exited. Shaw exited. Everyone got off the damn bus.

Kerr asserted himself in every way. By the time the tournament moved to Madrid for the medal round, he had become valuable as a perimeter threat, with eighteen three-pointers in thirty-six attempts, especially important in countering the zone defenses popular in international play. He was solidly in the guard rotation with Smith, Bogues, and Amaker. The guy who couldn't beg his way into a scholarship in 1983 was on the court in crunch time in a major international tournament three years later as the United States protected a lead in the July 17 semifinals against Brazil. Now his world lined up perfectly: finish off Brazil, play for the gold three nights later, return to a Tucson more proud of its Wildcats than ever, transition into the highly anticipated 1986–1987 as a senior, graduate, and move into sports administration.

In the closing minutes against Brazil, he was the dependable ball handler who could help run out the clock and make clutch free throws if the opponent chose to foul. With a little more than four minutes remaining and the United States up by eleven, Kerr saw an opening in the lane, dribbled to about ten feet from the basket, and pulled up. His weight shifted in midair to pass to an open Charles Smith, before spotting a defender stepping in front of Smith. Kerr recalibrated for an awkward shot in the same instant, but had no time to adjust his body. He landed off-balance on his right leg and collapsed in immediate and obvious pain, with 4:07 remaining, feeling the inside of the knee joint explode. Kerr let out a scream that teammate David Robinson, watching from the bench, called "one of the most horrifying sounds I've ever heard."

The diagnosis came so fast that the American squad was still at Madrid Sports Palace when Kerr was told not only that he needed reconstructive knee surgery that would end his senior season with the Wildcats before it began, but that he might never play again. The team doctor, Tim Taft, was certain after the U.S. victory to the point of saying, "To most athletes performing at such high competition levels, an injury like this is career ending. He will never have 100 percent strength in that knee again." Taft injected the disclaimer that he could not predict the future. But the certainty that the leg would never fully recover had Kerr in tears an hour after the final buzzer as he sat in the first row on the passenger side of the team bus. When he spotted the two reporters who had crossed an ocean to chronicle the Arizona contingent board for the same ride back to the downtown hotel, Kerr invited Hansen and Jack Rickard of the *Tucson Citizen* to his room for interviews. He was aware even in a state of emotional crumbling that fans at home wanted details and that the conversation would help Hansen's and Rickard's stories.

When Hansen knocked on the door and heard a shout from the other side to come in, Kerr was on the phone with his mother. Hang out a few minutes, Kerr told him. Returning to the call, Steve repeated Taft's dour prognosis of a career in danger and talked another ten minutes with Ann, crying through most of it. Kerr spent twenty more minutes with Hansen after he hung up and detailed his plan to head to Tucson almost immediately, the next morning, and have surgery at St. Mary's Hospital. The mood in the lobby to see him off was equally somber, with more tears and a hug from Bobbi Olson. The words "career ending" were ringing in his mind.

The July 21 surgery to repair a torn anterior cruciate ligament and a torn medial collateral ligament, leaving a six-inch scar across the knee, was such a big deal in Tucson that it required a post-op press conference at St. Mary's. The orthopedic surgeon who handled the procedure offered the calming news that "I think there's every chance for Steve to return to basketball," as good an update as supporters, including his girlfriend Margot Brennan in attendance, could have hoped to receive. In a ceremony to deliver additional good cheer, Olson and Elliott presented the patient with his gold medal and the game ball from the victory over the Soviet Union. Kerr was able to watch most of the tape-delay TV broadcast from the couch in his apartment with a supportive heart the day before the operation, until the game ended and being able to only witness the celebration became an emotional jab.

Behind the scenes, he couldn't get away from layers of pain. "I dream about it a lot, that specific play," he said in a hospital interview three days after the surgery. "I sleep a lot during the day, and I think you sleep pretty lightly then. I'll just kind of be dozing off and I envision myself jogging down court all by myself, and suddenly the leg gives out. The natural reflex is to jerk the leg real fast, except that I'm in bed and it really hurts when I do that. I've been doing that a lot." At least Kerr could look forward to going to Pacific Palisades as part of a schedule of light rehabilitation in Southern California until he returned to Tucson in late August for the new school year and, he hoped, resumed running in February. If all went well, he would be able to play basketball two months after that, a timetable that prompted Kerr to send a handwritten note to the *Daily Star* a few weeks after the operation with the request that it be published as a letter to the editor in a Sunday edition to thank the hundreds of people who had reached out with get-well cards. "P.S.," he wrote at the end, "I'll be back in 1987–88 to help the Cats to our third straight Pac-10 title."

As much as the Wildcats could cling to the encouraging prognosis that Kerr had a good chance to play again, it didn't do them any good when the 1986–1987 season started with three defeats in five games while their emotional leader watched from the bench. Losing once by a point, another time by five, and another by eight was an immediate indication of Kerr's value as the difference between continuing to build into a national power and Arizona falling out of the AP top twenty after a week. The Wildcats' 18-12 season and third consecutive first-round tournament exit included eight losses after leading in the second half and replacement point guard Kenny Lofton averaging as many turnovers in 26.2 minutes as Kerr did in 38.4 the season before. (Later in 1987, Olson, remembering Lofton's play in a team softball game, suggested Arizona baseball coach Jerry Kindall look at him. Kindall agreed that Lofton was raw but had potential. A little more than a year later, Lofton was drafted by the Houston Astros. Four years after Olson's tip, Lofton began a major league career that grew into six All-Star appearances, four Gold Gloves as an outfielder, and six times finishing first or second in the American League in steals.)

"We were close, we were competitive, but we lacked the leadership and the decision making that we needed," Olson wrote. "Too many times the wrong player had the ball at the end of the game. In an early-season game at UNLV, for example, we were up thirteen points and still lost 92–87, and Vegas went to the Final Four that year. So we were good, just not good enough. It's impossible to even guess how much better we would have been with Kerr. That was the season the NCAA instituted the three-point basket and he was our best three-point shooter."

Kerr spent what would have been his senior season as a de facto assistant coach, helping Olson and the staff when possible in his first exposure to that layer of the game after playing with the intelligence of a coach on the court. Indeed, when asked what he would do if he couldn't play again, Kerr grinned and said, "I'll just have them fire Coach Olson and take his job." As his recovery progressed on schedule, Kerr, still with limited mobility, was cleared to begin shooting early in the season. Usually, he was the first Wildcat at practice and would stay so long after that he had to be ordered off the court.

"I keep thinking that there's a reason this happened," Kerr said during the forced layoff. "Maybe it's a premonition. My dream has always been to make it to the Final Four. Next year we should be great. Maybe this is a blessing in that regard."

Kerr turned the 1986–1987 season into the unofficial head start of his plan to finish his college eligibility while starting graduate school in sports administration and then entering coaching as Olson's graduate assistant, the lowest rung on the staff. Remaining a constant presence by continuing to travel with the team and attending every game was also the reminder of how much he was missed, until, finally, the 81–65 loss at UCLA pushed him over the edge. Even after returning to the hotel in Marina del Rey, supposedly with enough time since the end of the game to decompress, Kerr in the lobby waiting for the elevator to go to his room was still visibly upset, venting about Arizona's lack of toughness. He seemed more angry about the soft showing than the Wildcats who played. None of these guys wants to go out and kick somebody's ass, he said. It was as if he was determined to not let it happen when he got back.

CHAPTER 5

Steeeeeve Kerrrrr!!!

Greg Hansen raised the possibility of a 30-0 regular season in an *Arizona Daily Star* column as 1987–1988 began, a suggestion that moved USC coach George Raveling to hold a reproduction of the printed madness above his six-six frame while speaking at Pac-10 Media Day. "I wanted to photocopy this article as the condition of surrender," Raveling said when his turn came in a ballroom at the Marriott near Los Angeles International Airport. "I figure I have nothing but a prayer." The audience, mostly reporters, laughed. "I'm drafting a letter to Commissioner Tom Hansen to suggest that we rename the conference the Pac-9," Raveling continued. "None of the rest of us are good enough to compete with an elite team like Arizona."

The team prompting religion and white-flag retreat took the court to a standing ovation merely for the annual intrasquad scrimmage in McKale Center, the Red-Blue Game. "A lot of it was for Steve," teammate Matt Muehlebach said. "Like, he's back. You could feel that connection when he ran out. From that second on, it felt like something good was about to happen." Just the possibility of having Kerr healthy again and part of a starting lineup with McMillan in the backcourt and Elliott, Tolbert, and Anthony Cook on the front line sent excitement coursing through Tucson as 1987–1988 dawned. Even losing a recruiting bid for promising San Antonio high school senior Shaquille O'Neal after O'Neal placed the Wildcats among his finalists couldn't diminish energy so palpable that, Olson learned years later, Kerr and Fraser once discussed buying seats behind the Wildcat bench to flip for a profit.

Another home exhibition, against the Soviet Union, followed before the official return in the November 27 season opener against Duquesne as part of the Great Alaska Shootout, Kerr's first real game in sixteen months. In early practices, Olson observed, Kerr looked "great," but the coach held off on a true assessment until Arizona had a contest that counted. As the Wildcats landed in Anchorage with the sun setting at 4:00 P.M., Olson considered the comeback of his trusty point guard, back as a team captain, the key to the season just beginning. If Kerr reclaimed his former stature, Olson believed, he would be the leader and three-point threat lacking the season before.

Dismissing Duquesne with ease as Kerr made five of six shots overall and two of three behind the arc in his first game with the three-point line helped Arizona set up an important read against number-nine Michigan with Gary Grant, a physical defender with a bright NBA future. Grant's teammates expected him to use his athleticism to erase another slow point guard, after years of watching the same outcome in individual matchups against other decent talent. Instead, Kerr made five of six shots, while Grant went three of fourteen, rubbed in a late three-pointer by pointing at Grant, and Arizona crushed a very good roster 79–64. Plus, Arizona "was so locked in together," Wolverines center Mark Hughes said. "They cheered so much for each other. 'Way to go, Sean! Nice job!' 'Way to go, Steve!' We're looking at each other like, 'What?' That was a little bit weird for us, being a Big Ten, crack-'em, tough, gritty team and those guys are doing a lot of yay-yay-yay cheering for their guys." Once, with a free hour on a game day, the Wildcats went outside for a snowball fight that became another bonding moment, with the bonus revelation of watching Lofton fire the icy hand-made pellets. "The best chemistry of any team I have ever been on," Kerr said.

Beating Michigan and its roster of seven players bound for the NBA emboldened Elliott to trash-talk Arizona's next opponent, number-one-ranked Syracuse, and star center Rony Seikaly, an All-America candidate. Seikaly is "not that tough," Elliott said, adding,

"I think our front line is better than theirs. I'd take Michigan's starting five over theirs." The surroundings may have been the greater
concern for Syracuse at the start of the day on November 30—a 7.5
earthquake rocked Anchorage and sent Seikaly running from his
hotel room into the hallway with a certainty, assistant coach Bernie
Fine said, that the world was coming to an end. By the end of the
same day, though, the Wildcats had another upset victory, two wins
over a top-ten team in three days, and Kerr had another big game
against a highly rated point guard, Sherman Douglas. UA won the
Shootout title as Kerr, Elliott, and Tolbert made all-tournament.
"When we came up here," Olson said, "I thought we were a good
ball club. But I had to see what we could do against this type of competition. Needless to say, I'm happy with the results."

Not only was Kerr immediately playing so well that it seemed
he had gone from the 1986–1987 season into 1987–1988 under normal circumstances, the national attention from Arizona's proving-
ground start left him finally sensing that "people have completely
accepted me as a person, not just as a victim. This is a great feeling
to be on a team with this kind of potential. I hope we can keep it
going all year." He got another emotional boost when the Wildcats
finally played a home game, December 4 against Cal State Long
Beach, and took the court to a deafening roar of support, a backing
around campus that had grown to include UA freshman Andrew
Kerr. It was, Tucson native Elliott later said, a magical time for the
program.

A trip to Iowa, then, fit perfectly, with the number-three-ranked
Hawkeyes the best measuring stick yet for the Wildcats and Arizona
up to number four just in time for Olson's homecoming. Aware that
many fans still felt betrayed by the decision to leave for Arizona,
he was admittedly nervous about getting a harsh reception during
pregame introductions and had taken the unusual step of closing
practice the day before. The concern increased once the session began and the starters were shut down by the UA reserves, who were
simulating the Iowa press as the scout team. "You can tell coach
really wants this one more than he's ever wanted a game," Kerr

said. "Usually the assistants do some things. Not today. Coach O ran the whole practice."

Helpful levity came after the morning shootaround the next day when Olson spotted Kerr and John Feinstein of the *Washington Post* in conversation in the motel coffee shop, a talk that would last hours. The coach told Feinstein not to keep Kerr much longer. The Wildcats did, after all, have a game that night. "We do?" Kerr said between sips of soda. "I'd completely forgotten." Olson couldn't help but laugh. "I knew Steve could handle it," he said of not ending the interview on the spot, as he would have with most players on a game day. "Steve can handle most things."

Olson got the ideal outcome of a warm greeting inside Carver-Hawkeye Arena and a 66–59 win behind fifteen points, six assists, and only one turnover in forty minutes from Kerr. Kerr turned out to be so full of energy, despite his coach's concerns earlier in the day, that he shook a fist in the face of his Iowa defender, B. J. Armstrong, after a three-pointer in the first half. On a night of obvious relief from Olson, the Wildcats even handled the actual Iowa press without difficulty.

It was about 2:00 A.M. by the time Greg Hansen and his *Arizona Daily Star* colleague Jay Gonzales finished their stories, went out for beers, and headed to their rooms at the Highlander Motel, the team headquarters as well. Walking down the hallway on the floor where the players were also staying, Hansen heard Anthony Cook call out.

"Hey, do you want to see the most popular man in Tucson?"

Hansen, intrigued, walked toward Cook.

"Come on in," Arizona's starting power forward said.

Entering the room, Hansen was directed to the bathroom to find Kerr drunk enough to turn his body rebellious, collapsed in alcohol-induced disrepair, on the floor except for his head propped against the bowl. The most popular man in Tucson needed all his strength to reach a hand up and flip off the amused reporter in a moment of defiance joined with surrender. By the time Gonzales came to see for himself, Kerr was on his right side in the fetal position on one of the beds, head on the bedclothes, with no pillow, knees drawn up nearly to his chin, and his hands in fists also under his chin. Slowly, as if it required all his strength, the limp mess that was one of the best players in the country extended his left hand and flipped off Gonzales as well.

The season was seven games old, all victories, and already turning into nonstop celebration. The "Steeeeeve Kerrrrr" call that PA announcer Roger Sedlmayer started years before had become a McKale party anthem, and it gained exclamation points in the 1987–1988 frenzy. At 9-0 on December 22, Arizona moved to number one in the country for the first time in school history just as the Pac-10 schedule was opening, an ascension followed by a thirty-four-point win over Washington State, a twenty-point victory over Michigan State, and finally a 91–85 triumph over number-nine Duke on December 30. In thirty-three days, the Wildcats had beaten four top-ten teams, three on the road, and Kerr had been named conference Player of the Week twice. The appraisal from the latest victim, Duke guard Quin Snyder, was that "more than anything, to me it was leadership that separated him. And obviously if you're a great player, it's easier to lead."

The leader was in such a good mood after the game that night that when he was handed a phone in the locker room for a segment on a Tucson radio show and asked for a New Year's resolution, he replied, "Yeah, as a matter of fact, the whole team has made one. We've resolved to work really hard to try to help Coach Olson kick this heroin habit of his because it's really been getting us all down lately." Even Kerr realized he went too far with that one, although Olson took no offense and shrugged it off as harmless mirth by a player mature enough when necessary.

Accurately reading the mood in town as UA basketball soared to new heights of civic pride, Mike Elliott, host of the morning show on Tucson's top-forty radio station KRQ, wrote a song to spin out as long as the insanity of early 1987–1988 lasted. Some players, after all, were being greeted by standing ovations when they walked into classrooms. He hoped to at least get the starting five to handle vocals and have reserve guard Harvey Mason Jr., a budding musician and the son of a prominent jazz drummer and producer, write the score. Not only did the younger Mason agree, and then complete the task in one night, but all the Wildcats, not just the opening lineup, jumped in with enthusiasm. The school and the conference signed off once Elliott gladly inserted lines into the original script that would make a portion of the song an antidrug message and not simply a salute to the rising basketball tide in the Southwest.

It was an ideal proposition for the loose Wildcats and especially their point guard who never sought the spotlight but knew how to grab on tight when one came along. And the timing was perfect, with interest in town higher than ever and the team building a national profile. Reporters parachuted in from major markets to profile an emerging program, the coach doing basketball miracle work, the star small forward who rejected recruiting pitches from monument programs to play for the hometown team, and Kerr, the feel-good tale of overcoming devastating adversity. "Oh my God," one of the visitors, Dick Weiss of the *Philadelphia Daily News,* said. "You had to fall in love with them." Locally, Tucson thrilled to a tune about the current team with music and singing by the current team, until it was the most-requested song at the station after only eight days.

What would have been amusing enough turned into an even greater lark when the idea grew all the way into a rap video, following the craze popularized by the Chicago Bears' "Super Bowl Shuffle" in 1985. Mason arranged a studio for the dual recording and video shoot—a converted gardening shed at a house in Tucson— and Mike Elliott lined up a film crew. He arrived to find players standing outside and Tolbert offering bottles of beer pulled from the pockets of very baggy shorts. When the two-hour session was complete, Mason mastered the song and the tapes were sent to Los Angeles, where a friend of Elliott's spliced in game and atmosphere clips from McKale Center to complete the video. "They were having so much fun," Elliott said. "You could tell that this team had great chemistry. It wasn't like Lute had assembled a bunch of guys who were good players and didn't like each other or who were indifferent. These guys loved each other."

In pink shorts and a long-sleeve blue shirt over a gray shirt, using sunglasses inside for mood, swaying amid a group behind one
of the microphones, Kerr was set up for his solo one minute and
fifty-five seconds into the video with "Give Kerr the ball, give Kerr
a hand." "I'll drill it in from three-point laaaand," he followed up,
dragging out the close in a flat tone.

Only the timing was unfortunate: "Wild About the Cats" was released soon after the first defeat, January 2 at New Mexico. It turned
into a local sensation anyway as part of the sugar rush of the 12-1
start that moved Oregon State coach Ralph Miller to blasphemy. To
find a team comparable to UA, Miller said, daring to reach for the
ultimate comparison, "You have to go back to some of John Wood-
en's teams of the mid-70s." As if to prove that the Albuquerque setback was a temporary loss of direction, Arizona won the next eight,
capped by a home victory over number-thirteen Illinois with Nick
Anderson and Kendall Gill. "Wild About the Cats" continued to get
regular play on KRQ, and players spotted around town were asked
for impromptu jams.

Ann Kerr's visit to see her two youngest sons during the win
streak was perfectly timed. Not only had Steve's celebrity status in
town grown to include life as a rap star, but the comeback from
his injury was going so well that Olson began insisting Kerr was
quicker than before it happened. The cold days of Alaska in November and Iowa in December that sent an ache through the re-
paired right knee turned out to be short term, early setbacks caused
by temporary life in the refrigerated section more than an urgent
warning. Now, in late January, the Wildcats were scheduled for a
warm-weather finish to the regular season in Tucson, the Bay Area,
Los Angeles, and Tempe, followed by a possible return to L.A. for
the start of the NCAA tournament and, if that went well, to Seattle. Another Midwest swing, to Missouri, was possible, except it
wouldn't happen until April.

In the most encouraging of all midseason evaluations, Kerr had
made it all the way back to become "the glue that holds this team
together," Olson said. "He provides leadership on both ends of the

court and he's the smartest player that I've ever coached or ever seen. I think he's the best point guard in the country." On another occasion, Olson called Kerr "the best leader I've ever seen. If he told this team that green was orange, they would all believe him." ("You want to know why I'm the leader?" Kerr responded. "It's simple. Last summer we went to France. I speak French. The other guys don't. Every time they wanted to hit on a girl, they needed me to interpret. That's when I became the leader.")

He began to consider the possibility of an NBA future for the first time, if only the glancing career of a couple seasons. While Olson offered tepid agreement—"but he has to go with the right team," one that "recognizes all the things he can do"—it became clear that the knee injury was already, strangely, one of the best things to happen to him. Exactly the opposite of career-threatening, as feared on the sorrowful bus ride to the Madrid hotel bound for uncertainty and a teary phone call with his mother, the night of July 17, 1986, was the godsend of adjusting Kerr's timeline. By missing the next Arizona campaign, he grew bigger and older, to twenty-two years old for 1987–1988. Though Kerr would have had the benefit of a season with the three-point line either way, endless hours of rehabilitation built the stronger leg muscles critical for a long-range shooter. His subsequent play and leadership then ignited the joyride of a team that was as close as it was successful, turning him into the most popular member of the most popular team in Tucson history. On a personal level, he got a second season around and a first season playing with Tolbert and Jud Buechler, important months in what would become two of the best friendships of his life.

Ann's up-close view of the joyous bedlam Steve helped create lasted four days, before she left January 22 as people were getting to know an inordinate amount about her third child. His first memories were of wanting to play basketball or baseball. He learned to read by scanning the sports section in the newspaper. In a region gone mad for its basketball team, he already had the big-picture perspective shaped by tragedy that would stay with him into future careers—"Don't get me wrong. Being No. 1 is terrific. But in a larger, more meaningful context, it's really no big deal." He was never a very good traveler. He could be lazy. Even that he hated getting out of bed in the morning. Everyone from the *New York Times* to *People* magazine spotlighted him. Feinstein, the *Washington Post* writer, made Kerr a focus of *A Season Inside,* his book tracking 1987–1988 nationally. "People knew all about him," Tom Duddleston, a primary liaison between the team and the media, eventually concluded. "I mean, everything about him."

"It's nice that people like me the way they do," Kerr told Feinstein during one of many interviews that would lead to a lifelong friendship. "But to tell you the truth, sometimes I get tired of it. I mean, if I hear or read one more time that I'm Huck Finn or Tom Sawyer, I'll throw up. I'm like any other guy my age. I like to have fun. I like to drink a few beers, and there are times when I'm an asshole. When my family reads all this stuff about how great I am, they think it's really funny." Still, "I'm trying to enjoy every minute of this. Because I know nothing like this will ever happen again in my life. This is an ultimate, something that will only happen once."

Being asked by *Daily Cal* assistant sports editor Michael Silver, his partner at the Palisades school paper, to write a guest column ahead of Arizona's trip to the University of California in February was practically Kerr's ideal way to maximize the fame. He would be published again, an opportunity he rarely missed, and be awarded close to a free pass on content and tone. If there was any direction from Silver, it was to go full "Riptide" on the hippy image of Berkeley that remained from its days as a center of 1960s campus protests and the counterculture.

Daily Cal staffers reading along or typing the story into a computer couldn't stop laughing at the takedown Kerr faxed to the office, sentence after sentence ridiculing the Cal stereotype. They could barely get through a paragraph without needing to stop. Cal fans were the most obnoxious in the conference, he wrote, and members of the school band wearing straw hats at games were countermen at Shakey's Pizza. Also, "To the earthy-looking, Birkenstock-wearing girl who, during one game two years ago, repeatedly yelled, 'Kerr, what kind of hair spray do you use?' I say . . . Before you and all the rest of Berkeley ask for advice on hair spray, try thinking about the simple basics of personal hygiene—like showering."

Kerr took the court to a predictable strain of boos, as he undoubtedly anticipated and gladly accepted. With one star Cal point guard, Kevin Johnson, in the NBA and the next, Jason Kidd, not arriving until 1992, Kerr and the Wildcats were unfazed by the hostile fans in close quarters to the court and won by twelve.

From taunting an entire city to beating UCLA in Pauley Pavilion to a final visit to Arizona State on February 25, the road schedule late in 1987–1988 fell into place as an unofficial Kerr farewell tour. He already considered Tempe a different last stop than the others, a place he didn't enjoy even though the Wildcats, in a reversal of previous roles, ruled the rivalry since he arrived in Tucson and had reached national heights as he prepared to leave. "The only game their fans even come to is ours," he said. "They draw terribly except when they play us and then the fans come in with a chip on their shoulder. It's never any fun playing there like it is at other places." There had even been occasional heartless comments about Malcolm's murder from ASU backers in previous visits.

On February 25, about a dozen college-age Arizona State supporters turned especially cruel. "PLO! PLO! PLO!" they chanted, even though the PLO had no known role in his father's assassination, soon after Arizona took the court for warm-ups a little less than an hour before tipoff. "Hey, Kerr, where's your dad?" He also heard, "Your father's history," and the demand, "Go back to Beirut!" It was bad enough that other Arizona State fans, defending Kerr, shouted at the wretched dozen to shut up.

Kerr, believing they were drunk, tried to ignore the inhumanity, but it was impossible in a gym still near-empty. He took a couple more shots, his body shaking and turning numb, before dropping the ball, conceding defeat, and moving to a sideline to sit on the bench, where he burst into tears. A couple fans came to apologize while teammates consoled him and considered going into the stands to confront "the scum of the earth," as he called the hecklers, but the Wildcats instead gathered their wounded leader and returned to the locker room, as usual, for final instructions from Olson. Soon back on the court, Kerr could immediately feel the difference, how, unlike most games, he was not initially looking to pass to get other players involved. "This time, I wanted to shoot." Arizona players and coaches, he said, were "really pissed, including me. For the first time in my life I actually found myself thinking about what I was going to say to the press about something that had happened. I just wanted to *get* those people somehow."

When he made his first shot, a three, an especially amped Kerr shook a fist at the crowd. Five more behind the line followed in the opening half alone en route to twenty-two points in a 101–73 victory that left Kerr practically apologetic for taking his rage out on an opponent that had nothing to do with the ugliness. "But I was just so angry I wanted to beat them by 50." Watching on TV in his dorm room in Forbes Hall at the University of Illinois, three weeks after the Illini lost in Tucson, sophomore guard Anderson could practically feel Kerr's pain in sympathy, saying over and over to himself how cruel the hecklers had been. Hundreds of letters of support arrived within days, some from disgusted Arizona State students and faculty and one from athletic director Charles Harris, with copies sent to six coaches and administrators at both schools.

"Dear Steve," Harris began. "It is with sincere regret that I write this letter. I would like to extend my apologies to you for the mental anguish that you had to endure because of the disillusioned few at the University Activities Center last Saturday. I refuse to refer to them as fans because they do not dignify the term.

"We do not condone that type of behavior from our ticket-holders. I certainly hope they will realize from this unfortunate incident that it does affect people in horrible ways.

"Again, please accept my apologies for you and your family, the Wildcat basketball team and the University of Arizona. All of us respect and admire you and hope that this can be a friendly rivalry for years to come."

While Kerr appreciated the gesture, he accurately attributed the incident to a small group of fans and did not think the school or program owed him an apology. His response to Harris's note praised ASU players and coaches—"They're all good guys"—though with a final play against the rival: It will probably be tough to recruit with that kind of publicity, intentionally or unintentionally spinning the ugly night into an issue for top high school prospects to consider. Beyond that, there was no lasting effect.

The regular season ended uneventfully from there, with easy home wins over Washington State and Washington before three more breezy victories in the conference tournament inside the McKale noise factory. By the time the NCAA tournament opened against Cornell on March 18 in Los Angeles, the Wildcats were 31-2, winners of eleven in a row, and extremely confident, none more than the senior point guard returning to his hometown. "We'll be playing five Steve Kerrs," the original said. "We ought to be able to handle them." He even laughed at the mention of Cornell. Living up to expectations, Arizona rolled by forty, then beat Seton Hall by twenty-nine to advance to the Sweet 16 in Seattle. There, in a second Olson reunion with Iowa, the top-seeded team in the West Regional won by twenty.

Kerr slept fitfully the night before Arizona would play North Carolina, with a trip to the Final Four on the line, churning in bed as he imagined the different scenarios. When he woke in the morning, Kerr began to pray: Please, God, let us win. "I've never done that before in my life," he said. "But then I can't remember ever wanting something so much in my life."

Kerr was still unsettled ninety minutes prior to tip-off, as he stood on the court before the crowd poured into the Kingdome. Suddenly struck as the opening lineups were introduced that it could be his last game, he felt his stomach twisting. The start of the game offered no comfort, with North Carolina controlling the tempo, forcing Arizona to play slow and taking a 28–26 edge into halftime. Olson implored his team to be more aggressive. When the Wildcats were and got the preferred faster pace, they began to pull away. The 70–52 victory and a trip to Kansas City for the Final Four secured, coming out with the other starters in the final minute was "the greatest feeling I had ever felt in my life."

Returning to Tucson hours later, the Wildcats bused to McKale Center, with Bobbi Olson dancing in the aisle, before they arrived to find some thirteen thousand revelers lying in wait, exploding when the team walked in. Each player spoke. Kerr went last, his speech preceded by the obligatory "Steeeeeve Kerrrrr!!!" welcome. "Hi," he deadpanned in response, "my name is Steve Kerr." The last thing he remembered was the party at his apartment complex and joining about thirty others in the pool with their clothes on.

The Final Four buildup almost instantly became so enveloping that mail arrived faster than he could wade through the stacks, his roommate had to screen phone calls, and practices were the only refuge. Leaving Tucson for Kansas City four days later was like making a successful getaway. Even better, as Kerr learned in a call to his mother the night of the North Carolina game, Ann and John would be there to see Arizona play Oklahoma, after traveling on first-class tickets courtesy of the president of Royal Jordanian Airlines, an American University trustee with Ann. Fully embracing the new breathing room, Kerr appeared at a group news conference Friday and responded to a question about Final Four nerves by grabbing the microphone and pretending he could not hold it still, with his hand shaking in fear of the semifinals. He felt great at practice at Kemper Arena, comfortable and with a shot in rhythm, while watching Elliott and Tolbert miss a lot and thinking they might be tight.

Back at Kemper on Saturday, his shot still felt good in pregame warmups. So did his first couple of attempts in the game, only to rim out. The third missed badly. Kerr failed on five of his first six attempts under constant harassment from Mookie Blaylock and Ricky Grace as Oklahoma squeezed Arizona with defense, controlled the tempo, created turnovers, and forced several Wildcats, not just Kerr, into quick shots. He started to press. The Sooners' game plan to pick him up full court, the same pressure defense they had successfully deployed all season, and wear him down was off to a good start. "These motherfuckers cannot score on us," Grace boasted in the locker room at halftime as Oklahoma owned a 39–27 lead.

Arizona rallied in the second half, even with Kerr continuing to flail. He missed three-pointer after three-pointer, until he was drowning in the worst game of his life. Watching from the arena with his team set to face the winner in the championship game two nights later, Kansas assistant coach Alvin Gentry, who had scouted Palisades senior Steve Kerr for Colorado, thought the Wildcats were getting good shots. Kerr most of all was missing the same tries he had made countless times before. When Oklahoma finished the 86–78 victory, he had made two of thirteen shots, including two of twelve behind the arc.

He would carry the pain of the night with him the rest of his life, still practically cringing decades later at the memory. Kerr would, he later often said, trade two or three future NBA championships for a win over Oklahoma and the chance to give his storybook college career and dream teammates an appropriate finish. Worse, his mom and older brother had come all the way from the Middle East just to watch the personal debacle. "My mother could have stayed in Cairo and seen better basketball," Steve said.

Olson couldn't help but make the connection. "This was one of the very few games in Steve's entire career that she was able to attend," he wrote. "I coached Steve for five years and I never saw him have an off day shooting, so I have to believe that the fact that his mother was at the game affected his performance. I think he was trying so hard to have a perfect game for his mother. After he missed his first few shots the pressure just grew and grew. Shooting is as much mental as physical; sometimes it seems like a great player can almost will the ball into the basket, and I think Steve's desire was so strong that it took him out of his natural game." To Kerr, he had two good launches at the start and never found his rhythm again. "I wanted to win that game and win the national championship so much, and I probably was trying too hard."

The locker room after the game was as sad as any Olson would ever experience. A lot of players had tears in their eyes and their heads down as he told them he was proud of them and there was no shame losing to a quality opponent like Oklahoma. He called the team together for a final huddle. They wept, "just kind of hanging on to one another for a while," Kerr remembered, torn up most of all that the incredible journey was over. One of the favorite teams of his life would never be together again. Standing in the hallway a few minutes later, Olson choked up at the realization that his time with Kerr was over. "In the five years I've known him," the coach said, "I wouldn't change one thing."

Kerr was still an open emotional wound the next morning as he walked with his mother into the ballroom at the Hyatt Regency, the downtown media hotel, for the U.S. Basketball Writers Association banquet. The recipient of the group's Most Courageous Award, for overcoming tragedy and a career-threatening injury to emerge as one of the best players in the nation, would rarely in his life as a gifted speaker be as challenged to make remarks as he was that day, with the pain of defeat still fresh and his father's death returned to the forefront. True to the personality that had already emerged, Kerr opted against the gentle thank-you remarks that would have been acceptable and even understandable. Hurting or not and knowing he was essentially delivering a national farewell to college basketball, he wanted to acknowledge everything the sport had done for him.

From among the Arizona contingent in the audience, Duddleston, well acquainted with Kerr's grace in public settings after five seasons, could feel Kerr struggle with his emotions. While the tears were not unusual—he twice cried on the court before games, after all—choking up this time seemed to render him uncharacteristically disorganized. Once Kerr gathered himself, though, he spoke with uncommon sincerity and poise for a student. Detailing the treasures of his close relationship with Malcolm, sometimes still through tears, and humbly explaining that he never could have imagined the career that had ended hours before he brought some in the audience to tears as well. That included Jay Gonzales, even though the *Arizona Daily Star* reporter already knew the story well.

Another USBWA member, Tom Shatel of the *Kansas City Star,* was struck by the thought that he was listening to a future senator or governor.

"I've enjoyed every moment of my career at Arizona," Kerr said behind a microphone while unsuccessfully holding back the watery emotions. "I'll remember it forever."

The Wildcats landed in Tucson to a hero's welcome of convertibles that paraded them from the airport to the campus as fans lined parts of the route, Another twenty-five thousand backers waited inside the football stadium. When someone played "Wild about the Cats" with the team on a stage, it turned into an impromptu performance of each player taking the mic to sing his line. Kerr appeared to give in to the party moment as much as anyone, still feeling the disappointment of Kansas City, but also not about to let his final act as a University of Arizona basketball player quietly slip away.

Kerr never got over the Oklahoma loss. Beyond that, though, he had endured the initial contempt of teammates disgusted at having to play with a guy who couldn't handle pickup games, the phone call in the middle of the January night that started the worst time of his life, and being told that a knee injury had probably just ended his career. Five years at the University of Arizona, an opportunity he didn't deserve and then nearly turned away from when it did come, changed his life for the better in immeasurable ways. He was named second-team All-America as a senior, developed into a pro prospect to his great surprise, met Margot Brennan and several others who would remain among his closest friends, and got an unofficial start in coaching under a future Hall of Famer. Kerr was so consistent that final season that Olson assistant Kevin O'Neill said he "never had a bad practice." Sean Elliott, forever a favorite teammate, was the greatest talent in program history, but Kerr left as the best-loved Wildcat in any sport, a standing that held up thirty years later.

"I don't like it when people say I've had bad breaks," he said as his Arizona career neared an end. "I've been one of the luckiest people in the world. The knee injury taught me perseverance. And my father's death has helped me put things in their true perspective.

I realize now, like I never did before, how things can be cut short suddenly. That's why I play basketball. I love playing as much as anything on earth. And if you don't do the things in life that you really want to do, then life's really not worth living."

Maybe, he thought in moments of dreaming big, he could last a season or two in the NBA.

CHAPTER 6

This Guy Can't Play

The 1988 Olympic basketball trials began May 18 in Colorado Springs, Colorado, with ninety-two candidates, secrecy, and disinformation. Executives from sneaker companies and NBA scouts cramming for the draft were welcome, but the media was barred. Organizers spun the explanation that players would be too busy to conduct interviews, but everyone understood the real reason: naming John Thompson coach meant accepting his Georgetown method of building a wall around the team to prepare for the Summer Games in South Korea four months later.

Returning to basketball much sooner than normal, without the usual summer break, would be especially beneficial to candidate Steve Kerr after the emotional welts from the Oklahoma game. Six weeks between the Final Four and the first phase of Olympic tryouts was enough time to rest after a season of mounting pressure, but not so much that he could spiral into months of self-loathing. Reporting to Colorado Springs and having the opportunity to represent the United States again, with the chance to make it to the end of a major international tournament this time, forced him to focus on the future, not the personal hell of Kansas City on April 2.

Plus, Kerr was growing increasingly optimistic about being picked in the June 28 draft and knew the trials would be the perfect setting to reclaim whatever ground he lost with the worst game of his life. While going two of thirteen from the field and appearing to wilt under the Final Four heat lamp had been a hit to his NBA stock, he had also played well enough against elite competition the rest of 1987–1988 that one dreadful night would not end the dream.

There had been too many good nights. Concerns about his shooting were the least of the worries as scouts debated his future in May and June. The fluctuation in his draft stock would depend more on front-office evaluations of his size (tall enough, but too weak), his ball handling (decent for college, but the inability to create for himself and others would hurt at the next level), defense (poor), and athleticism (average).

To Cavaliers general manager Wayne Embry, "He was limited somewhat in his playing ability, but there was something about him aside from his shooting. You start there, with what everyone could see. But getting to know him, we detected through our background checks that he was a person of very high character." From close proximity, Phoenix general manager Jerry Colangelo concluded: "Half a step slow, not a great physical talent, very smart, could really shoot the ball, great character." Philadelphia scout Bob Weinhauer noted Kerr "got better every game I saw him play," high praise and an especially important insight considering front offices loved prospects on an upward trajectory. Weinhauer had the perspective to know for sure—he was the Arizona State coach who watched freshman Kerr several times, who was on the opposing bench and went into the Arizona locker room after Kerr's surreal performance two nights after Malcolm's death, and in early summer 1988 was tracking the U.S. Olympic hopefuls in a series of exhibition games in Europe.

Weinhauer's focus may have been on guards who could shoot as he tagged along through France, Norway, and Austria, but guards with star potential. Rex Chapman, Mitch Richmond, and Hersey Hawkins were possibilities for the 76ers with the third pick. Kerr was just hoping to be one of the seventy-five selections over three rounds at the Felt Forum in New York. He formulated alternatives just in case, most prominently signing in Europe, an easy culture adjustment for him, and then returning to join Olson's staff. Or maybe he would immediately start on the career that did have a chance to succeed and become an Olson assistant while taking another year of grad school.

If anything, Kerr put down deeper local roots after the season. Unlike the many pro candidates around the country who stopped attending classes and focused on draft prep, Kerr remained a campus regular. He worked an internship in the sports information department, typing football rosters into the office computer to be formatted as reference material for the media in the upcoming season, and accepted an invitation to join a baseball team that included several others from the Athletic Department, until someone pointed out that an NBA hopeful risking injury to leg out a triple in a rec league game might not be wise. Still, Kerr seemed to be settling in to make Tucson a permanent home.

Being told in a phone call from a reporter that he had been picked fiftieth by the Suns, then, was as encouraging as it was strange. The draft coverage Kerr had been watching at home in Pacific Palisades ended when the network switched to a *Gomer Pyle: USMC* rerun. He was at least slightly familiar with Phoenix and would be just an hour flight from girlfriend Margot Brennan, who was working at an advertising agency in Los Angeles. The relationship that started with a blind date their sophomore year, arranged by Bruce Fraser, had remained serious across the miles and years. A match for Steve as warm, considerate, and outwardly feisty as he was mostly in sports, Margot, also the child of a college professor, had long established herself as supportive and protective by the time Steve phoned her in L.A. with the news.

Choosing a popular player with area ties would have prompted speculation anyway about the motivation to take a slow point guard who couldn't defend, but assumptions flew into overdrive at a time Phoenix was desperate for positive publicity. Two months earlier, three current and two former Suns, one a member of the mayor's task force on drug abuse, were indicted by a Maricopa County grand jury investigating cocaine trafficking, while two others avoided charges after being given immunity in exchange for testimony against teammates. Plus, *Sports Illustrated* reported, Phoenix police had requested a tape of the Suns-Bucks game in February as part of an investigation into gambling that also included wiretaps at a local bar frequented by players. The league was concerned enough to come to Arizona in March for a secret meeting with team officials, the police, county authorities, and detectives handling the gambling investigation, although no charges were filed. The franchise was so badly stained that even Margot later conceded the Suns took her boyfriend with an impeccable reputation "probably because they had a lot of issues with the drug stuff."

Just as much evidence existed that the Suns made the decision for basketball reasons, most of all that GM Colangelo valued late selections after watching Jeff Hornacek go from the number forty-six pick two years before to the opening lineup. And although Hornacek could play some point guard, Phoenix needed a dedicated backup for Kevin Johnson, acquired four months earlier in a trade with Cleveland, as part of the roster fumigation. Eager to move past the blight of the previous season, which had been a toxic mess on the court as well with a 28-54 record, Colangelo hired Cotton Fitzsimmons as coach, signed Tom Chambers as a free agent, and drafted Dan Majerle in the first round. Colangelo needed contributors, not local favorites. "Certainly we were all aware of how popular Steve Kerr was, and it certainly wasn't going to hurt us if he were to be drafted by us," Colangelo said. "And if he were to make it, that's just a plus-plus." But "the pick was not predicated on just popularity. I wouldn't have done that."

Hornacek was very much on Colangelo's mind as the general manager scouted Arizona and noted the similarities to Kerr. The comparisons went back to high school. Hornacek had barely been recruited out of La Grange, Illinois, before going to Iowa State as a walk-on and developing into a college star beyond all expectations. Both lacked athleticism, both were seen as point guards but would prove to be at their best playing off the ball, both had great instincts on the court and the highest of character, and both not only lasted until near the end of the second round but weren't even close to Phoenix's priority in that second round. The Suns took Joe Ward and Rafael Addison in 1986 before Hornacek went forty-sixth, just as they selected Andrew Lang at twenty-eight and Dean Garrett at thirty-eight before picking Kerr with the fiftieth choice. Hornacek's early NBA success was a factor in Colangelo taking Kerr.

Kerr's Olympic hopes lasted through Colorado Springs and the eight-day European tour before he was cut seven days after the draft. His path forward in the NBA, meanwhile, again hinged at least in part on Kevin Johnson, the point guard Olson most wanted in 1983 recruiting, before Johnson's decision to attend California left a roster spot open for Kerr as the might-as-well last resort. In the fall of 1988, Johnson was still a much better prospect and had the advantage of a season of NBA experience after finishing college in four years, without a redshirt campaign. He was also faster and more of a true point guard who created opportunities for teammates, and he came with an impeccable reputation of his own. "He was polite; oh my God, was he polite," Johnson's high school principal raved. "He was a fine, fine young man and a good student." He developed such a close relationship with the coach and the coach's wife that some in the organization tagged him Kevin Fitzsimmons. Kerr was not expected to challenge for the starting job anyway, not against that daunting backdrop or in any other reality, but constantly practicing against Johnson with jets in his legs could also immediately expose Kerr as a wasted pick with no future.

He was so far from making an impact, in fact, that one of Kerr's early NBA decisions was to deconstruct his shot, the best part of his game and the primary reason he was picked as high as number fifty in June. "I'd spot up and take my little shot, and I got sick of seeing it swatted into the fourth row," he said. A lot of the moves that worked in high school and college had little success against the elite competition, guards who were almost always bigger or faster and certainly more experienced. He watched Hornacek, Mark Price, and Craig Hodges and tried to build the same quick release that offset their lack of quickness, even if it meant elevating and finding the basket in midjump. Trying to develop another counter, Kerr schooled himself to look at the court to get the defender to relax, then quickly rise for the release once the ball came.

In what would become the Kerr methodology for the rest of his career, each technique was honed by repetitions after practice and pregame warm-ups so focused that teammates and opponents took notice. Dismissing the idea of volume work, he preferred approximately two hundred attempts before games, but a concentrated two hundred, all from spots where he might get the ball in a few hours. "He practiced the shots he would get if he got in the game," Jeff Turner remembered decades later of his brief time with Kerr in Orlando. "He knew from practice and everything, 'If I'm getting in, here's where I'm gonna be.' No goofing around. It was serious." Only when the serious work got done in practice did he join the shooting games. "But everything had to be done first," Turner said. "All the work had to be put in first." Soon Kerr was "one of the guys that was just so efficient with his shot," said Jim Les, a frequent head-to-head opponent in the similar role of shooting specialist off the bench. "There was no wasted movement, no wasted motion. By the time he caught the ball, he was already into his shooting motion, so it put a premium on trying to get there on the catch and contest."

Kerr related to Hornacek in particular, for the same reasons Colangelo made the comparison before the draft, only Kerr went further. When he tried a mind trick in the 1990s that called for pretending to be another player in workouts in hopes a substitute identity would curb his overthinking, he chose Hornacek. Kerr loved that Hornacek's repertoire stretched to flip shots and other attacks in addition to their shared ability as perimeter threats who could handle limited duty at point guard. Watching his imaginary self made Kerr realize he could expand his offense and, more important, be more aggressive in looking to score, a problem as his professional career began with little opportunity on the veteran Suns. He likewise found joy in imitating another guard as part of the scout team that helped the best players prepare for the upcoming opponent.

"I was always the shooter on the scout team," Kerr said, "and that was the greatest feeling of freedom because I had to be whoever— Hersey Hawkins. *We gotta guard this guy, he's going to light it up. . . .* Well, I'm the guy! And I'd totally get out of my own way. But then

I'd stop and think, 'How pathetic is that? Why don't I act like that all the time?'"

When the new Suns started 15-10, far ahead of their pace the previous season, Kerr moved to the background. He didn't make his pro debut until the twenty-first game and didn't reach double digits in minutes until the twenty-fourth. Johnson was regularly playing high thirties to low forties, leaving little time for anyone else, and certainly not a limited rookie on a roster in win-now mode after the depths of the previous campaign. Assistant coaches Paul Westphal and Lionel Hollins could make him look bad in one-on-one or two-on-two after practice. "He couldn't guard us," said Westphal, thirty-eight years old and five seasons into retirement. "We were too quick for him even then."

By the time the regular season closed with the Phoenix Suns redeemed at 55-27, Johnson had averaged 39.2 minutes, the third-most in the league en route to being voted the league's Most Improved Player. Kerr averaged six minutes in twenty-six regular season games, and none in the playoffs as the Suns lost in the Western Conference finals. He took more than two three-pointers in a contest only once.

Kerr was frustrated enough, despite reaching a level he didn't think possible just two seasons before, that he told Bruce Fraser he would rather be in Fraser's role as a graduate assistant to Lute Olson than riding the Suns bench. It didn't help that Kerr before the season had turned down an offer to play in Germany, where he likely would have had a larger role given the weaker competition. If nothing else, Kerr showed himself in practice to be "a determined worker," forward Tyrone Corbin said. "I just remember him coming in and he knew who he was. He had to work extremely hard at developing a craft, first of all of being a shooter and being a point guard, and then learning how to manage the defensive areas on the floor with his size. But he could really shoot the ball." "He had to get stronger," another teammate, Eddie Johnson, said. "That was something that was evident that he had to do because he had good size. He could flat out shoot it. He wasn't afraid at all. He wasn't afraid to speak his mind. Very knowledgeable."

In the loudest statement of all, the Suns saw enough flicker of potential to sign Kerr to another one-year contract. Twelve days later, though, with the Cavaliers looking to add shooting and Embry an admirer since before the draft, Cleveland sent a second-round pick to Phoenix to acquire Kerr. "He had one thing that's appealing to all of us," Embry said. "That's the ability to make shots."

As much of a change as Ohio and the oncoming winter slam would be after eight seasons of Southern California shoreline and Arizona desert, joining the Cavaliers became his latest lucky break. There was a path in Cleveland to a meaningful role most of all, as the backup to Mark Price at point guard, and a meaningful role on a team that had just won fifty-seven games at that. Low-key Lenny Wilkens, although a contrast to the gregarious Cotton Fitzsimmons, was highly regarded as a coach who instilled confidence in players, connected with veterans and prospects, and delivered results. Embry had liked Kerr since before the draft and made the trade to acquire another shooter who could contribute to a long playoff run, not a roster filler whose biggest contribution would be as a practice sparring partner, and certainly not as a publicity move in a worrisome time for the franchise. Against a backdrop filled with positives and in a locker room where most of the best players were also the best people, Kerr had surpassed his NBA life expectancy.

Meeting Craig Ehlo one of the first days in Cleveland, before most of his new teammates had arrived in town for training camp, was especially fortuitous. Ehlo had likewise come out of the Pacific 10 Conference, from Washington State, and was a perimeter threat as well, though he was a more traditional shooting guard than Kerr as a shooter forced by slight stature to play point guard. The Cavaliers were also Ehlo's second stop after failing to gain much traction in his first NBA home, Houston. He had been the number forty-eight pick in 1983, five years before Kerr went fiftieth. When Ehlo told his new teammate and kindred spirit in the autumn of 1989 that he was usually on the practice court by 10:00 A.M., Kerr, not surprisingly, was there for the next session.

It was just the two of them on the court of the sixth floor of the

Richfield Coliseum, the home arena in the southern suburbs, shooting and talking, shooting and talking, the start to a lifelong friendship. They joked about Kerr's ill-fated recruiting visit to Gonzaga, a
story Ehlo knew well with the Spokane campus just seventy-five
miles from Washington State, and they swapped memories of the
Pac-10 stops. Kerr was up front in acknowledging his shortcomings,
the same skepticism around the league that he was too slow and his
ball handling was too shaky to play point guard. Kerr asked a lot
about Price, the man ahead of him on the depth chart. What kind
of guy is he? Is he mean? Although Ehlo could not know this within
hours of meeting Kerr, the answer that would eventually become
obvious to everyone was that Price and Kerr were almost identi-
cal in personality, quality people and ideal teammates who had no
problem whiplashing to menacing on the court.

The understudy learned that for himself once all the Cavaliers
gathered for training camp and Price turned territorial, just as he
did when other point guards joined the team in previous years. As
if wanting to send a message to the newcomer and Wilkens before anyone had the chance to consider taking away his minutes,
Price went hard at Kerr in two-a-days, just as his competitive streak
would drive Price to tell teammates other times that he would chew
up and spit out any potential threats at point guard. It didn't matter
that there was no realistic way a second-year player just thrilled to
be in the league would threaten the standing of an All-Star coming
off a season of 18.9 points, 8.4 assists, and 36.4 minutes. Far from
being offended, Kerr could appreciate as much as anyone the flashpoint when a polite, easygoing guy steps on the court, not to mention welcoming that constantly charging into the Price buzz saw
of surgical playmaking, shooting, and tenacity would make Kerr
better.

When the regular season began November 3 at Chicago with
Price briefly sidelined by a sprained ankle, Kerr started for the first
time as a pro and played forty-one minutes, more than double his
previous best. Back in a reserve role the next game, he logged just
twelve minutes, but then broke twenty for four games in a row,

still had a presence with nineteen for one night, and then spiked to thirty-eight, thirty-two, thirty-nine, and thirty-seven minutes from late November into early December. It was a dream sequence that became a constant flow of opportunity for Kerr as one of the most visible members of the second unit backup center Paul Mokeski nicknamed the Bomb Squad for its dependability in tight situations.

In Kerr, Mokeski with eleven seasons of experience saw a skilled perimeter threat but also a young player held back by a lack of confidence. Kerr, Mokeski believed, was overthinking situations and twisting himself in knots with spasms of self-doubt, to where it was harming a career barely getting started. "When we played together in practice," Mokeski said, "he would just let it fly. He could obviously shoot the basketball and be very effective that way. Then in games he would pass up shots. I would be on him to just shoot it. 'No one's going to get mad. Everyone knows you can shoot. Just shoot it. If it goes in or not, it doesn't matter. You need to shoot it.'" Mokeski delivered the same message on several occasions as a friendship developed and Kerr began referring to him as Uncle Mo. There was no way for either to know how much Mokeski would later regret the advice.

Kerr was making a successful transition to his new life on the whole, though, handling a windfall of minutes amid Mokeski's concerns about reaching his potential and even managing the first slap of an Ohio winter. The day Uncle Mo borrowed the gear of a TV cameraman in the locker room for interviews after practice, Kerr gladly stepped into the role of the rube with a warm-weather résumé transported to a frozen land, dressing in pants, shirt, sweatshirt, heavy jacket, and stocking cap pulled low until only his eyes were visible. On the court, Kerr was especially effective behind the three-point line, quickly making Embry look good for having spent only a second-round pick to acquire a contributor.

"When I got to the NBA, my shooting kept me in the league early," Kerr said. "But I really kept working because I knew I wasn't as talented as other guys. I actually got to be a reasonably good defender. It *hurt* to play defense, physically hurt, because I wasn't very big or very strong and I had to fight through screens all the time and I got knocked around. But I have a pretty good pain threshold, so I was able to deal with it."

Nothing that season worked more in his favor than Embry trading Ron Harper and three draft picks to the Clippers for Reggie Williams and Danny Ferry on November 16. Swapping the starting shooting guard for two forwards created minutes in the backcourt just as Kerr was proving worthy of added responsibility by turning into one of the best three-point shooters in the league. Gaining an unexpectedly prominent role in the Bomb Squad also came with the good news of Ehlo being promoted to the opening lineup as Harper's replacement. What Kerr could not have realized was that Ferry's arrival in 1990–1991, after Ferry finished the season with his Italian team, would be the start of a valued friendship.

Kerr's first sustained success as a pro, doubling as the first indication that he could outlast his own projection of a career topping out at two seasons, also emerged as one of the few upbeat story lines in a season quickly being lost to injury and manpower problems. The Cavaliers were 6-11 as they flew from Los Angeles to Sacramento the morning of December 8. The beat writers who had driven the 135 miles to Reno in previous seasons with an off day in Sacramento this time aimed for South Lake Tahoe and the casinos of neighbor city Stateline, just steps across the California-Nevada border. Mokeski was instantly intrigued when he heard the plans. As a child in the Canoga Park section of Los Angeles, Mokeski and his family practically made Tahoe an annual destination for summer vacations from grade school through high school. A predawn departure and at least eight hours on the road, depending on stops, was usually followed by a week in a large shared cabin among the pines. He had long ago come to appreciate the mountains, the clear air and the blue jewel of a lake, and as an adult he added the tables on the Nevada side to his favorite activities. A couple years before, while playing for the Milwaukee Bucks, Mokeski gathered a few teammates for the same run now under discussion. This time, he called over one of the writers, Joe Menzer of the *News-Herald,* at the end of practice. Get the biggest car you can rent and two cases of beer, Mokeski instructed.

By the time Menzer took a taxi to the airport, claimed a Lincoln Continental from the counter, purchased beer, put one case in a cooler with ice in the backseat and the auxiliary in the trunk, and drove to the team hotel across the street from the state capitol to meet his group, the traveling party had grown to five. Unable to drink alcohol while on anti-inflammatories for a strained groin, Ehlo volunteered to be the designated driver. Uncle Mo commandeered the passenger seat. Kerr, Menzer, and Burt Graeff of the *Cleveland Plain Dealer* climbed into the back and distributed canned beverages on the 100-mile drive in late afternoon. With conversation and beer flowing as the Lincoln left downtown and began gobbling Highway 50 asphalt into the mountains of northeast California, the talk centered on the gambling ahead. Kerr the overthinker broke down his blackjack strategies.

Once inside a Stateline casino, Kerr set up at an inexpensive table with Ehlo, Menzer, and Graeff while Mokeski headed for roulette. When Mokeski wandered back to report he was up $900, Ehlo didn't believe him and decided to see for himself. It was just Kerr and the two reporters when Kerr stopped the dealer in the process of taking his chips after a hand, pointing out he had twenty. "Yes," the dealer responded, "and I have twenty-one, and that's called blackjack."

Kerr erupted. "That's bullshit, man." He pushed back from the table and stormed off.

Chagrined, he soon cooled down to concede he had miscounted the dealer's cards, and got embarrassed when the error was pointed out in front of his friends. The kid pitcher who would spike his glove in frustration on the mound had refused to back down in competition at the cheap tables of Stateline, Nevada. Flustered and cornered by the truth, he bolted.

They spent a few hours in Stateline and absorbed only mild financial hits before the return trip with the beer from the trunk in use, until Menzer requested a stop on the freeway shoulder to relieve himself. Directing Ehlo to maneuver the car to aim the high beams at the reporter in midrelease on the side of the road at about 7,300 feet, as Menzer shivered through wind gusts that reached twenty-three miles per hour and temperatures that eventually dipped into the high twenties, the four in the toasty Lincoln busted up. They pulled back into the Hyatt parking lot at about 2:00 A.M.

It was like Kerr's second season was turning into one long personal joyride, albeit amid continued bad news in the standings. He was still getting big minutes when the Cavaliers went to Orlando on January 6 and Kerr started making early three-pointers, each punctuated by a solitary "Steeeeeve Kerrrrr!!!" from about twenty-five rows up at midcourt. Mike Elliott, his friend from the Tucson morning radio show and the creator of the popular Arizona rap video, had moved to Orlando and came out to say hello, much to Kerr's delight, after Kerr spotted him near the court at halftime. Kerr made five of six behind the arc that night. When the Cavaliers visited the Lakers at the Forum, about fifteen miles from Pacific Palisades, he played forty-three minutes, his most ever as a pro.

Kerr established himself, and created a much-needed confidence boost, by leading the league in three-point shooting at 50.7 percent, while averaging 21.3 minutes and playing seventy-eight games. All were valuable statements even on a wounded 42-40 team. Kerr's life solidified beyond basketball when he married Margot in Tucson in the offseason, with Olson among the attendees and Ann and Susie briefly in tears as they celebrated another family milestone without Malcolm. Proving she was an ideal match for Steve in sense of humor as well, Margot asked her new husband if they were crying because his father was not there or because he was marrying her.

Being miscast as a point guard continued to hurt him as 1990–1991 began, though, and the role where Kerr had the greatest impact, as a perimeter threat, remained a minor emphasis in the days before the three-pointer grew into a priority weapon. Even with another dependable showing at 45.2 percent, his role dropped from 21.3 minutes a game in his debut season as a Cavalier to 15.9. Completing the mood, the downgrade came as Cleveland finished 33-49 and in sixth place in the Central Division, the only time Kerr would play for a losing team in the NBA. Embry then investing both 1991 draft picks on guards became the latest bad sign.

Kerr did have a prominent role early in 1991–1992, and then again at the end before Cleveland advanced to the Eastern Conference finals against the Bulls. Michael Jordan's disgust for the Cavaliers had been boiling for years, ever since he went to the basket in the first quarter of a March 28, 1990, game in Richfield, was jarred by what he considered a cheap shot from John Williams, and came down hard on his tailbone, to the cheers of the home fans applauding the crash landing. "Boy," he was still saying years later, "that fucking burned me." Jordan snarled his way to sixty-nine points, eighteen rebounds, six assists, and four steals in fifty minutes of an overtime victory that night and was still in retaliation mode as the Eastern Conference finals opened May 19 in Chicago Stadium. That he had already inflicted considerable revenge by hitting a buzzer-beater to eliminate Cleveland in the first round of the 1989 playoffs was not enough retribution for Jordan and his boundless levels of competitive rage. Wanting more three years later to the month, he had thirty-three points, seven assists, and six rebounds in the opener and thirty-six points, nine assists, and six rebounds in Game 3, sandwiched around a bad outing when he missed fifteen of twenty-two shots while committing six turnovers. He was bound for another big scoring night in Game 4, eventually thirty-five points, when Ferry was ejected for throwing two punches at Jordan, a move the Bulls felt was designed to instigate a response from their star that might lead to a suspension. Jordan did not comply.

Instead, Ferry was fined $5,000 as the Bulls, seeking their own justice, painted a target on him for Game 5. Chicago had all but drawn retaliation on paper and made it part of the playbook, until backup power forward Stacey King finally saw Ferry break free from defender Will Perdue and head to the basket for an uncontested score in the fourth quarter of a contest heading toward an easy Bulls win. King could not remember who he was guarding and in the moment didn't care. *I'm getting this motherfucker,* he thought after spotting his victim in the open. The collision that followed with 1:02 remaining "was bush league," Kerr said, likely especially enraged because the intended was a good friend. "We expected them to retaliate for the Ferry-Jordan incident, but nothing like that."

King asserted the fake cover story that he went at Ferry to stop a layup, not for payback, and always insisted it was a lawful move to make a play on the ball, not a cheap shot, but payback was exactly what he and the Bulls had in mind. Planting a hard forearm to Ferry's head resulted in King being called for a flagrant foul, an ejection, and a spike of tension on the court that drove Kerr to approach King with a fury among the cluster of players from both teams. Giving up eight inches and fifty-five pounds, the Cavaliers guard who played all of three minutes that night and did not get into three of the eventual six games confronted King, his neck tilted up.

"You motherfucker!" Kerr screamed. "You cheap-shot motherfucker!"

"Get the fuck out of my face!" King fired back, before extending his left arm to clutch Kerr's neck. Four years after enduring the worst game of his life against Oklahoma and Stacey King, in new cities in a new league and with new postseason stakes, and certainly with the new perspective of being the farthest thing from a star guard and team leader, Kerr was in physical conflict with the same big man. King began to squeeze, until others pushed them apart and King was forced to release his quarry. Even on opposing sides in the scuffle at close quarters, though, King gained valuable future insight into Kerr as "the only one, really, seriously, the only one of the Cleveland Cavaliers that actually really wanted to defend his teammate. He showed some fight."

Easily the longest season of Kerr's career so far ended with a Chicago victory in Game 6 two nights later, a reminder how tenuous his future with the Cavaliers had become. Though he loved the idea of staying in Cleveland, there was an unmistakable message in his playing just 20 minutes in the series, about one-fourth of Terrell Brandon's time as the backup point guard, and averaging 12.4 minutes in the entire playoffs. The important accompanying development that would become key to his future—the Bulls advancing to face the Suns in the championship series, John Paxson taking a pass from Jordan to hit the shot that clinched the title after years of coach Phil Jackson urging Jordan to trust the mortals on the roster—did Kerr no good heading into the summer of '92.

When the next season started with Kerr barely playing, Embry began trade talks to reduce the backcourt logjam, but also with the hope of finding Kerr a new home that would offer a good chance at success. Embry made a point of it for one of his favorites, a player who had endeared himself to every level of the organization and had just become a father for the first time with the birth of Nicholas on November 9 in Cleveland. In a rare moment of sharing his thinking with someone beyond the Bulls' walls, secretive general manager Jerry Krause confided to a rival executive that he could see Kerr having success in Chicago as part of the unique triangle offense, but Krause stopped at actually scraping together spare change to acquire Cleveland's very available third-string point guard. Embry began to focus his attention on Orlando, reasoning that Kerr would have endless open looks on the perimeter playing with rookie Shaquille O'Neal.

Weeks passed from the first conversation between good friends Embry and Magic GM Pat Williams and completion of the deal on December 2, an inordinate amount of time for a minor transaction and a telling sign of how much the Magic searched for alternatives before resigning themselves to settling for Kerr. Strangely, considering the reputation that preceded him and would follow, shooting wasn't Kerr's primary appeal, not even with the added importance in Orlando of a perimeter game to keep defenses honest as O'Neal instantly became a commanding presence inside. Williams and Coach Matt Goukas were looking for depth at point guard behind Scott Skiles, and Embry did a convincing selling job on the dual benefits of Kerr as a quality guy who could handle that exact role. Embry was right about one part.

Kerr was plainly sweating his future seven months before free agency when Menzer, the *News-Herald* beat writer, called Kerr at his condominium in suburban Brecksville the night of the deal. "Man,

Joe," he said on the way out of town, "if I can just get one more contract, my family will be set and I can go on to whatever I'm going to do next." Menzer could hear the tension in his voice as Kerr talked through his realization that the end was coming mixed with the hope he could last another season, 1993–1994, to build the bank account for Margot and infant Nick. That Orlando presented a good opportunity in the moment—a chance to play right away, an ideal shooter's scenario of playing off the double teams O'Neal was receiving, college buddy Tolbert on the roster—offered little emotional comfort in the moment.

It took Williams about a week after Kerr arrived in Orlando to realize his mistake. Goukas was so taken aback by Kerr's poor play that he quickly dropped him from the rotation as Williams likewise watched his hope for a backup point guard get devoured with such ease and frequency that even he, the man who made the deal, could not build a case to give Kerr another chance. "This guy can't play, this guy can't play," Goukas was heard to tell his assistant coaches several times in disgust on the bench.

While Magic staffers noticed Kerr's frustration, especially when he was sent into the game only to soon be yanked back, he never spoke out against his coach. The smart, practical Kerr, aware that a bad season was problem enough months before free agency but that a bad season compounded by a bad attitude would be worse, won out over the feisty Kerr. He would sometimes show brief disapproval by throwing his hands in the air while dropping back on the bench after the latest quick hook, but he remained largely quiet as his role diminished. He showed up early to practice and stayed late anyway.

Kerr at least had the good fortune of getting into each game as the Magic played the Bulls three times in six weeks, even if the January 16 appearance was just two minutes and he took a combined two shots in the three outings. It was a reminder, if nothing else, to Phil Jackson and the Chicago front office that he was still in the league. And the chance to return to Cleveland around the same time provided the fun of seeing a janitor's closet labeled the

Steve Kerr Interview Room, a tweak courtesy of Cavs PR boss and friend Bob Price. "Yeah, you guys are real funny," Kerr said amid the smiles, his own included.

His real contribution came in a new role as a leader for the first time as a pro. He'd had little opportunity to lead on the veteran Cavaliers, and obviously none as a Suns rookie. In Orlando, twenty-seven-year-old Kerr, midway through his fifth season, was practically elderly on a roster that revolved around the twenty-year-old rookie O'Neal along with Dennis Scott, twenty-four, and Nick Anderson, twenty-five. "The things that he did, a lot of guys tried to do the same thing," Anderson said. "'Let me model myself after him.' It wasn't more him trying to show anybody anything. Look at how Steve Kerr carries himself on the court and off the court. A lot of guys, they just tried to model after him." Equipment manager Rodney Powell noted how, "even though he was young, they still looked up to him." Kerr at the same time connected with older teammates Skiles and Jeff Turner and continued his friendship with Tolbert.

Kerr and Tolbert were joined by personality and background, two Southern California products who landed in Tucson, entered the NBA the same season, and remained grounded while building a career. Perhaps because a boyish appearance allowed him to seem more mischievous than troublemaker, Kerr became an Olson favorite despite radio hijinks about the coach on heroin while Tolbert dearly tested Olson's patience. Tolbert didn't practice hard, and hid in a fountain when the staff wasn't looking to avoid doing the entire campus run with the Wildcats, before rejoining teammates as the group passed for another lap. In the reunion season with the Magic, he arrived in shorts and a T-shirt when Kerr got a Magic group on the course at high-end Sherwood Country Club during a Los Angeles stop. Tolbert had to visit the pro shop before being allowed to tee off. A similar wardrobe repair was required before a round at the conservative Country Club of Orlando.

Management decided long before the end of the season that Kerr had no future with the Magic, or likely with the entire league.

There wasn't even an internal conversation about a possible return in 1993–1994, let alone actual negotiations on a new deal once Kerr became a free agent on July 1. He was twenty-seven and sinking so fast that Orlando's minor investment in him still felt like an overpay.

Though he had no false illusions about his standing among the twenty-seven franchises, Kerr's psyche was under greater attack than at any time since his Arizona teammates had turned freshman Steve Kerr into chum in preseason pickup games. At least his first pro season had been in relatively familiar territory, Phoenix, and just being on the Suns had been a joy ride after the previous years of thinking he had no chance to make the NBA. Cleveland had brought him a decent role for three seasons, with the stability of being in the same place. Now, though, getting dumped by Orlando meant Kerr had a wife and young son and was staring at the prospect of joining a third team in ten months.

He was admittedly close to the end, his hopes of squeezing out one more contract appearing doomed. It was college recruiting all over again. Returning to Tucson for the off-season, Kerr appeared at Sean Elliott's fundraiser for Big Brothers Big Sisters and before a crowd that still considered him a local legend turned his plight into a punch line. I'm twenty-seven years old, he told the audience, and my career is over. "I'm done," one onlooker remembered him saying, and, "I don't know what I'm gonna do." While obviously his famous self-deprecating humor was in full bloom and this was not an official retirement announcement, people in attendance who knew him felt it was also Kerr accepting an unavoidable truth.

When his fears over the lack of interest in him around the league became real in July, Kerr considered calling Olson to see if Arizona would take him in once more, this time as an assistant coach. In typical Kerr fashion, he worked the problem through in advance to a logical conclusion. If this was the end of his playing career, he rationalized, Tucson was the ideal landing spot: he knew he fit into the program, he was beloved around town, and he could learn a new career from one of the best. The move would mark an instant shift from very little career certainty as a player to more security

than any beginning coach could dream of having. It made so much
sense.

That the ultimate planner started down this path in his mind
showed how serious he was about walking away from the NBA after five seasons. That he did not follow through and actually approach Olson was just as telling. Beyond the obvious point that his
decision showed how much he still loved being on the court, his
determination to stay in uniform when the feeling from NBA executives clearly was not mutual was an early public sign of a change in
Steve Kerr, a personality shift as he was about to turn twenty-eight
that would alter the rest of his life for the better.

Refusing to concede defeat was typical Kerr determination.
Brandishing that much confidence with little reason for optimism,
of course, was not. In the strangest of times to attempt to pick his
spot, he compiled a list of teams that needed a player who could
shoot, who had experience, who would play for cheap, and who
was willing to accept a bench role. Remaining self-assured as an
unwanted free agent required ignoring the reality of the deafening
silence from teams as July faded into August and August turned
into September in a replay of life as a Palisades senior, seemingly invisible as the basketball world whooshed past.

Including Chicago among the ideal landing spots was equal parts
sensible and ludicrous. The Bulls had just won fifty-seven games
and a third consecutive championship, finished with the second-
best three-point percentage in the league, and would return most
of the same roster for 1993–1994. They had veterans Michael Jordan, B. J. Armstrong, and John Paxson in the backcourt, and what
chance did Kerr have of cracking that rotation if he couldn't get
minutes for 41-41 Orlando? On the other hand, the depth chart
was just thin enough that a fourth guard couldn't hurt, especially
one with a low-risk contract. There was no such thing as too much
shooting to draw defenses away from Jordan and Scottie Pippen,
and Kerr's reputation for professionalism signaled that he would be
a solid citizen even with a small role. Plus, the Bulls in win-now
mode wanted established players able to make an immediate contri-

bution, not unproven prospects needing time to develop, and Kerr had the additional credibility of having made two playoff runs in Cleveland, seventeen games in all. As potential new teammate Stacey King could attest, Kerr would not back down once he got there.

He reasoned it out all the way to how his game was similar to Paxson's, evidence to Kerr that he was an obvious fit for Phil Jackson's triangle offense that relied heavily on perimeter scoring to space the offense and create openings for Jordan and Pippen. "He told me, 'If I can make that team, my career will be extended by a lot,'" Olson said. "'I'm not a point guard, never was, but if they can get me the ball, I'll hit shots and make a place for myself with a great team.' He had it all mapped out. He weighs things, and he always has." Plus, Kerr would be twenty-eight years old on opening night with a clean medical record, compared to Paxson who was thirty-three, heading into the final season of his contract, and coming off an injury-plagued 1992–1993 season. Not merely immediate insurance, Kerr could sell himself as the eventual replacement for the aging, hobbling backup.

His agent, Mark Bartelstein, called the Bulls to press the case, hoping to hear back from Krause at some point early in free agency to detail why the team with three consecutive titles and Michael Jordan needed the player who couldn't get on the court with a lottery team. Months passed without a response as Kerr had conversations with the Hawks, Pacers, Mavericks, and hometown Clippers, but no appealing offers. He glanced at Europe as an option, but did not want to leave the NBA and also remembered the insight from Cleveland teammate Ferry that his game deteriorated in the one season he spent in Italy.

"I never had any illusions about being a star in the league," Kerr said. "I just wanted to be in the league."

That Kerr did not realize Krause was already a fan was understandable. The point man on Bulls roster decisions had long been mocked for taking secrecy to the extreme of sitting in distant reaches of college arenas to avoid being spotted and having Chicago's draft plans decoded. Sleuth, he was derisively tagged, with a trench coat and everything else that went with the spy look. Krause shared little with anyone outside the organization, and sometimes not even within it, but he confided in an executive with another team on multiple occasions he thought Kerr fit on the Bulls. Why Krause did not make it happen as Cleveland shopped Kerr at a low price, and then ignored the approach from the Kerr camp early in free agency, was never clear.

Both got what they wanted when Kerr signed a one-year deal with the Bulls for the league minimum of $150,000 on September 29. Ironically, the player once told his career was over because of injury had sold himself as the healthy reserve guard. To Margot, her husband "with really nowhere to go" had "probably basically begged his way onto the Bulls." More pointedly, he had failed forward, going from months of being unwanted to ending up with his first choice. Kerr would be in what he considered the ideal system to revive his career and could safely assume playoff money would follow as an additional financial bump.

It had been such a wearying few months for Jordan—a torrent of questions about his gambling and his father's murder in July—that, from the Bulls' perspective, another relief option couldn't hurt. Jackson assured Kerr before the deal that he had a great chance to make the team, while Krause went as far as allowing that Kerr had a chance, minus the emphasis. "We have a non-guaranteed spot. Steve wanted a shot."

He was about to get one.

CHAPTER 7

OKP

Phil Jackson had sensed a problem months before as the pressure to be Michael Jordan drove the greatest player in the world toward early retirement. Not merely understanding his star's need to walk away in the fall of 1993 as the demands melded with the fresh trauma of James Jordan's murder, Jackson supported the decision, to his own obvious detriment. He floated the compromise that Jordan skip the regular season and return for the playoffs, a suggestion Jordan rejected, but Jackson mostly saw his role as encouraging Jordan to weigh the decision from every angle. That vein of discussion stretched all the way to Jackson, the son of Pentecostal preachers, asserting that quitting was wrong because it would deprive millions of the gift God had given Jordan. "For some reason," Jordan replied, "God is telling me to move on, and I must move on. People have to learn nothing lasts forever."

When Jordan made his departure official with an October 6 press conference at the Berto Center, the Bulls' training facility in suburban Deerfield, what the smoking crater in the middle of the locker room meant for roster filler Steve Kerr was not exactly a primary concern. He had signed a week earlier as an insurance policy that might never be needed, not a central part of the solution to a basketball disaster response. As days passed, though, and attention turned to plotting the next wobbly steps, an idea that would have been laughable on September 29 suddenly became all too real for a dazed organization staring into the unknown: the guy who had to hustle a minimum contract might have gone from luxury to necessity.

The seismic setback to the franchise could be celebrated, quietly, as Kerr's personal gain, even once the Bulls signed another guard, Pete Myers, the day after Jordan quit. Between Paxson's uncertain health, Jordan's exit, and Kerr's fit in the triangle, he was already closer to the Jackson analysis of having a great chance to make the team. "Boy, it's all about timing, isn't it?" he and center Bill Wennington, another free-agent arrival, agreed in conversation the first day of camp. The difference was that Kerr, unlike most everyone around him, benefited from Jordan's retirement.

Taking nothing for granted, not after months of being traded, dropped from the rotation, and pondering a career change, Kerr sweated out each shift in wind direction. "Steve would get the newspaper and look for Phil's comments," Margot said. "'Yeah, Steve Kerr had a good practice today.' He'd feel excited about that." Their Chicago existence was so tenuous that the couple and eleven-month-old Nick rented one room at the Residence Inn next to the Berto Center and regularly informed the front desk whether their stay would be extended another week. If the weather was bad or his wife needed the car, Steve and his equipment bag would commute by train from the same northern suburbs to downtown for home games, then hop into a cab for the short finish to Chicago Stadium.

Jackson remained so sure of another trip to the playoffs that he made a secret prediction before the start of what countless others figured, or hoped, would be painful retaliation for all the success that had come before. Forty-nine wins was a reasonable goal, Jackson jotted down, even if he wasn't confident enough to share the forecast. He believed that the team spirit built in recent years would carry the Bulls through the transition and that Chicago still had enough central figures from the title teams to remain dangerous. He liked the late addition of Myers, a reliable guard who could defend and pass, and regarded another new arrival, rookie forward Toni Kukoc, as an intriguing prospect who could shoot and handle the ball, albeit while questioning whether Kukoc was tough enough to go from European star to key contributor in the physical NBA. Kerr and Wennington were farther down Jackson's reasons to believe the Bulls would remain relevant.

That Tex Winter saw greater possibilities in Kerr's arrival mattered far beyond his title as assistant coach. Morice Fredrick Winter—born in panhandle Texas—was teammates with future Hall of Famers Bill Sharman and Alex Hannum at USC, played basketball against UCLA standout Jackie Robinson, appeared destined for the 1948 Helsinki Olympics in the pole vault before an injury, and became a head coach at twenty-eight. For decades, he was one of the most respected strategists of the college game. In the fall of 1993, he was best known as the innovator of the triangle offense that Jackson had already deployed through three championships, an approach that needed outside shooting and smart players able to make quick adjustments in midplay. In Kerr, Winter had the potential for both.

Winter had added credibility as a favorite of both Jackson and Krause, enviable for job security, but increasingly uncomfortable while stuck in the middle of the Jackson-Krause relationship turning toxic. Winter, Jackson said, is "the one person in the entire organization who can speak his piece." It was Krause who wanted Winter's innovative mind on the bench in Chicago in the first place, under Doug Collins, and it was Jackson who embraced Tex's presence when Jackson replaced Collins in 1989. As the Bulls took the first uneasy steps into the neck-high marsh of life after Michael Jordan, it was Winter who was among the first to be open to the possibility that Kerr could be a key part of the recovery.

Kerr's introduction to the only Bulls he knew firsthand was colored by the strangeness of Jordan occasionally showing up to watch practice, a tangible, lurking reminder of the void when no one needed reminding. As Chicago rebranded itself, Jackson appeared to take greater control. "I think it really sort of became Phil's team at that point," Kerr observed. "Even though I wasn't there before that, I'm sure Phil was dominant and his presence was felt before that, but it really became Phil's team after Michael retired because it had to be." Scottie Pippen, the new best player, wasn't going to step into that void. "He was everybody's favorite teammate, but one of the reasons for that was he was vulnerable," Kerr said. "And Phil was not vulnerable." That was an opportunity for the recent arrival as well. Kerr was never going to be a forceful voice with the Bulls, but growing into a leadership role, playing with a veteran group in Cleveland, and becoming a mentor while passing through Orlando showed he was comfortable as a locker-room presence.

Then came the real reminder of who was missing, in the home opener with the ring ceremony that included spectator Michael Jordan sitting courtside. He told the crowd he would always be a Bull and would support "my teammates" to the fullest, then watched a gruesome 95–71 loss to Miami. Some fans lasted only until midway through the third quarter before leaving. "What better way for the players to learn they could no longer count on Michael to bail them out than to lose by such historic proportions with the man himself sitting in the front row?" Jackson reasoned.

Kerr was not a consistent shooter the first month and did not score enough as the season progressed to help Jackson address the biggest strategic concern, replacing Jordan's offense, but Kerr at least quickly established himself as part of the rotation, an accomplishment after his Orlando flameout. It didn't take long for Krause to break into spin mode, to the surprise of no one acquainted with his insufferable need to be credited for even the smallest moves. Boasting about signing a fourth guard available to the world all off-season contradicted the reality that Krause had spent much of that time ignoring the free agent furiously waving his arms to get the Bulls' attention. Krause may have played with semantics to turn it into being interested in Kerr all along in his latest bit of mangled revisionist history.

Everyone around the Bulls recognized it as classic Krause and a reflection of his bottomless hunger to be appreciated. He was right, though, to believe he deserved greater praise for building most of the roster around Jordan. He had hired Jackson as an assistant and later head coach, drafted Pippen out of tiny Central Arkansas, and had added several important complementary parts through trades, the draft, and free agency. Part of the problem was that he was a public-relations disaster, mocked by players, ruthless to Jordan in particular for being five-eight and 260 pounds and too often wearing rumpled clothes with remnants of recent meals still attached. Jordan called him Crumbs, with humiliation in mind, not the cutting sense of humor typical in professional locker rooms, and led the team in mooing when Krause entered their sanctuary. Others hummed the "Green Acres" theme. To Kerr, it was "very uncomfortable." "Can you imagine James Worthy treating Jerry West this way?" Jud Buechler once told him.

Worse, Krause was viewed as the villain who wanted to show the world he could compose a championship roster without Jordan, and the sooner the better. He knew too well the cautionary tale of the Celtics of the Larry Bird years choosing loyalty over wins, hanging on to former superstars too long and paying for it with a lengthy rebuild. Krause's intentions were obvious to many even with Jordan still in the fold and titles flowing. He wanted marquee billing on a team with a player whose popularity was charted on a global scale. Krause wasn't even popular in his own locker room. It was an unwinnable game.

The 1993–1994 season, then, was his big chance. Although Kerr signed when Jordan was still part of the basketball constellation, Krause privately boasted of Kerr as an ideal fit for the Bulls, someone with high character and the intelligence to quickly pick up the complicated triangle offense, who could contribute at least one important skill (shooting) and handle pressure. Repeating one of his pet phrases, Krause would say that Kerr was OKP. Our Kinda People.

It was meant as high praise, even if Kerr hadn't been OKP enough to be signed in July or August or nearly all of September. Krause was mostly right too. Bouncy Kerr, with his breezy, genial personality, may have been the antithesis of Sleuth alienating the roster and cloaking the front office in secrecy, and Kerr would never be a suck-up genuflecting before the personnel boss, but Kerr had been a company man every stop of his career. He filled enough other requirements to be a proper Bull worthy of an acronym.

The longer the season went, the more secure Kerr's spot on the team became and the more Jackson's preseason prediction turned accurate. As Jordan signed to play minor league baseball for the Chicago White Sox, also owned by Jerry Reinsdorf, the Bulls and their veteran roster remained as relevant as the coach had expected. Even as they took an understandable giant step backward on offense, they remained one of the better defenses. The ominous beginning of the home opener gave way to so much forward progress that the Bulls reached forty-nine wins, Jackson's secret number, with almost three weeks to spare.

Chicago's eventual 55-27 finish was third-best in the Eastern Conference and just two fewer wins than the season before. Pippen, Armstrong, and Horace Grant were All-Stars while Pippen was also voted first-team All-NBA and first-team All-Defense. He had successfully moved, it seemed, out of MJ's shadow. Kerr's contribution was important as well: he played all eighty-two games with a career high in minutes, shots attempted, shots made, and points. He took such full advantage of the opportunity that would not have come with Jordan in uniform that the numbers in these four categories would hold up as the best of his fifteen seasons. And the playoff money did come as the Bulls reached the East semifinals before losing to the Knicks, a series that included Pippen refusing to take the court for the final 1.8 seconds of Game 3 to protest Jackson calling the last play for Kukoc.

Even with that unforgivable moment, which would scar the rest of Pippen's career, 1993–1994 and their response to adversity had been a startling success for the Bulls—and for their new key reserve. Kerr had gone from unwanted to major factor within two months and just as quickly built a relationship with Jackson that would become important to both. "Steve and Phil had, I think, a special bond where they really understood each other," Wennington said. "Steve being a cerebral player and Phil being very cerebral himself, they had that intellectual connection that worked well for them."

"This is a thinking man," trainer Chip Schaefer said of Kerr, "in an industry where there aren't a lot of those around. I think that's always made him kind of rare. There's so much more to him. I think that people that are well rounded . . . there's just so much more to them than athletics. A passion for basketball, without question, which Phil has and Steve has. But sometimes you've got to step away from it and have other interests, music and art and literature and all these other things, and I think that's where they really connected as well-rounded intellectual people."

In production and relationships, Kerr's first Chicago campaign vindicated his vision the previous summer that the Jackson system would be an ideal showcase, all the way to Paxson retiring in the 1994 off-season, just as Kerr had plotted while installing himself as the successor. The unusual surge of confidence in pushing forward rather than retiring or heading to Europe a defeated man would prove to be a turning point in his life. Kerr, of all people, came to represent franchise stability after one season as the Bulls feuded mightily, even with Krause spared the biting Jordan commentary on appearance and appetite. Paxson and Jordan were gone, Krause failed in his attempt to trade Pippen for draft picks Krause coveted for the rebuild, and a new front opened as Jackson turned insubordinate against his boss. The coach was so unconcerned about his contempt becoming public that he unloaded in an interview with writer Roland Lazenby for an article to be published around the start of training camp. When Lazenby showed Jackson the story about to be filed, to make sure Jackson grasped the severity of his comments, Jackson made one change. Where Lazenby had written that Krause weighed 260 pounds, Jackson crossed out that number and substituted 280.

When Jordan returned to the court for Pippen's charity game at Chicago Stadium in September in a final run before the team moved across the street and their old home was demolished, the off-season turned from difficult to cruel, as locals were teased by the vision of Jordan on hardwood again. The night came complete with Jordan bending down on all fours to kiss the floor in personal farewell, before he doused comeback speculation in postgame comments that he would never play organized basketball again. His uniform number 23 was retired in "A Salute to Michael" event on

September 1, with plans for a bronze statue to be erected outside the United Center. Krause got booed so badly by the crowd on what was supposed to be an upbeat night of celebrating a great career that his wife broke out in tears.

Jackson wasn't convinced it was the end. The same instincts that suggested to him in the summer of 1993 that Jordan might walk away from the NBA, months before it happened, led Jackson in the fall of 1994 to sense hints of an equally dramatic comeback. Then, while the baseball strike did not directly impact Jordan and his fellow minor leaguers, the biggest name became worried he would be used as a draw when spring training began in Arizona and, worse, that he would get a chance to make the majors only as a replacement player if the work stoppage dragged into late April. Refusing to consider that, he announced his retirement from baseball on March 10, 1995.

A potential Jordan basketball return had been a topic of conversation for weeks within the Bulls as rumors flew and players acquired since his retirement grew openly excited at the possibility of their new teammate. They were "like kids almost in how they felt about it," Schaefer said of a dinner with Kerr, Luc Longley, and Larry Krystkowiak as speculation became constant. "I remember sitting there and listening to those guys and thinking, *Boy, you have no idea how hard it is playing with him.*"

They knew of the demon competitor from afar, of course, but even opponents didn't have the full view, nor did any Bull who played only during the retirement seasons. "He came to practice some, occasionally, but he was really unapproachable for those of us who didn't play with him, just because of who he was and his presence," Kerr said. "He's kind of an intimidating guy, as you know, especially if you don't know him. You just don't wander over to Michael Jordan and say, 'Hey, what's up?' He was like this looming presence. None of us knew him very well." Working alongside Jordan had to be experienced to be understood.

To Jordan through the years, Longley lacked a killer instinct and

Will Perdue was "Will Vanderbilt," because he wasn't good enough to have the surname of a Big Ten school, by any spelling. Jordan called Horace Grant "Dummy," sometimes to his face, and once screamed at him, "You're an idiot. You've screwed up every play we ever ran. You're too stupid to even remember the plays. We ought to get rid of you." (Jordan wasn't alone in his harsh criticism. Jackson considered Grant's psyche so fragile that he was "actually afraid of people" on the court and once started to cry during an argument with the coach.) Dennis Hopson and Steve Colter both wilted so badly under Jordan's unrelenting expectations in practice that they had to be traded, broken spirits in tow. Kukoc, Jordan said, loved the fame, "but he doesn't like to work." So great was his frustration with Kukoc's untapped potential, unlike the anger he felt toward others for lack of dependability, that exasperation "makes me just want to choke the shit out of Toni and say, 'Man, you have a hell of an opportunity; just take it.'" Even Scottie Pippen came under fire to a degree. As much as Jordan appreciated his running mate, he also said Pippen was "lost" in the lead role during the retirement and that "he wants someone beside him. He's like a little brother."

Jordan would later get on Kerr for missing a shot or lack of aggressiveness, just as teammates in previous stops had encouraged him to be more assertive in looking to score, but nothing like the savage personal attacks unleashed on other Bulls. He had no serious issues with Kerr, the player who didn't have nearly the skill set of Kukoc or many around the league but who also focused daily on wringing out every drop of ability. "Kerr has heart," Jordan came to say. "He gets the maximum out of what he has." Ever the diplomat, or the realist who understood Jordan was right even if he wasn't, Kerr flipped the Jordan method of verbal beatings into the public assessment that Jordan tearing through teammates "may be a good thing," because "he forces us to fight and be competitive, to fight through those weaknesses and not accept them, to work on them, and to improve ourselves." Never mind that Grant had been good enough to start for Bulls title teams in 1991, '92, and '93, or that it would be impossible to imagine Kerr as a general manager or a coach, allowing anything close to the same divisive running commentary, let alone spinning it into a positive.

The worst venom was saved, of course, for Krause. Their relationship had been bad since the general manager mandated Jordan rest an injured foot in 1985–1986, telling him, as Jordan remembered it, "You're Bulls property now, and we tell you what to do." Jordan never forgot hearing himself called "property," or the feeling of being talked down to rather than supported in a frustrating second season, even when Krause built a championship roster around him. The tension between them became more palpable when Chicago traded Jordan favorite Charles Oakley to New York two years later for Bill Cartwright, then surged again when Jordan saw Cartwright as limited by deteriorating skills, followed by prime Jordan target Horace Grant taking Oakley's job at power forward. Krause not only stood by the Oakley-Cartwright deal, he called it one of his favorite trades ever.

In the second week of March 1994, though, there was only silence amid frenzied speculation about Jordan rejoining the Bulls. With stock in companies he had endorsement deals with jumping a collective $2 billion within days, Jackson finally had to tell Jordan not to attend practice on March 16—the media stakeout around the Berto Center, just in case Jordan suddenly appeared in uniform, had gotten too unwieldy. It was the same thing the next night at home against the Bucks. Finally, after turning down different versions of potential press releases, Jordan took a piece of paper and wrote his own very succinct unretirement announcement in front of agent David Falk on March 18, to be typed on Falk Associates Management Enterprises letterhead and faxed by the director of media services in FAME's Washington office: "I'm back."

Kerr at last would get the chance he had expected when he signed in the fall of 1993—to play with Jordan and, more important, to play off Jordan. The Kerr vision all along, the reason the player essentially unwanted by the entire league had aimed impossibly high to decide he could contribute to the best team, was that Kerr-Jordan would be a mutually beneficial relationship. As any realist would have known, and Kerr had surely always been that, the arrival of the new shooting guard would cost him minutes, but with the continued belief he could make jump shots that would force defenses to guard him on the perimeter and give Jordan and Pippen more space to operate. The presence of Jordan and Pippen, in return, would guarantee Kerr more open looks than he'd have with any other team. In a perfect bit of timing, he'd gotten the season and a half without Jordan to prove his value to Jackson, a large opportunity that might not have come without Jordan's retirement, and then got the ideal role he had originally imagined as a Jordan complement.

While thrilled with the new addition, Kerr was also quickly taken aback at the new reality of daily life around a walking force of nature who would eat his own. Jordan asserted himself with a fierceness that shocked the same Kerr who had traveled dangerous lands, played against adults as a teenager on a dirt court, yelled at peers to get off the bus to visit a tourist attraction in Spain, and tried to brawl with Stacey King despite giving away eight inches and fifty-five pounds. "We had no idea," Kerr recalled decades later. "He was so intense . . . and condescending in many ways. None of us felt comfortable. On a daily basis, he would dominate practice, not physically, but emotionally and in an intimidating fashion. He was going to make us compete, whether we wanted to or not, you know." It was exactly as Schaefer had predicted at dinner weeks before. On days players were tired, Kerr said, Jordan "would ridicule us and cajole us and . . . you know, just yell at us. It was tough. It was hard to deal with."

That Jordan demanded the same of himself, especially in the early weeks of the comeback, helped Kerr understand Jordan's motivation as pure: he was there to win, period, and anyone who got in the way did so at their own peril. It would have been adjustment enough for anyone living it for the first time. Kerr, though, had an added acclimation of previously only knowing sunshine, from high school camaraderie to rah-rah Arizona to the NBA of the encouraging Suns, the supportive Cavaliers, the youthful energy of the

Magic, and finally the previous Bulls with Jackson as the dominant personality. All his earlier stops had been nurturing. Michael Jordan didn't do nurturing.

The comeback that began in earnest on March 19 in Indianapolis, with the Bulls at 34-31, challenged Jordan physically, with the awareness that returning to greatness required relying on different muscle memory from what he'd built for baseball. Still trying to reach peak game condition about a week later, he stayed after practice in Deerfield to run extra sprints with no prompting from anyone, an uncommon move for an NBA player so late in the season but necessary for Michael Jordan as he stared himself down in the same way he challenged all those around him. Some teammates were shooting, some were warming down with stretches, as he chugged through one set along a sideline and then another, starting and finishing at the end where Kerr and Buechler were working on free throws. Unprompted and without comment, they set down the balls and joined Jordan on the baseline before the next dash. The other Bulls still around followed their lead and ran as well.

The playoffs opened a month later with the Bulls at 47-35 and Kerr as a key piece after playing all eighty-two games again and leading the league in three-point percentage a second time. Most significantly, he remained a trusted Jackson regular even after Jordan stepped back into his previous large role. When a 3–1 victory over Charlotte in the opening round was followed by a split of the first two road games against the Magic, and with Jordan scoring thirty-eight points in Game 2, Chicago had reason to feel encouraged that everything around their hero, not just his playing time, was reverting to the dynasty days. Even the sight of him on the ground in Game 1, desperately reaching in a losing battle to recover the ball that had been poked away in a crucial moment, could have become a mostly forgotten footnote with a strong finish to the series. Instead, the Bulls were shoved into the off-season with three losses in the next four games and the image became permanent.

Jordan went into the summer embarrassed, a development that would become especially relevant to Kerr in multiple ways, even if neither he nor Jordan could have realized it as their strange 1994–1995 ended. Kerr, as the Chicago representative in the players' union, turned his attention to the labor dispute that led to the first lockout in NBA history after Houston beat Orlando in the Finals. He was a dream appointee, embracing the role most every peer in the league would try to avoid in a union drowned by apathy and an ideal communicator to keep teammates updated and deliver the union perspective to the press if necessary. "Since you have Michael Jordan on the team, that attracts a lot of media and so consequently the issues became a little bit more prominent in Chicago," union head Charles Grantham said. "If there was anything going on between management and labor, they were constantly talking to that team about it. Steve did an excellent job of managing that." Jordan emerging as an opponent was tougher to handle.

Jordan, as part of a small group of superstars, was pushing for an agreement with owners that would remove the cap on maximum salaries. Most players in the league, including Kerr, the epitome of the NBA middle-class, argued for an outcome that would benefit the majority but cost the Jordan faction. When the dispute was settled in September, in time for a full schedule, the cap remained.

The response when the Bulls reconvened for training camp was Jordan churning in a competitive rage that surpassed even his usual demonic approach, as if he had spent the entire summer since the Orlando series pacing and swearing revenge. Jordan was thirty-two, had gone the eternity of two and a half years without a title, had fumbled away a game against the Magic in a rare embarrassment, was mostly surrounded by teammates who hadn't earned his trust, and cared little that his lack of respect for Krause was common knowledge. Jordan in the twilight, entering his eleventh basketball season, knew he was running out of time.

Never one for patience anyway, Jordan's sense of urgency was particularly obvious while consumed by an internal brushfire during early workouts in Deerfield. "I got a glimpse of it right away," Kerr said. "Camp was insane, how competitive and intense it was. Michael was coming off the comeback when he hadn't played that well in the playoffs, at least as far as his standards were concerned. He was out to prove a point and get his game back in order. So every practice was like a war." From Jordan's perspective, "a lot of these guys have come from programs who have never experienced the stages of being a champion. I'm just speeding up the process." His tough love so dominated the first days of 1995–1996 that even Dennis Rodman, arriving with his hair dyed red and black to match the team colors, quickly faded into the background.

Kerr was especially exposed to the wrath of Jordan, perhaps more than any Bull. Although entering his third season in Chicago, appreciated by the coaching staff, accepted by the front office, an initiated OKP and everything, he was still new to Jordan after just twenty-seven games together. It didn't matter what he had shown everyone else—Kerr had to acquit himself before the toughest judge of all. Not only that, he had to do it amid Jordan's lingering irritation from the lockout. On top of everything, Kerr and Jordan usually played the same position, shooting guard. They were face-to-face in practice, combatants more than teammates given Jordan's fury.

The turbulence of emotions was already routine by the third day of camp as Jackson went from the court to his office for the annual conference call with reporters around the country to preview the season, a mandatory commitment for all head coaches. The scrimmage continued with starters versus reserves, the first unit getting away with physical play and Jordan hammering away with uncalled fouls and trash talk. Kerr was fed up. "Phil's absence definitely led to a situation where it was a little out of control," he would recall.

Jordan mouthed off, and Kerr, no MJ in savaging opponents with words but also well acquainted with inner rage, fired back. Kerr got the ball, was fouled again by Jordan, and used his off arm to throw an elbow at the defender. Jordan locked in on his prey. A play later, Kerr cut through the lane and was met by a forearm shiver. He responded in kind. Jordan instantly went after him with such ferocity that another reserve, Buechler, compared it to a velociraptor attack in *Jurassic Park*.

"I had no chance," Kerr said. "It was just mayhem. We were screaming at each other, and our teammates, thank God, they all ran in and pulled us apart. But I ended up with a black eye. Apparently, I got punched. I don't even remember getting hit."

Jordan stormed out of practice and left the building. Jackson returned in time to speak with Kerr, urging him to do his part to mend the conflict, as if Kerr wanted a long-running battle with anyone in the organization and would risk ruining a dream role on a winning team. (Not to mention it was impossible to imagine the sunshine personality seriously feuding with anyone.) Either way, he was smart enough to know what making a permanent enemy of Michael Jordan meant for career longevity in Chicago.

The uncertainty of what would happen next became moot as soon as the victim returned home to an apologetic message from Jordan on his answering machine. King, among others, was "very shocked" at Jordan's contrition because "I've seen Michael punch guys before and never apologize." The difference this time was that "Steve fought back and other guys didn't fight back," King said. "You ask guys. 'Well, I was scared I would get traded.' You're getting your manhood tested. Steve got his manhood tested and it was like, 'Hey, this shit ain't happening, bro. I don't care if you beat me 100 times. I'm coming back 101 times.' That's how Steve is and that's why he got Michael's respect, because Michael saw in him that he had some dog in him."

Actually, Kerr was very worried about getting traded or cut. When another Bull called Sam Smith of the *Chicago Tribune* to relay the developments that took place out of sight of the media, apparently hoping word would get out and more people would finally realize Jordan was a bully who created conflict with many teammates, Smith phoned Kerr at home. Kerr confirmed the details and walked Smith through what happened, then made the unusual request of asking one of the most respected reporters in the league to not report the news of Michael Jordan giving a teammate a black eye. Look, Kerr told him, I'm just barely hanging on trying to make this team, and I obviously have got to deal with this guy.

Kerr had no way to know he was overreacting and that, if any-thing, as would soon become clear, the brawl turned Jordan into an admirer. But his worry was understandable in the moment. Kerr had no standing with the Bulls to survive a power play with any-one, let alone Michael Jordan and his fist. Either way, Smith agreed to the request, a decision he would never regret. He liked Kerr and they had become friendly, for one thing, and Smith felt a personal obligation not to harm his career.

When reporters saw the evidence on his face the next day, Kerr brushed it off with various versions of "Things happen" or that he caught an accidental elbow. The truth was that "everything was still a little uncomfortable" for him, complete with a shiner as a re-minder. Smith eventually layered the real account into big-picture stories about Jordan meshing with new teammates going through their first training camp together, and the confrontation that might have been months in the making ended faster than it had devel-oped. But while Kerr would spend decades joking about losing the only fistfight of his life quickly and badly, the actual impact was life-alteringly serious and remained an important development, even a turning point, long after the color around his right eye faded: he had earned Jordan's trust, an accomplishment that could not be over-stated.

In the history of surreal Steve Kerr days, it would be hard to top the serpentine hours of flicking matches around a flammable Michael Jordan, getting punched in the face, receiving an apology from a cruel competitor who apologized to no one, and ultimately gaining entry past the velvet rope and into the Jordan realm. Kerr naturally would eventually go out of his way to tweak himself for getting mauled—"By the way, I kicked MJ's ass," he quipped twenty-three years later in an aside to a conversation without anyone bring-ing it up. In the 1995–1996 season, though, Jordan said the pouncing "helped us tremendously," and Jackson likewise came to see it as a bonding moment, "a turning point for the team." Part was that Jor-dan could now feel better about at least some of his supporting cast in coming to see "Kerr has heart" and "he gets the maximum out of what he has," and part was that Jordan admitted regret and showed a maturity that had not always existed.

Just as the knee injury in the 1986 world championships that threatened to end his career in college became good news, getting pummeled by Michael Jordan would turn out to be one of the best things to ever happen to Steve Kerr. He couldn't keep up in skill or athleticism, and had bounced from team to team, while Jordan reigned as the face of the entire league, but standing up to the schoolyard bully whose mere presence intimidated others put Kerr on Jordan's level in willingness to sacrifice everything to win. That the statement came in practice, Jordan's private gladiator arena, may have meant even more, because the showdown could not have happened in a game. Kerr proved he was fearless, and Michael Jordan prized fearless.

When the maniacal level of intensity carried into the regular season, against actual opponents, and with Jordan's game sharpened by a summer and training camp to prepare, the Bulls reasserted their place in the league. Kerr slumped early, but the Bulls were so overwhelming—three winning streaks of at least five games in the first twenty contests, a 23-2 mark by Christmas, a 14-0 January—that the usual speculation of great possibilities quickly became whether they could break the record of sixty-nine wins in a season set by the Lakers of 1971–1972. For all the competition opponents were providing, Chicago might as well chase ghosts. "Best team I've ever seen," said Laker Magic Johnson, two games into his own comeback after retiring in 1991. "They're as good as our championship teams were. They're better than their three title teams. They're scary, man."

Jordan, asked about living in an otherworldly zone, said, "It's like every move, every step, every decision you make, it's the right decision." The Bulls so dominated the opening three months, in fact, that Jackson grew worried. Concerned they might be peaking too soon and that it would be impossible to maintain the tidal wave of energy through a playoff run as well, he considered holding key players out of games to purposely knock his team out of rhythm.

Jackson got unwanted assists when Pippen missed five games because of knee tendinitis and Rodman was suspended six games for
head-butting a referee, but that did little to halt the speeding train
that was dragged all the way down to a 12-2 March. "So many guys
have never been in this position before," Jordan said of the new
supporting cast that hadn't been around for his pre-retirement title
run. "That's what makes me feel good. Steve Kerr, Randy Brown,
Luc, Jud. It's great for them."

Jordan's favorite among the newcomers didn't find his offensive
rhythm until early December, about a month into the season and
a couple weeks after his search for answers prompted Kerr to get
strategically drunk on the team flight from Chicago to Orlando.
He plotted out his drinking, cutting loose and inviting the kind of
severe hangover the next day that would make it too painful to continue to overthink and press on his shot. Running around a resort
golf course in the dark and being held over a sprinkler by Wennington and Longley was not in the Arizona version, nor was Jackson
telling the players they were idiots. Once Kerr started to build momentum, though, the recovery from the slow start took him all the
way to second in the league in three-point percentage at 51.5 percent, while the Bulls set the record with seventy-two wins.

It wasn't until the playoffs, Jordan said, that he became aware
of their tragic connection, two and a half years after Kerr arrived
in town and fourteen months after they became teammates, even
though Jordan considered himself a hoops junkie and the Kerr back-
story had been retold several times in the local media and national
press. Jordan appeared stunned when *Chicago Sun-Times* columnist
Rick Telander noted that Kerr's father had also been killed by a
pistol, just as gunfire cost another Bull, Pete Myers, his father in
1978 and former Jordan teammate Scott Williams lost his parents
in a murder-suicide shooting. "I never knew," Jordan said of Kerr.
"I knew of his closeness to his mother, but I didn't know what happened to his father. He never said anything, and I never asked."

On an off day during the second round against the Knicks, Jordan
turned contemplative on the spot. "I'd be pretty sure he does feel

the same things I do," he said. "Not having a father figure around to help you with family decisions—now you just have to live off what you attained before it happened. The difference is I had my father until I was 32. I was a grown man and had determined my path. He, I guess, was what, still in high school? and had to do a lot of growing up. I think about my dad. Sometimes before a game, I'll think 'Should I be aggressive at the start or passive?' He always said, 'Show leadership. Be aggressive.'"

There is no indication that either of them brought it up in the ensuing decades and indeed, while Jordan's rarified level of respect since the practice fight was well known and Kerr spoke of MJ in reverential terms, the two were more business associates than buddies. Beyond team activities—games, practices, travel—they lived in separate universes. Kerr hoofed it to home games via public transportation while Jordan often big-shot his way into the city by cruising the shoulder of the Kennedy Expressway to beat rush-hour traffic, usually with basketballs or Bulls tickets tucked away in case he got stopped. Jordan hadn't flown commercial in about seven years. He lamented being a prisoner of fame who could not stroll Lake Shore Drive without risking a mob scene.

Jordan and Kerr had both dreamed of going to UCLA, but were snubbed in recruiting and not so much as invited for a campus visit, even though Jordan was a major prospect coming out of Wilmington, North Carolina. (The two could have been college teammates in Los Angeles, along with Reggie Miller, for at least one year, depending on whether Jordan kept to his North Carolina timeline of entering the draft after his junior season.) Beyond that, one worked to be a dependable contributor and the other couldn't walk down a Chicago boulevard without hell breaking loose. As Kerr was among the first to say, business associate was as close as most Bulls were going to get to Jordan.

That was true even as Kerr observed his teammate mellow during the season, once order had been restored to the Jordan universe and no one dared doubt him, and as Jordan spoke of wanting to bring Kerr, Brown, Longley, and Buechler into the championship fraternity. Pushing with his usual ferocity on the court, Jordan led Chicago to easy playoff wins against Miami and New York before the ultimate redemption of dominating Orlando with a meaningful contribution from Kerr. He was in the finals for the first time, against Seattle.

SuperSonics coach George Karl had already hired Brendan Malone, the Detroit assistant during the Pistons' demolition-derby days against Jordan, to scout Chicago in the playoffs. Working every angle, Karl, like Jordan a North Carolina product, brought the lady who cooked for Tar Heel basketball players for thirty years to Seattle for Game 4. Jordan appeared rattled when he saw her siding with the enemy, exactly the payoff Karl wanted, followed by Jordan missing thirteen of nineteen shots and the Bulls losing by twenty-one. The Sonics also won Game 5, before Kerr became a champion for the first time with the Game 6 victory on June 16—Father's Day. "So that made it especially poignant, I'm sure for Michael and I know for me," he said. "Father's Day is still a little bit tough for me every year. Michael's dad had been by his side for every other great moment in his basketball career, so I have no doubt that's what he was feeling that night—his absence. I can certainly relate to that feeling."

Jordan had the release of falling to the United Center hardwood and clutching the ball close to his chest while an arena full of celebrants watched. Inside the locker room a few minutes later, as many of his teammates partied on the court, a television camera captured him face down on the carpet and sobbing. The camera captured no such scene for Kerr, who, forever willing to put his sentiments on display, looked joyful standing on the scorer's table with other Bulls as "Sweet Home Chicago" fired from the loudspeakers. Nick joined him for the father-son moment that was seen.

Kerr vowed soon after reaching the locker room to always remember 1996 as a special Father's Day, as if it was possible to forget clinching a championship on any date. But he offered no indication of matching Jordan's conflicted emotions: elation at the title countered by the sorrow of missing the man who would have been just as delighted. Margot, among the wives nearby, had a cigar in one hand and her clothes drenched in champagne.

Jordan had blended himself into the perfect combination of lethal talent and embracing teammates that Jackson had wished through years of prodding, an evolution apparent through Kerr most of all. Jordan "is such a fierce competitor that he brings everybody beyond their individual levels," Jack Ramsay, a Hall of Fame coach working as an ESPN analyst, observed during the postseason. "I watched Steve Kerr, who had the reputation of being a no-defense guy, a good spot-up shooter. Now you watch him, he's out there playing defense, challenging everybody that he plays, he's right in their face. He may get beaten, but he's not going to back down from the chore. He now puts the ball on the floor and creates his own shot. That's something he never did before. Michael's influence on all those players is tremendous."

Kerr was so understatedly valuable the first full season with Jordan that Winter, the triangle architect, came to regard the simple act of sending Kerr into the game as a weapon. Kerr didn't even have to make a shot, Winter would say. Just having him on the court was enough to inject a new layer of fear into defenses already dealing with Jordan and Pippen. The role player was making life easier for future Hall of Famers, not just the other way around, a stunning compliment that would remain among the highest praise of Kerr's career.

CHAPTER 8

"I'll Be Ready"

Steve Kerr smelled of the worst of Atlantic City, an unforgettable, awful reek as he spilled off the rented tour bus and into the lobby of the stately Four Seasons in Philadelphia at 9:30 A.M. His body aching from the ravages of alcohol was proof that the all-nighter with Buechler, Rodman, and several Rodman acquaintances, some voluptuous, had been a success. Most important, the 120-mile round trip to coastal New Jersey seemed to achieve the goal of helping Rodman reconnect with the team after his third suspension of 1996–1997.

Jackson had not only watched the party on wheels pull up just before he saw Kerr and Buechler in the hotel's lobby restaurant, the coach had signed off on it in advance. The two players approached him and laid out a plan to nurse Rodman's spirits. Jackson agreed and even encouraged second-year forward Jason Caffey to tag along. "Dennis had sort of been away from us, in a spiritual sense, and Phil felt we needed to bring him back in, which in Dennis's case means going out and getting hammered," Kerr said. He also couldn't help but wonder, "How many other NBA coaches would tell one of their young players to go out and get shitfaced with Dennis Rodman?" Jackson's only regret was the worthless practice after the return, so bad that he called it off after forty minutes, followed by a loss to the 18-44 Nets the next night.

Kerr's first season as a champion was frequently devoted to the emotional rescue of others, and especially the teammates with the biggest names. Gluttony runs with Rodman were uncommon, just

as most Bulls rarely visited his alternate universe and saw his cos-
tumed antics as a shy and socially awkward lost soul overcompen-
sating to a sometimes alarming level. Kerr, like Jordan and Jackson,
didn't even attend Rodman's postgame birthday party late the
previous season at a Chicago club, where the NBA crowd mixed
with rockers and the guest of honor in a guarded upstairs lounge
and Eddie Vedder of Pearl Jam led the house in singing "Happy
Birthday." But having long understood the value of locker-room
chemistry, and appreciating adult beverages and the occasional casino trip, he and Buechler suggested the Atlantic City errand in the
name of team bonding.

The more conventional approach was aiding Jordan and Pippen
by constantly, for years, going out of his way to be accessible to the
media, whether staying after practice to stand before the TV cameras or circulating in the locker room to speak with writers needing
a pregame interview to make an early deadline. Kerr and Wennington, most notably, became the Bulls who took questions so that famous others could avoid another bank of lights and recorders. Being
an unlimited source of lengthy answers, keen insights, and snarky
commentary the "Riptide" columnist would have appreciated was
Kerr giving Jordan and Pippen one less thing to sweat.

It had always been a comfortable role—the college freshman
who resolutely stayed in the Arizona locker room and took postgame questions about the murder of his father days before, the
Cleveland newcomer who almost immediately volunteered to handle any interview requests, and the Orlando temp who exchanged
ideas with the front office on media procedures. The dynasty Bulls
were different-level press madness, yet Kerr remained helpful even
after becoming an established contributor and champion. K. C.
Johnson of the *Chicago Tribune* finally informed Kerr he should get a
co-byline after regularly contributing insights, or at least a portion
of Johnson's salary.

"Steve understood everything," said writer Roland Lazenby, a
frequent presence as the author of books and magazine articles on
the Bulls. "He cared on a different level, but he also just could lay

back and find amusement in things. His sense of humor was a huge part of it. But he was never snide. Not an iota. He had a way of illuminating things. He was sort of like a surgeon in that regard. It was just instinct. He knew how to help reporters and people who were smart enough to talk to them, he knew how to help illuminate without really violating a lot of the fundamental trust. It was never about him. If there's a guy in the NBA who's more self-deprecating, I'd like to know who it is. He just had that way."

By 1996–1997, with interest in the Bulls stronger than ever, the intangible contributions from Kerr and Wennington became both real and humorous. Equipment manager John Ligmanowski had taken to turning in their direction anytime the light of a TV camera flicked on, crossing his arms across his chest, placing his fingers at his shoulders, and quickly flapping his hands, jabbing them for being moths forever ready to fly toward brightness. It was no surprise that Wennington and Kerr had become friends: they had similar personalities, were both smart and mature, and both had the experience of living abroad, immersed in the game but aware of a real world beyond the court. They had even joined the Bulls as free agents the same September day in 1993. The reserve guard and the reserve center joked to themselves about their unplanned role with the media and teased each other about being the last players at practice some days because, Wennington said, "no one else would talk."

Wennington finally made it official with a visit to a Chicago shop to purchase a trophy, two feet tall, to be presented to the other at any time, even during an interview, in an attempt to mock the recipient. He had it engraved: MOTH OF THE YEAR. The award moved back and forth for two campaigns, changing ownership every couple weeks or so in acknowledgment of a particularly notable dash to the light, a continuous inside joke of so many exchanges they lost count and later lost track of the trophy itself. Sometimes the hardware would be handed off, other times the new winner would find it placed in his locker without comment.

Kerr continued to likewise distinguish himself on the court, a contribution more important than ever as Harper returned from off-season knee surgery and Jackson worried about the toll of Pippen playing in the 1996 Atlanta Olympics. Plus, Jordan would turn thirty-four just after midseason. Jackson's need to prioritize rest for the stars guaranteed continued opportunities for thirty-one-year-old Kerr, an opening he again capitalized on by remaining a dependable shooter who played all eighty-two games for the fourth time in as many years in Chicago. There was even the trinket of winning the three-point contest during All-Star weekend in a particularly enjoyable return to Cleveland.

Wennington remembered it "being a little bit of a rebellious period for him, where he was just going out and relaxing a little bit more, which was uncharacteristic of him. Very. I don't remember it lasting more than a whole year. It wasn't even a whole year. But it was a happy year. He was doing good. He kind of came out and understood that's the way it was." At other times in his career, pushing himself to play without self-imposed stress, just as Mokeski had urged in Cleveland practices to let it fly, Kerr wrote "F.I." on his game shoes to remind himself to just "Fuck It." Going for the Kerr version of completely cutting loose, he grew a goatee, only to look back years later on the facial hair as practically the unhinged act of a maniac. "It sounds crazy. But I grew a goatee."

"He was—I don't want to say tightly wound, but really intense and was really hard on himself," Wennington said. "He was his own worst enemy when he was out there. He loosened up a little bit. I think Phil got on him a couple times about doing things, not taking open shots and doing things. That bothered [Jackson]. But I think [Kerr] came to that point where he said, 'Hey, you know what? Hey, I've just got to go out and do it. It doesn't matter.'"

He headed into the first postseason as a defending champion especially dependable at 53.3 percent from the field, the best of his nine years and a mark that would hold up as a career high, along with second-best in the league in three-point accuracy. Everything was so falling into place that Arizona won the national championship on March 31, the same time the Bulls were 62-9 en route to 69-13. A 3–0 sweep of the Washington Bullets in the first round of the playoffs came next, then a 4–1 victory over the Atlanta Hawks, with Kerr a combined nineteen of thirty-seven overall (51.4 percent) and ten of twenty (50 percent) on threes. He seemed so locked in that it was easy to dismiss the 33.3 percent in the five games of the Eastern Conference finals against the Miami Heat as a momentary lapse in a good run.

When that was followed by an equally dismal start to the championship series against Utah, though, his woes quickly accelerated into his worst basketball moment since the Final Four nine years earlier. Kerr played seven minutes in the opener in Chicago and didn't take a shot. He got a better chance with nineteen minutes in Game 2, but converted just two of six attempts, before the temporary relief of three baskets in six tries in Game 3 in Salt Lake City. His mood then took a hard turn toward darkness. The Bulls as a whole were on the verge of tearing apart, with Jackson having been given permission in the final months of his contract to speak with potential new employers, Jordan blasting away at Krause especially hard in the playoffs, and a tough series against the veteran Jazz. But no one was closer to the brink of emotional breakdown than Kerr.

He had an encouraging beginning to Game 4 when he made his first attempt, an eighteen-footer, in a much more hostile atmosphere than the Bulls had dealt with the year before in Seattle. Utah was an overflowing pandemonium of fans, music, and a revving motorcycle spewing exhaust as it slowly motored on the court for pregame introductions. Nearly twenty thousand people had come to a private air terminal at 2:30 in the morning ten days earlier to greet their returning heroes after they won the Western Conference crown in Houston. The noise trapped inside the Delta Center for games, especially playoff games, was the continuation of one of the best home-court advantages in the league.

Kerr went from converting the first shot to missing everything. Four more tries went astray, all three-pointers, a pair in the second quarter and a pair in the fourth, the last that could have turned a 74–73 deficit into a 76–74 lead with twenty-nine seconds remaining. Only Jordan's historic Game 5 while ill—thirty-eight points and seven rebounds in forty-four weakened minutes, in one of the landmark days of his life—allowed the Bulls to return to Chicago up 3–2.

By 1997, the new arrival who in 1993 had scanned local papers at the Residence Inn to find the nugget of an encouraging comment from Jackson, had banned sports sections from his Lake Forest home, even before the Finals, "because he's so sensitive to criticism," Margot said. The nadir of the championship series in particular had turned into his professional version of Arizona-Oklahoma '88, a playoff emotional descent that continued until Margot, as she would later relate, could barely get her husband to leave the bedroom. "Why can't I ever make a shot that matters?" he lamented to her. Unlike the bratty temper of his youth or the fits of rage on display later in life, Kerr's frustration after missing fourteen of twenty-one shots and scoring nineteen points the first five games manifested as a deep funk.

His coach, on the other hand, did not waver. Dispatching Kerr from the bench late in the first quarter of Game 6 to give Jordan a rest was a continuation of the confidence Jackson had shown from their first conversations, and tangible proof of Kerr's major role. Jackson even left Kerr in when Jordan returned and stayed with Kerr over Harper the entire second period despite Kerr's collecting more fouls (two) than baskets (zero). After Kerr sat the third quarter, Jackson went to him again in the fourth, even though Kerr had contributed only two free throws to the scoring. He finally made two shots, a seventeen-footer with 10:50 remaining and a three-pointer from twenty-four feet with 8:52 left. Most tellingly, especially after Kerr followed the two baskets with two misses, Jackson prepared to send him out again in an 86–86 game as the Bulls called time-out with twenty-eight seconds remaining.

With "Mony, Mony" by Tommy James and the Shondells blasting as a traditional time-out rocker at home games, ricocheting off walls and bodies, Jordan turned to Kerr in the huddle and predicted that John Stockton would leave Kerr to help double-team him. Kerr, one seat to Jordan's left, flicked a quick single poke with his right index finger back at him.

"If he comes off," Kerr said with unflinching certainty, "I'll be ready."

Jordan got the ball from Pippen with eleven seconds remaining, then penetrated a few steps to the free throw line on the left side. Stockton left Kerr for the double team, as Jordan expected. Kerr was two of four in the game, eight of twenty-four in the series, and thirty-two of seventy-six in the playoffs, but the Jazz were not reacting to Kerr's slump. It was Michael Jordan in the closing moments with a championship on the line, Utah wasn't going to leave Bryon Russell alone on that island. With Russell and Stockton trying to surround Jordan, Kerr ran toward his teammate at about three-quarter speed, timing the approach perfectly to be in position at the free throw line if a pass came. Jordan left his feet with no shot, spotted an option, and flipped the pass to his right to Kerr.

The ball launching from Kerr's right hand with a flick of the wrist and arcing in midair with one second on the shot clock was nothing less than a freakish intersection of his life, the commitment to preparation and especially the people in the scene. Stockton, who took Kerr apart on the recruiting trip to Gonzaga in a way that stamped Kerr with the certainty he could not make it in major-college hoops, had left him unguarded. Hornacek, the player Kerr emulated during visualization exercises, looked on helplessly. Buechler the connection to beloved Arizona. Jordan and Jackson, representatives of how much his unlikely career progression had become a dream sequence.

Also fittingly, the greatest moment of his playing career, the thunderclap he would eventually see as the tipping point that created his future, came via the slightly flawed shooting technique he had long ago come to accept. This time, it was a slight drift to the left at the release and his right leg scissoring slightly farther forward than the left. "I'm far from a textbook shooter," Kerr once said of his mechanics. "My left hand is more on the ball than maybe it should be. I wouldn't pick my shot to show to kids. There are guys with beautiful shots. Eddie Johnson. Mark Price. Dell Curry. Sometimes I shoot almost a knuckleball." This one had good backspin, and it certainly was the kind of jumper—midrange, straight away, coming to the ball to take defensive pressure off Jordan—he had practiced thousands of times. There was the bonus, or the irony, that the catch-and-shoot specialist most dangerous with his feet set, his weight balanced, the chance to square up to the basket and able to squeeze off a quick release, was turning immortal in Bulls-crazy Chicago through several seconds of constant motion.

Oh shit, Hornacek thought to himself from about ten feet away as the ball took flight, *that's going in.*

The moment of the swish, for an 88–86 lead with five seconds remaining, generated no outward reaction from Kerr. As a party broke out around him in the stands, and likely for miles beyond the United Center, he again aimed a stiletto index finger, this time the left, at Jordan, seeming to acknowledge keeping his promise from the huddle. Stone-faced, he accepted a high-ten from Jordan and walked to the bench for the Jazz time-out, as if leaving the court after a good practice. There was a left-handed high-five with Dennis Rodman as Rodman jogged past, a quick embrace with Randy Brown, and a pat on the back of the head from Buechler, plus other quick embraces, before Kerr rubbed a folded white towel over his face and the top of his head. But it was mostly business among the Bulls and the new hero while understanding Utah had enough time—five seconds—for a high-percentage response.

Midcourt about twenty rows up after flying from Sacramento for the game, a seat he talked his brother with season tickets into surrendering, former Kerr opponent and Chicago native Jim Les sprang up. Les had likewise come to the league from far back in the pack, as an unathletic late-second-round pick who carved out seven seasons in the same era as a shooting specialist with smarts. Now he was admiring one of his kind in a superstar's moment. Cavaliers general manager Wayne Embry cheered the player who had long been one of his favorites. In his hometown of Lubbock, Texas, Craig

Ehlo called his former Cavaliers teammate within minutes to leave a congratulatory message. "There are certain players you subconsciously root for throughout your career, as long as they're not doing it against you," said Milwaukee Bucks assistant Bob Weinhauer, the Arizona State coach when Kerr played following Malcolm's death.

The real celebration began minutes later as the Jazz came out of a time-out and threw away their attempted response to Kerr's dagger, a bad pass that led to a Kukoc dunk and the final 90–86 margin. Jordan even hugged Krause, what appeared to be a heartfelt embrace and not an obligatory clutch. Few, though, bathed in the delirium more than Kerr, who had ridden deep into the valley before emerging as a most improbable icon for a city, all within the same series. How close he came to decades of burning through whatever stomach lining had not been consumed in nine years by the Final Four despondency, if the wide-open look clanked away and the Bulls lost Game 6 five nights after the crucial miss in Salt Lake City.

"Steve's been fighting with himself because of Game 4," Jordan said. "He kept his head in the pillow for hours because he let the team down, because everyone knows he's probably one of the best shooters in the game, and he had the opportunity to pick us up and give us a lift, and he was very disappointed." When the teammate whose grit he already respected didn't flinch from the moment in Game 6, Jordan was moved to say, "Tonight Steve Kerr earned his wings from my perspective, because I had faith in him, and I passed him the ball, and he knocked down the shot. I'm glad he redeemed himself, because if he'd have missed that shot, I don't think he could have slept all summer long. I'm very happy for Steve Kerr."

Nothing had changed by the time they reconvened three days later for the victory parade through the city that culminated with the Bulls onstage in Grant Park, 319 acres of gardens, museums, landmarks, and, June 16, 1997, comedian Steve Kerr. Jackson, for one, never felt comfortable at the same outdoor parties thrown almost annually and would describe himself as phobic about large crowds to the point of getting queasy in uncontrolled, nongame settings. And Jordan slyly used the occasion to deliver a serious

message in an unserious tone, that owner Jerry Reinsdorf should
bring the team back for 1997–1998. Reinsdorf, robbed of the opportunity to appear gracious in making the offer himself, was offended.
He didn't like the feeling of being leveraged, or the appearance of
anyone, even Michael Jordan, dictating terms.

Kerr took control at the podium. "A lot of people have been asking
me about the shot the other night and there've been some miscon-
ceptions about what actually happened," he began in beige shorts
and black commemorative T-shirt matching the casual mood. "I
wanted to clear it up. When we called time-out with twenty-five
seconds to go, we went into the huddle and Phil told Michael, he
said, 'Michael, I want you to take the last shot.' And Michael said,
'You know, Phil, I don't feel real comfortable in these situations, so
maybe we oughta go in another direction.' And Scottie came in and
he said, 'You know, Phil, Michael said in his commercial that, you
know, he's been asked to do this twenty-six times and he's failed. So
why don't we go to Steve.'"

The crowd roared in delight, and the Bulls stretched across the
stage in a row behind him, including Jordan and Jackson, laughed
and applauded. "So I thought to myself, 'Well, I guess I gotta bail
Michael out again.'" He gave a half-shrug and a quick smile. "But
I've been carrying him all year, so, you know, what's one more time.
Anyway, the shot went in, and that's my story and I'm sticking to it."
With perfect mic-drop timing, he spun left and walked away from
the podium.

There would be few better definitions of Kerr than the brief timeline of fighting through adversity, preparing for a moment, handling pressure, and then flipping the success into a gag. In time, he
would come to view the winning basket as the tipping point for all
the good that followed in his professional life—name recognition
he never imagined, which led to networks wanting him after retirement, which kept him in the public eye to create opportunities
in management or coaching. It probably isn't true. Kerr already had
a long enough résumé as a player and was so good with a microphone and camera, from the other side, that broadcasting bosses

could see a natural as an analyst. And enough teams had by late on the magical night of June 13, 1997, already sized him up as having a bright future on the sideline or as a general manager. The innate way of connecting with people, the way he understood the game at a high level, the professionalism and work ethic made it so, not the straightaway seventeen-footer.

There was the additional payoff of another contract, at $750,000 nearly three times the league minimum for veterans, as the Bulls endured another contentious summer of free agency and the strange dynamic of a front office that appeared to be forced into keeping a championship team together. When it wasn't dealing with free agency, management was trying to trade Pippen to the Celtics for draft picks, with an eye on recent high school graduate Tracy McGrady in particular, knowing Pippen had one season left on his deal and no desire to return. "There's more bullshit flying around this team than a dairy in a tornado," was how Longley put it. "There's always something going on. Dennis is always doing his thing, or something's going on. Michael's retiring, or Jerry's making noise. We've had more controversy or circumstance around this team in the past three years, so we've had a lot of practice at putting things out of our mind." The latest was Krause's declaration that 1997–1998 would be Jackson's last in Chicago, triggering the Jordan response that he would retire rather than play for another coach.

"In Chicago, everywhere we go, people are asking us, 'How can they possibly think about breaking this team up?'" Kerr said, speaking out against management for one of the few times in his life. "And frankly, we don't have any answers for that." Later in the season, he would join teammates in condemning the decision to trade Jason Caffey. Krause being misquoted on media day about organizations, not players, winning championships increased the friction and drove his image to new lows, wrongly in this case. Not merely seen as the general manager strangely looking forward to ending a dynasty still in motion, he could now additionally be viewed as the guy driving Michael Jordan from the game.

Kerr and the Bulls, minus injured Pippen and unsigned Rodman, were in a bad mood when they boarded the 747 normally used by the Rolling Stones for tours and headed to Paris for a preseason tournament against teams from Italy, Argentina, Greece, Spain, and France. "In certain ways, it's not much of a reward," Jackson said of his practice routine being interrupted to showcase the Bulls as an NBA marketing tool. "JORDAN AWAITED LIKE A KING," blared the headline in the country's major sports daily, *L'Equipe*. "Michael Jordan is in Paris," the paper *France-Soir* fawned. "That's better than the Pope. It's God in person." "The young Parisians lucky enough to get into [the arena] must have dreamed beautiful dreams, for their hero had been everything they could have hoped for," another writer passed along. That Jordan was seen wearing a beret meant "We shall be able to call him Michel."

The thirteen-year-old North Korean known as Pak Un, said to be the son of an official at the embassy in Bern, Switzerland, was driven the 375 miles from the Swiss capital to see his beloved Bulls. In time, friends he made in the West would talk of seeing photos of the shy student posing with Kukoc and Kobe Bryant, on separate occasions and in unknown locations, and a room filled with basketball memorabilia in his apartment at 10 Kirchstrasse in the town of Liebefeld. Pak had a collection of Nikes and drew pencil sketches of Jordan. Although it was unclear whether he watched the October 17 win over French club Paris PSG Racing or Chicago beating Greek squad Olympiacos the next day for the championship as Kerr scored ten points, or both, his presence inside Palais Omnisports de Paris-Bercy would be noted decades later, once it became known that the teenager studying in Switzerland was future North Korean dictator Kim Jong-Un.

Returning to the United States and coming together again once Rodman re-signed in time for the start of the regular season brought the realization that 1997–1998 would be the last season together for the original core with five titles (Jordan, Pippen, and Jackson) and the second wave that had been part of two titles (Kerr, Harper, Rodman, Wennington, and Buechler). "The finality of it gave the season a certain resonance that bonded the team closely together," Jackson wrote. "It felt as if we were on a sacred mission, driven by a force that went beyond fame, glory, and all the other spoils of victory. We were doing this one for the pure joy of playing together one more time. It felt magical."

It was the most difficult of the three full seasons on the court since Jordan returned anyway, with an inability to win close games and an early 8-6 mark for the strange sight of the Bulls in eighth place. Additionally, Pippen got drunk on the flight from Sacramento to Seattle and launched into a tirade against Krause during the bus ride to the hotel. As Christmas approached and Jackson pondered his tradition of giving books, he considered *Any Idiot Can Manage* for Krause. "But in the end," Jackson said, "I didn't buy him anything because I couldn't find it in myself to give him something of value."

Kerr's contribution to the gloom was a cracked femur that cost him ten games in November and December. He was back about a month when Derrick Coleman of the 76ers landed on Kerr after a block attempt, resulting in a broken left clavicle and twenty-nine games lost. Worse, Kerr had the added frustration of believing Coleman could have avoided the hard contact. After playing eighty-two regular-season contests the previous four seasons, he would make it into only fifty in 1997–1998, the fewest since 1991–1992 as a Cavalier, joined by the disappointment of dropping to 45.4 percent overall and 43.8 percent on threes.

He could at least be encouraged that he was returning with enough time—the final quarter of the schedule—to reclaim rhythm and conditioning before the playoffs. Starting the comeback March 8 against the Knicks at Madison Square Garden, with a Manhattan energy that made it one of Kerr's favorite stops, was a bonus. He shot the first time he touched the ball, after entering late in the first quarter, such a change from his usual approach of gently sliding into the flow of a game that reporters brought it up after the easy Bulls win. Kerr said he felt like Wennington, referencing his fellow Moth who was typically so eager to launch that Jordan had tagged him "trampoline hands." Kerr made the inaugural attempt and three in all in five tries while Jackson ran him back into shape with twenty-six minutes in the first game action he'd seen in seven weeks.

"That's one of the things about injuries, you have a lot of time to think," Kerr said. "I really thought about my situation here and my future, and I realized that early in the season I was probably pressing a little bit because of the uncertainty over next year, me being a free agent and nobody knowing what was happening with the team. I realized that I was gonna have probably 20 games left and then the playoffs. And then, who knows? That might be it. So I better enjoy it and be aggressive and try to have as much fun as I can when I do come back."

His coach had a similar mindset. Wanting to appreciate what little time the group appeared to have left, Jackson scheduled a meeting before the playoffs and asked players and staff members in advance to write a paragraph on the impact of the season and the team on their lives, anything from their own words to lyrics from a song to a spiritual verse. Choosing to gather in the video room in the training facility signaled a special level of importance as the spot Jackson had informally renamed the "tribal room," in tribute to the Native American beliefs he admired. He even added the decorating touches of a bear-claw necklace, an owl feather, and photos of a newborn white buffalo, among other items, and he would bang a drum to alert players to gather.

Half the participants followed the instructions and arrived with written sentiments, including Jordan in the form of, in Jackson's words, a "very moving" poem that praised the team's dedication and expressed hope that the bond would last forever. Kerr was shocked at the gentle words from a velociraptor. His contribution—unwritten—was to share the thrill of becoming a father to Madeleine while with the Bulls and bringing four-year-old basketball fan Nick to meet Jordan, Pippen, and Rodman in the locker room. The pieces of paper were crumpled and dropped in a coffee can after each reading, the lights were flicked off and Jackson ultimately lit the wads on fire. Kerr was one of many brought to tears. "I'll never forget that moment," Jackson later wrote. "The quiet aura in the room. The fire burning in the darkness. The intense intimacy we felt sitting silently together and watching the flames die down. I don't think the bond among us had ever been stronger."

The vibes carried over to the court as the Bulls opened the playoffs by eliminating the Nets 3–0 and the Hornets 4–1 before beating the Pacers in the first two games of the East finals. When Indiana pushed back by evening the series, Chicago responded to its first postseason test by winning two of the last three to advance to a rematch with the Jazz in the championship series, this time with Utah on ten days' rest and with home-court advantage. The noise in the return to the Delta Center, Jackson said, was "astonishing" and "beyond the realm of tolerance. Last year, I'd go back to my room and my ears would ring for hours. They toned down the motorcycle sounds some, but the introduction is the worst—the bombs, the flares, the balloons bursting in sequence." Worried about permanent ear damage, he wore earplugs.

Invisible in the 1997 Finals until the last ticks, Kerr was everywhere a year later. In Game 1, Jackson left him in to defend Stockton and paid for the gamble when Stockton got Kerr in the lane and made a nine-footer with nine seconds remaining for the winning points, a portion of Stockton's seven points in overtime that turned into a Gonzaga recruiting visit. Two days later, down a point with forty-eight seconds remaining, Kerr missed a twenty-five-footer in front of the Jazz bench, only to move in to collect the long rebound between six-nine Malone and six-seven Russell. "That's true desire," Jordan said. Kerr then quickly spotted Jordan open under the basket and delivered the pass that gave the Bulls an 87–86 edge and a key moment in the 93–88 Chicago victory that evened the series.

Just like the year before, Kerr was on the court for the final Bulls possession, except this time Jordan finished off the Jazz by himself with an iconic seventeen-footer over Russell with five seconds remaining. Kerr didn't have to bail him out again.

"My story is not quite as exciting this year, but I'll share it with you anyway," Kerr said at the latest Grant Park party, looking out over the sea of people. "When we called time-out, we were down three with forty-five seconds left. I kinda thought to myself, this would be a great chance at a three-pointer to tie the game. And I mentioned that to Phil. And Phil looked at me with this disgusted look and he said, 'Steve, let's face it. Last year was a fluke. Get the ball to Michael and get the hell out of his way.' So that's what I did. You know what happened. You know the rest. And for what it's worth, I thought I did a fantastic job of getting out of his way." With that, Kerr turned and went back to his seat on the stage.

The improbable last contribution, an offensive rebound-turned-assist, was a fitting ending after an unlikely five seasons in Chicago that almost didn't happen and then turned into three titles. Joining the Bulls changed the history of the unwanted reserve trying to claw out one more contract, from the long-term implications of connecting with Jackson to hitting the shot to clinch the '97 title that Kerr was certain put his life on a new course. As the search for the next opportunity began amid the looming breakup of a championship roster, it was hard to avoid the strange reality that for all the eventual Hall of Famers in the organization, it was possible that no one gained more from the second Jordan run than Steve Kerr.

CHAPTER 9

Civil Action 01-1994

Things were going so right for Steve Kerr by the summer of 1998, in the wake of a third consecutive title and a hero's play for the second finals in a row, that even the NBA-wide blight of a lockout could be spun into a personal positive. While he was blocked from signing a new contract with league business shuttered as the labor dispute stretched from July into September and, like his peers, could begin missing paychecks, rest had become a priority as well. Even being limited to 50 appearances in 1997–1998 because of injuries, Kerr still totaled 272 games the previous three campaigns counting the postseason, a heavy workload for anyone, but especially someone turning thirty-three. Fifty-eight of those games were in the playoffs alone, practically an extra season, and his 58 were against the best competition in the tensest of situations. While the reason for the extended break was unwanted, the timing was perfect.

The league indefinitely postponed training camp on September 24, about a week ahead of the planned opening, scrubbed twenty-four exhibition games, and then canceled the remainder of the preseason on October 5. When a negotiating session three days later resulted in little progress, the first two weeks of the regular season were dropped. Grandfathered in as the Bulls' representative despite being a free agent, Kerr was among two hundred players at a union meeting on October 22 in Las Vegas, a six-hour gathering at Caesars Palace that notably included former teammates Jordan and O'Neal in an attempted statement of solidarity for an organization usually clouded in apathy. Kerr reported a session unlike any in his four years in the role, with "guys yelling and screaming in there and showing a lot of emotion, and that's very important," but they were no closer to a solution.

Owners and players did not reach an agreement until January 6, the day before the league's so-called drop-dead date to cancel the entire season, with everyone understanding that the entire operation would now have to be thrown into overdrive to jam in even a shortened schedule. Abbreviated training camps, fifty games instead of eighty-two, and, in an issue for Kerr, a small window for roster moves before the start of preseason. But even that wasn't a problem in the end. Hoping to leverage his career surge in Chicago into a three-year deal worth $3.5 million, Kerr ended up with the jackpot of five years and $11 million from the Spurs as part of a trade and cast his MVP vote before a single practice: "My agent, Mark Bartelstein." In another sign of how much the basketball world had turned in his favor, never would Kerr be more rested for the playoffs than with a truncated slate when he needed it most.

Back in Chicago, Krause was finally getting his chance to sledgehammer a championship team and start over. Once Jordan announced his second retirement on January 13 at a press conference on the United Center floor, with the caveat of being 99.9 percent sure he had played for the last time, enough of an opening for speculation, the Bulls scattered: Kerr to the Spurs on January 21, longtime friend Buechler to the Pistons the next day, Pippen to the Rockets hours later, and Longley to the Suns a day after that. Rodman was released January 21 but remained unsigned as camps opened. Tim Floyd replaced Jackson. Co-Moth Wennington, Harper, and Krause favorite Kukoc were left behind as opponents salivated at the impending revenge. "For all the years they destroyed people, it's payback time," Timberwolves forward Sam Mitchell said. "And people aren't going to care that Michael Jordan and Scottie Pippen aren't there. All they're going to see is that Chicago Bulls jersey, and if you can beat them by 50, beat 'em by 60. They're going to get drilled."

The change could not have been more dramatic for Kerr in particular from the emotional mayhem of Chicago infighting to an organization noted for serenity compared to most any team and especially contrasted to what he had just witnessed for five seasons. San Antonio was the ultimate in low maintenance, even in its stars. David Robinson had the maturity and discipline of his Naval Academy schooling and Tim Duncan the island tranquility of his Caribbean upbringing, personalities that made Kerr seem Rodmanesque. As if that wasn't happy landing enough, the Spurs also had one of his favorite teammates ever, former Arizona star Sean Elliott. And there was no chance of reliving the Krause-Jackson verbal combat because Gregg Popovich held both roles, coach and general manager.

While Kerr never publicly maligned the Bulls' madhouse of self-mutilation, not with the gratitude for all the franchise and the city had done for him, he quickly conceded San Antonio was an easier existence. It had nothing to do with downshifting to the pace of southern Texas—he was as practiced as anyone in the league at adjusting to new settings after a life of bounding among the crowds of Los Angeles, hiking through endless sands in Egypt, of a Chicago commuter existence or Tucson framed by desert, of the South of France or Cleveland. The team, not the market size, made it welcoming as a return to an environment devoid of daily toxins. Kerr was a perfect fit in a setting that prized humility, intelligence, and humor.

Just as noteworthy, he was for the first time since high school joining a team without needing to prove he belonged. His arrival at every place since Palisades had practically required a name tag for identification—the last recruit, the late draft pick, the two trades for second-round choices, the guy thrilled to get a minimum contract. His arrival on the Spurs was different, even with the concern that the player who built his career on three-point shooting had joined a coach and general manager who considered that weapon a cheap gimmick. "I hate it," Popovich would say, even years later, long after it had become accepted around the league. "To me, it's not basketball, but you gotta use it. If you don't use it, you're in big trouble. But you sort of feel like it's cheating." Popovich was at least open to being forced into relying on an occasional three as air support to keep defenses from collapsing on big men Duncan and Robinson inside.

The potential concern quickly dissipated when Kerr played close to or more than twenty minutes a game once the season finally began February 5, about thirteen weeks later than usual. Feeling uncomfortable in Popovich's offense was the problem, hardly unusual for a player on a new team and especially in the unique circumstances of a compressed training camp, but also a red flag not to be ignored. If he didn't make shots, he didn't play. Not needing anyone to remind him, Kerr pulled assistant coach Mike Budenholzer aside during an early four-game trip through the East and Midwest, part of a stretch of Kerr making just fifteen of forty-four shots overall and six of twenty-three three-pointers. (In a sign the basketball gods remained at least partly on his side, his best game by far in the frustrating time came, in a sympathetic twist, in the Chicago homecoming.)

At Kerr's suggestion, bordering on insistence, the pair went to Budenholzer's hotel room, fed in VHS tapes, and dissected Kerr's few games as a Spur as the patient scanned the TV screen for clues as to what he was doing wrong. "Timing and detail and really wanting to dig in," Budenholzer called it, "almost like a coach." They went from Play to Pause to Play to Pause countless times, back and forth, deconstructing Kerr on offense and defense, no possible adjustment too minor, until Budenholzer saw a player so invested and so self-aware the memory would stand out for decades.

Kerr was paying for the greased calendar, especially the reduced training camp, as the bad fit grew so pronounced that it was easy to see the signing as a bad idea for both sides and not merely a slow start. Kerr loved, then and forever, the Phil Jackson attack based on ball movement and constant motion, even if it meant restricting the offensive blowtorch of Michael Jordan. San Antonio's system centered on throwing the ball inside to Duncan and Robinson and staying out of the way. While he naturally filed no public complaints, some of those close to Kerr spoke in whispered tones of the newcomer growing increasingly frustrated at what he considered a flawed approach. "He hated it," one person who heard the feedback said. "He thought it was terrible. He completely disagreed." With Kerr a Jackson loyalist in every way and missing the Chicago game plan, the relationship with Popovich did not start well.

Kerr's drain on the offense would have been more obvious except the Spurs as a whole were in disarray at 6-8 and internally bunkering into crisis mode after the fourteen-point home loss to the Jazz as the calendar turned to March. The short schedule was working against them, allowing much less time than usual to recover and find a playoff rhythm as a visit to Houston loomed as unusually meaningful for an early-season contest. It was enough to drive constant speculation on Popovich's future in his second full season as coach, talk fanned by Doc Rivers's presence as an analyst on local broadcasts. Rivers had been a popular and well-respected point guard before retiring in 1996 after most of two campaigns as a backup in San Antonio. For years he had been seen as a future coach, somewhere, and now he was in the very unwanted position of mortician waiting to be told to begin work. Kerr and other players felt the tension.

Avery Johnson, the starting point guard, called a March 1 team meeting in Houston to deliver the pep talk that changed the rest of Kerr's life. Johnson viewed Popovich much the same way Kerr regarded Phil Jackson, as the coach who rescued a laboring career that turned into the unimaginable riches of championships and millions of dollars in contracts. The only difference was Popovich's impact was as an assistant coach while they were with the Warriors. Jackson had already proven himself by the time Kerr arrived in Chicago, compared to Popovich with no credibility in the role. To Johnson, gathering the Spurs to rally support and urge players to pull together was part of his job as one of the team's emotional leaders, but also personal.

The response of a seventeen-point win over the Rockets the next night brought temporary relief. When that was followed by another resounding road victory, by sixteen at Dallas, the Spurs were back at .500 for the first time since the opening week in what became the start of a nine-game winning streak on the way to eighteen victories in twenty games. Popovich was firmly back on stable ground, a key development for the Spurs and massive for the backup shooting guard who nearly lost what became one of the most important relationships of his life before it barely started.

Popovich was no child of North Dakota and Pentecostal preachers who waved sticks of lit sage to purify the locker room after a bad game. Kerr's new coach hailed from Merrillville, Indiana, ten miles south of urban Gary and forty-five miles southeast of Chicago. And Popovich was a military guy, Air Force Academy '70, who later in life displayed the reminder during national anthems with arms snapped tightly at his sides, toes of his dress shoes pointed at the forty-five-degree angle required by the military, heels touching to form the base of the V. His All-Star center would do the same, only in a basketball uniform, and sometimes think about death as the song played. Lieutenant j.g. (retired) David Robinson, Navy '87, would imagine battles and those who made the ultimate sacrifice.

Popovich and Jackson did, however, both put a priority on communication and invited the outside world into the locker room, in contrast to the basketball-only focus elsewhere. Even as Kerr bristled at Popovich's offense, he eventually found his new coach had the same gift as Jackson for connecting with people from diverse backgrounds. Kerr did not need to learn the skill himself after growing up with a comfort level in different cultures, but the common thread helped build what became a close relationship.

The comeback that started with the team meeting in Houston led to a 31-5 finish to the regular season and thirteen wins the first fourteen games of the playoffs, a late charge that included a 4–0 rout of the Lakers in the second round. Unemployed Phil Jackson followed along during a lonely cross-country drive to a speaking engagement in Pebble Beach, California. His past and future unknowingly converging as the desolate miles piled up, Jackson listened to Game 3 of the San Antonio–Los Angeles series on the radio and stopped in a bar in Clinton, Iowa, just in time to watch on TV as Chicago won the draft lottery and Jerry Krause celebrated

Steve Kerr and his mother, Ann, joined by family friend Najeeb Halaby, visit President Ronald Reagan and Vice President George H. W. Bush at the White House in 1984. Reagan invited the family to thank them for Malcolm Kerr's commitment to sharing American values in the Middle East before he was assassinated.

Kerr relaxes with—and on—his two older siblings, John and Susan, in a light moment during his senior season at the University of Arizona.

Left: Kerr's Arizona headshot, basketball in hand. *Right:* Lute Olson, Arizona's legendary head coach, who gave the lightly recruited Kerr a shot.

Getting into the spirit of Alaska during a photo shoot when Arizona played in Anchorage early in Kerr's senior season. The play of the Wildcats and their point guard served notice of great things ahead for 1987–1988.

The shot Kerr believes changed everything. The jumper beat the Jazz in the final seconds of Game 6 of the 1997 Finals, delivered another title to Chicago, and made him a bigger name than ever.

Kerr and Phil Jackson embrace as the Bulls celebrate winning the 1997 Finals, a poignant moment in a connection that would last long after their days together in Chicago. Jackson insisted from the beginning that Kerr would have a meaningful role, against all odds, and Kerr paid him back years later by hitting the shot that clinched the title.

The final legendary head coach for whom Kerr played, Gregg Popovich of the Spurs, delivers instructions to his veteran guard on the court.

Left: Kerr during his first season as Warriors coach. Lacking the traditional pedigree of previously being an assistant coach, Kerr relied in part on the wisdom gleaned while playing under Jackson and Popovich, two of the game's greats. *Right:* Kerr, soaked in champagne, and Draymond Green with the championship trophy after the Warriors won the 2017 Finals. The coach and his All-Star power forward clashed, but also developed a deep respect and tight bond.

President Barack Obama shows off his jumper for Kerr and the Warriors, who visited the White House in 2016 after their first championship.

onstage by "pumping his chubby little fist." Jackson laughed loud enough to draw attention, prompting fellow patrons to send over more beers than he could drink in a month and send their children home to collect Bulls paraphernalia for autographs. The next day he checked into a hotel in Laramie, Wyoming, to watch the fourth quarter of the Spurs completing the sweep, without Kerr getting into either game Jackson tracked, and became so disgusted by the Lakers' weak chemistry and lack of toughness that he couldn't help but visualize how he could transform them into champions.

When that led to a 4–1 victory over the Knicks and the first championship in Spurs history, Kerr became the lone non–Boston Celtic to win four consecutive titles and only the second from any organization with back-to-back crowns on different teams. But the drop to 16.7 minutes a game in the regular season, after averaging at least 22 all five years in Chicago, then 8.8 in the playoffs, made it his smallest contribution to a ring. Plus, he was now on the other side of Jackson's verbal jabs, having to hear the coach he so admired eventually denigrate the Spurs' accomplishment by calling winning in a shortened season an asterisk championship.

Jackson was in a small village in remote southwest Alaska, on a fly-fishing trip with his sons, when he learned his agent and the Lakers had reached a contract agreement to coach the team short on toughness and chemistry. The July 16 hiring came with Jackson in a decidedly different setting for the press conference, Beverly Hills, and as a welcome development that Kerr and the other former championship Bulls would finally have the reunions that had been mostly wiped out by the jumbled fifty-game calendar. In 1999, with Jordan retired, Jackson idling, and Rodman on the L.A. roster for such a short time that he missed all three Spurs-Lakers contests, Kerr crossed paths only with Pippen, who was with Houston, and Harper, a remnant in Chicago. In Kerr's second run in San Antonio, the schedule would return to eighty-two games, with at least two against every opponent and four versus the Western Conference, including Los Angeles and its new coach and new starting guard Harper.

Once the season started, Kerr had little to do except see old friends and build on positive relationships in San Antonio. He didn't break nine minutes until 1999–2000 was three weeks old, didn't appear in three consecutive games until a month had gone by, and usually played little or not at all. Popovich might not have used him anyway, as the previous campaign showed, but the defending champions winning at an impressive rate without him made it clear that Kerr was not needed. The season quickly became, and remained, an even bigger career setback than the one before, this time without the convenient explanation of transitioning to a new team.

Simply put, choosing San Antonio was a terrible basketball decision and one the free agent who succinctly mapped out why he once belonged in Chicago could have seen coming. It was understandable as a money grab after years of existing season to season, but he would never fit in a system whose coach prioritized what Kerr could not do (defense) and devalued his strength (perimeter shooting). The Spurs likewise had little use for Kerr, beyond wanting his championship mettle to help a roster that had been unable to reach the top, but the intangible cost them a five-year contract. Now that it was into a second season of Kerr turning invisible, the bad fit was obvious to all.

Jackson found his former key reserve "anguishing" when the Los Angeles coaching staff went to the Kerr home for dinner on January 31, the night before the Lakers faced the Spurs in the Alamodome. "But Steve was also going on thirty-four years old, his wife and kids loved San Antonio, and he was grateful for the security," Jackson noted. Proving Kerr divulged no secrets, or that the visitors were bad listeners, the Spurs won by twenty-four as he managed four minutes. Even the good news was turning bad—he got a real role in February, frequently breaking double digits in minutes and finally making three-pointers, only to suffer a torn cartilage in his right knee and undergo season-ending surgery on March 22.

Jay Howard's suggestion to Kerr to fill the time as he recovered was a new one: become a color commentator. Kerr had been an honorary member of the media for decades, from practically becoming the Arizona spokesman as a freshman to many polished studio appearances in Cleveland to such a deep understanding of the press that Orlando PR man Alex Martins asked his insights on how big events like the Final Four and NBA playoffs were covered. In Chicago, his willingness to help had been trophy-worthy. If you need anything, he told the media relations department early in every stop, don't hesitate to ask, wanting to help the team any way he could and genuinely interested in making life easier for writers and broadcasters. The former *Tideline* co–sports editor would stay loyal to his former calling.

Breaking down the action live, though, sitting courtside and wearing a headset, weaving quick-jab insights into Howard's fast-paced play-by-play was new. Kerr would be a Spur all other times, attending practices and meetings and heading to the locker room for halftime, and then share whatever he felt comfortable divulging from the radio spot on press row. When Howard approached Popovich for final approval, where an injured reserve with thirty-two appearances would be watching was far down his list of concerns as the Spurs prepared to face the Suns in the first round with Duncan also now lost to a torn knee cartilage.

"Well why the fuck do I care?" Popovich said.

As the season crashed down around the Spurs in a 3–1 loss to Phoenix, Kerr, in case he was testing himself for a future career, was a natural. It was like sitting next to a coach, Howard thought. Kerr broke down referees' decisions from the perspective of the players and talked through strategy without colliding with the game calls. When a subtraction error caused Howard to give the wrong margin on the air, Kerr, invoking the Lakers' Hall of Fame announcer he knew well as a former listener in Los Angeles, zinged Howard by noting how Chick Hearn would have gotten it right. And when he returned to the air after what turned out to be the final halftime speech of the season, Kerr passed along the homogenized message from Popovich to an overmatched squad that the Spurs should just go out and play the final two quarters as best they could and leave it up to the basketball gods. "He did it instinctively," Howard said.

"He just was so good at it that I never had to sit down before a game or after a game and say, 'Here's what we should have done.' Never had to do that. It was seamless." Kerr also asked for advice on how he could improve.

Though he still wasn't playing much the next season, at least his relationship with Popovich improved as they connected more on a personal level. The day Popovich divided the Spurs based on political preference for a scrimmage before the season, Republicans versus Democrats, and had the team watch a presidential debate together remained a favorite Kerr memory. "I think it is more truth than a trick," Popovich said of the approach Kerr would later emulate. "I guess it's just a personal belief that in the end basketball is not all that important compared to what really is meaningful to us in our lives. Your families, your friends, whatever you believe in. Those things sustain you and when things don't go well for a certain period of time, it's important for everybody to know that's when your integrity shows. That's where your character shows. You realize it's not about you. It's not 'poor me.' It's called life and you move on if you have any character at all. It's the way you would want to raise your kids. It's what you'd tell your kids if they were feeling sorry for themselves, so why can't it work for us too even though we're grown? It's basically that philosophy more than anything else." Kerr, for the third time in his life, after Arizona and the Bulls, had joined a team that did not appear to need him only to stumble into a lifetime partnership with the coach.

His relationship with San Antonio and its coach in particular was so good that Popovich extended to Kerr the unnecessary courtesy of giving him updates as trade talks with Portland developed in the summer of 2001, wanting to be sure Kerr would not be surprised if a deal happened. When it did on July 25, with Steve Smith going to the Spurs and Derek Anderson to the Trail Blazers as the headliners and Kerr a lesser piece, Popovich delivered the news in a phone call that touched on the popularity of all the Kerrs. He might not be able to go home, Popovich told Kerr, because his wife is going to be mad at the move that sent Margot and Steve away. So began one of the unique and difficult stretches of Kerr's life, even for someone with a coping mechanism steeled by the decades.

He had never experienced anything like the piranha tank of the Portland locker room because no one had, with players arrested or facing league discipline with such frequency that they were tagged as the Jail Blazers four years earlier, a label that stuck. "I'm always surprised that Portland people can actually root for their players, given the type of character they display on the floor, but they somehow manage," Phil Jackson chimed in. "Maybe it's the money that they're paying [that makes them] feel they owe allegiance to the team. And they carry the name of the town on their backs." Even Kerr had moments of mocking the image of his new club.

Plus, he would be alone in Portland after the decision that Margot and the kids would return to San Diego and a sense of stability, making 2000–2001 the double challenge of being on a team running amok and being away from his family much more than usual. On top of everything, he would have a rookie head coach so unprepared that Maurice Cheeks arrived at summer league in Las Vegas, saw notes on the grease board left behind by the previous team in the locker room and took in the message that players should defend, block out, and play tough. "We need to do this stuff," he told equipment manager Bob Medina, "Good points." Now Cheeks would be in charge of the marauders.

The living arrangement, though important, was just one pressing family issue as his mother and siblings spent months debating whether to file a civil lawsuit against Iran over Malcolm's murder. The decision to proceed was anything but a sterile call of the law, as evidenced by the anguish while the case moved forward. The family understood it would reopen searing wounds unlikely to bring anything in return. Even if the Kerrs won, the chances of Iran paying were slim, if not nonexistent. The government might even skip the proceedings rather than acknowledge the legitimacy of the case, possibly making the effort more frustrating and hurtful than the healing resolution the family desired. Steve, for one, favored skipping the emotional grinder. But Andrew was the one who rushed into Marquand House sobbing he wanted to get the guys who killed his dad, Andrew was the one who lived with Ann years afterward and heard her sobs, and Andrew was the one who came across a document linking Iran to the murder as part of his work with the National Security Council. Steve and the others inclined to avoid more heartache ultimately reasoned that supporting Andrew mattered more.

There was also the bigger picture for Ann of wanting "to think of it as the forces of good against the forces of evil." To her, Malcolm accepting the job that sent him down the tragic path in Beirut was standing up for what "we believe America is best at doing, our educational system, our moral values" and that, finally, "it was time to think about accountability." Andrew and Malcolm's brother Doug wanted someone, even the faceless someone of a government, being judged for the crime, but Ann was aiming for an emotional resolution. Principles were at stake. The family agreed to the legal approach in early September 2001, an early legal step, but one that Susie detected had already left them drained and exhausted, long before the proceedings actually began.

Thirty-six hours later, on September 11, Susan was enjoying a sunny afternoon at home in the English countryside while on the phone with John in Michigan, still struggling to grasp the legal gymnastics ahead but at least relieved that the family had agreed on a path forward. Their Washington lawyer, Mike Martinez, was in his office some three miles from the Pentagon on a day so blissful across the Atlantic that the only Kerr daughter was spending an hour with her youngest son picking apples from a neighbor's tree before driving to gather her other boys at school. Someone on the playground during the pickup told her the United States had been attacked, news so jolting that Susan quickly spiraled into a panic, thinking of the Kerrs and van de Vens as potential targets as well. "What if they come after us again?" she told a friend there.

In that chaotic instant, her mind raced to imagining the van de Ven's address being posted on the internet and Hezbollah gunmen infiltrating their village in eastern England, able to only briefly stop herself to realize an ongoing plot against the Kerr family was not part of a mass murder an ocean away. But the fingertip grasps on reality were rare. The other moments were consumed by fresh layers of anxiety as Susan and her sons drove home with bulletins pouring out of the radio and getting worse all the time. They heard the update that a plane had now crashed into a field in Pennsylvania. She was screaming hysterically, for the first time since Ann called in 1984 with the news that Malcolm had been shot.

Steve and the Trail Blazers were three weeks away from the start of training camp, and none of the Kerrs were on the East Coast of the United States under attack. "But each of us felt the same sickening, intimate knowledge of what the families of those killed now faced," Susan later wrote. "Though we had lost no one, the sense of trauma and unreality was uncannily like that which I remembered from all those years before." The direct impact on the family of the attacks was Andrew becoming more determined that the suit against Iran proceed, even if that meant going it alone, without his siblings and mother. It was an unnecessary vow. The action moved forward with five Kerrs in the immediate family, plus Malcolm's sister and the estate of his late sister.

Steve remained typically understated within the family— "nonconfrontational by nature," Susie described him—saying nothing even privately about the potential impact of 9/11 on the lawsuit taking an emotional toll before the trial began. He did, however, make a very public declaration while still in San Antonio by going to a restaurant with a Middle Eastern theme, ostensibly as a helpful boost in a lonely time for the business. Not long afterward, he appeared on a local radio show and asked listeners if they would reject the characterization of all Americans as Timothy McVeigh, the Oklahoma City bomber, a rhetorical question meant to point out that not all Arabs were terrorists. Around the same time, Ann invited a visiting professor from Yemen to stay in her guest room in Pacific Palisades, aware of the reception a man named Muhammad with dark skin and a beard would receive in a search for housing. Muhammad also devised a cover story for anyone who asked where he was from: Fiji.

Kerr v. Islamic Republic of Iran was filed September 20, 2001, in the U.S. District Court for the District of Columbia and assigned to Judge Thomas Penfield Jackson, a Reagan appointee in his eighteenth year on that bench. The complaint was translated into Farsi and forwarded to a Swiss envoy in Geneva for delivery to the Ministry of Information and Security in Tehran. No reply was received, no public comment was made.

The legal process moved slowly and privately as Kerr adapted to Portland. The Blazers had a strange roster dichotomy, with exemplary citizens like Chris Dudley, Mitchell Butler, Dale Davis, and Kerr running counter to the organization's renegade image. On the court, Cheeks went from being intrigued by Kerr's arrival as a trade throw-in—"Anytime you come from the Spurs it's going to have some special appeal to it," the coach said—to relying on Kerr and Pippen most of all among players to shape strategy. Cheeks solicited opinions on offensive sets, defensive alignments, and working with the unique personalities of the locker room. "I knew he was a good player and a veteran, and I knew he could probably help me make this transition a little easier because he had been around the game so long and won championships," Cheeks said. "And then once I got around him, I knew what kind of person he was, and I knew he was going to help me even more." He considered Kerr something of an untitled assistant coach.

Cheeks needed only until opening night, October 31 against Phil Jackson's Lakers, for confirmation. When Los Angeles called timeout in the second half, Cheeks turned to Kerr with the challenge to diagram the next Laker play. Kerr took the grease board, scribbled where Shaquille O'Neal would be, where Kobe Bryant would come around a pick, and how the set would develop. Events transpired exactly as Kerr predicted. Sixteen seasons later, Coach Steve Kerr would employ a similarly inclusive approach, getting input from every direction and took Cheeks's tactic further by selecting players to run time-outs.

His unofficial duties soon grew to include mentoring rookie Zach Randolph, the first-round pick who had brushes with the law as a teenager but was viewed by many around the league as a good guy influenced by the wrong crowd. The gifted power forward the Blazers got to know would be swayed by the harmful voices in the locker room, but was also a willing listener on the many occasions veterans Dudley and Kerr tried to steer him in a better direction. It soon became common to see the African American who grew up on welfare, the white guard from moneyed Pacific Palisades, and the white center and third-generation Yale graduate sitting together on the team plane. The time Kerr saw Randolph draped in a flashy necklace he asked how much it cost. "About $10,000," the rookie replied. Man, Kerr said, his sarcasm raging, I gotta get one.

On some level, they were trying to save Randolph from the bad influences among them at the start of what would become a seventeen-year career. "I don't know if that was conscious or subconscious," Dudley said. "But we just gravitated where we just were pulled toward each other and sat with each other and liked each other's company. We all had come from different places, different backgrounds, whatever. It was to Zach's credit too. He really wanted to learn. He wanted to understand the ways of the world, so to speak, in different areas. It just happened." Kerr, Cheeks observed, was "relatable to everybody. You would have not known he had four championships. The way he carried himself, the way he related to people, it was easy to see if he became a coach he was going to be a good coach." Later in the season, Kerr would be so impressive attempting to rally the Blazers during a bad stretch that speaking up forcefully in the huddle after a home shootaround despite a limited role in games likewise struck Dudley as the work of a future coach.

The Blazers finished 49-33 as Cheeks conceded his inexperience cost them five or six wins. Kerr enjoyed the season anyway, despite the same minor role as the season before in San Antonio and spending too much time away from Margot and the kids, and even despite the outlaw roster. In contrast to their unfortunate but well-earned image, the players got along in a way that would prompt him at the time and for years to come to defend the group as pleasurable to be around, a sentiment shared by many inside the locker room with mentions of Rasheed Wallace and Ruben Patterson as generous teammates, no matter how many issues they had in the real world. Kerr felt he, Dudley, Butler, and Rick Brunson "added some sanity to a situation that seemed a little insane the last couple years," and he made the best of the unwanted alone time by exploring Portland.

Kerr so enjoyed the team and the city that he hoped to return for the final season of his contract, 2002–2003, with the understanding it could also be his last before retiring. He called President Bob Whitsitt in midsummer to gauge whether the team felt the same way, hoping for enough stability to bring the family to Portland this time, and hung up with the strong sense he would remain a Blazer. Kerr reported being told his name had not come up in trade talks, that nothing was expected and to continue with plans for Margot, Nick, Maddy, and Matthew to move, but to check back in a couple weeks for an update before finalizing the relocation. Kerr never got that far. A week after the conversation with Whitsitt, the Trail Blazers dealt him to San Antonio as a minor piece in a larger deal fifty-three weeks after the Trail Blazers acquired him from San Antonio as a minor piece in a larger deal.

Kerr was surprised at the swap and angry at what to him felt like being double-crossed, without the courtesy of an update as the deal developed. That the family was all still together in San Diego, about two months before the start of camp, wasn't the point. He felt misled in a way that hadn't happened to him in basketball since the Gonzaga recruiting trip in 1983. Perhaps Kerr misheard Whitsitt, perhaps Whitsitt misspoke, and other Blazers would later back Kerr's account, but the bottom line should have been obvious to anyone and especially to a player always aware of his place in roster hierarchies: few players were off-limits in trade talks on a team with championship aspirations coming off back-to-back first-round losses, both three-game sweeps at that, and certainly not a thirty-six-year-old who averaged 11.9 minutes. Heading into the final season of the contract made Kerr even more appealing to potential suitors looking to shed salary or pick up a possible contributor without a long-term commitment. Kerr was so obviously a trade candidate that Whitsitt for years remembered agent Mark Bartelstein, while making it clear his client was happy in Portland, circling San Antonio as a preferred destination if a deal did happen.

As with Wayne Embry and the Cavaliers in 1992, Whitsitt held Kerr in such high personal regard that he wanted a destination that would offer a positive outcome, if a trade did happen. "I would trade guys to a bad situation because I've got to do what's right for the organization first," Whitsitt said. "But if I could do something that I thought was good for the good guys, I'd always try to do that. At least getting Steve Kerr back to a good situation made me feel a little better versus shipping him out for possibly his last year into the worst organization in the league, where they're going to win no games and it's a bad place to live." San Antonio was, of course, the definition of a good situation—Kerr knew and liked the city, knew and respected the coach in a franchise drenched in positives, knew the system, and the Spurs offered a better chance at another title than the Trail Blazers. Locker-room positives Tim Duncan, David Robinson, Danny Ferry, and Malik Rose were still on the roster and had been joined since the previous Kerr stay by Kevin Willis, Steve Smith, Bruce Bowen, Manu Ginobili, and Tony Parker, sixteen years after Parker's father hosted the Arizona basketball team in Challans, France, on its European summer tour.

If he had to be uprooted, the Spurs' embrace was an ideal place to recover from the frustration, even with the reality that a change in location might not lead to a larger role. If anything, arriving far down the backcourt depth chart, and with a coach who kept a tight hold on his veterans' minutes to ensure fresh legs for the playoffs meant Kerr could play less than in Portland. But San Antonio was a realistic title contender, an important consideration for a thirty-six-year-old with the chance to go out on top.

The regular season began with the same focus for Robinson, the Spurs legend likewise heading into what was understood to be his final trip through the NBA before retirement. In the victory lap that followed, Robinson received gifts from other teams as well as a $100,000 contribution from teammates and staff to the all-scholarship school he had created for underprivileged kids in San Antonio, and an annual $8,000 scholarship for twenty-five years to the same Carver Academy. Future winners of the league's Community Assist Award would receive the David Robinson Plaque, Commissioner David Stern announced in recognition of Robinson's exemplary citizenship. When the time came for tributes during his own presumed goodbye, Kerr deadpanned, he would get a six-pack and a bag of popcorn. Then, when the Spurs played in Cleveland on November 16 for what by all indications would be Kerr's final visit to his former home, Kerr and Danny Ferry, another ex-Cavalier heading into retirement, entered the locker room to find a six-pack of bottled beer on both their chairs and a bag of popcorn from a concession stand in their stalls. Their friend Bob Price, the Cleveland PR director, had made sure of it.

A month later, on December 16, still part of the rotation, Kerr played twenty-one minutes against the Clippers in Los Angeles and headed east while the Spurs' trip continued north to Seattle, with the understanding that anyone outside the team who asked where he was would be told he was missing games for personal reasons. Kerr said he did not want the attention that would come if word of a four-time NBA champion suing a country got out, and Popovich quickly agreed.

Civil Action 01-1994 began in the U.S. District Court for the District of Columbia the next day with Ann, Malcolm's four children, and his surviving sister, Dorothy Kerr Jessup, in attendance for the bench trial. Andrew's anger had subsided enough that he backed off the initial inclination to kill the perpetrators, knowing his father would disapprove, but he still liked the idea of shooting the murderers in a kneecap to let them endure the pain and then have to limp the rest of their lives, "the way we are." A trial, he conceded, was "probably" a better move.

The defense table was, as expected, empty as testimony began December 17. Going first on the second day, Ann said, "My children have each, I think, done remarkably. Each one has gone through this and somehow overcome it, and they have found life partners and made wonderful matches, and to me that is one of the most fulfilling things. And they have found careers that are very satisfying to them. A parent under any circumstances would want that, but particularly so under these circumstances, that what has happened hasn't held them back in these important life choices. They have been able to go ahead and do this."

Almost as soon as court reconvened for the third day, December 19, at 10:12 A.M., Steve was sworn in and took his turn on the witness stand with a startling personality choice given the somber task at hand.

"Can you briefly describe for the court your educational background?" Michael Martinez, the lead attorney for the family, asked early in the testimony, just as he had asked other witnesses to provide a snapshot introduction for the judge.

"Yeah," Kerr replied, "it won't take long."

There was laughter.

"I graduated with honors from Palisades Elementary School and—"

Laughter was again noted.

"—graduated from the University of Arizona in 1988."

"Okay," Martinez said. "And you received a degree, though, correct?"

"I did, yes," Kerr answered.

"All right. And can you tell the court your current occupation?"

"I'm an aging professional basketball player."

Later, when asked why he decided to participate in the suit, Kerr responded, "Well, because Andrew told me to." Turning serious, he added, "There were a couple of reasons. The main reason was when this was brought up as a family, I wanted to be part of the family. I wanted to support everyone. I didn't have a great interest in doing this. I didn't think I would get a great deal of satisfaction, given that there's nobody sitting over there at the defense table. There's nobody in the jury box. I wasn't sure if I would get much satisfaction. And there definitely still is something lacking for me since nobody's actually going to serve any time or pay the consequences in a way that they should. But I feel great about the fact that we have done this as a family. I feel great that I've come up and spoken, and I wanted to do it to support the family."

While receiving the desired satisfaction was impossible, Kerr did delight in the rare chance to hear memories of young Malcolm from Dorothy Kerr Jessup and used part of his time on the stand to pay tribute to Ann for "holding the family together, accomplishing so much with her own life and moving forward and being such a great mom and a great grandmother, and we love you, and we're lucky to have you. Thank you." In the end, he was happy the suit went forward and felt some good would come of it, regardless of the ruling and the frustration of staring at an empty defendants' table. Kerr stepped down after forty-six questions from the family's attorney and the judge, some basic to establish his background but mostly about growing up with Malcolm and the personal impact of the loss.

Agreeing with his older brother's sentiments, Andrew called the proceedings "a pretty impotent attempt at justice." Also, he added a moment later, "I want to say that I think it's really a testament to my parents that our family has done as well as it has, and that, you know, we really owe them a lot. I think a lot of people, a lot of families would have kind of scattered to the wind, and not only, I think, did we stick together, but, you know, we're very close, and that means a lot to have them."

Judge Jackson concluded the testimony portion of Civil Action 01-1994 at 3:38 P.M. on the third day with a statement: "Very well. The case is submitted. And let me say that I am deeply honored to have presided over this proceeding. I'm humbled and honored to have met this family. You are truly admirable people, and I will remember you."

The aging professional basketball player rejoined his team for the December 21 home contest against Michael Jordan and the Washington Wizards, logged seven minutes in what amounted to a conditioning session, and returned to his previous role of regularly breaking double digits off the bench. Jackson's ruling in *Kerr et al. v. Islamic Republic of Iran* came February 11, with the Spurs in Portland. The evidence, the judge stated, "amply demonstrates" that Hezbollah, sometimes known as Islamic Jihad, acted at the instigation of and with the logistical and financial support of the Iranian government. Based on compensatory damages and in part on the testimony of an economist who determined what Malcolm would have earned in salary and pension as AUB president for another thirteen years before retiring at sixty-five, Jackson awarded $8,025,296 to Ann as executrix of the Malcolm Kerr estate, $10 million to Ann directly, $3 million to each of the four Kerr children, and $1,500,000 each to Dorothy Kerr Jessup and the executrix for the late Marion Kerr Miller, Malcolm's other sister. Nineteen years and one month after the murder, the family, aware they would probably never see a dollar, at least had a measure of emotional satisfaction.

The longer the regular season went, the less Kerr played. The playoffs started with him locked on the bench for all six games against the Suns in the first round and for three of the six in the second round versus Phil Jackson and the Lakers, with all of six, two, and two minutes in the three times he was given directions to the court. And when the Western Conference finals against the Mavericks opened with Kerr sitting the first two contests and barely playing the next two—literally barely playing: three seconds late in Game 4 for his dependability from the line with Dallas forced to foul—Popovich grew weary of questions about Kerr not playing. When another came after Kerr was a spectator for all of Game 5, Popovich turned to Tom James, the director of media services standing nearby. "Do I really have to answer this shit?" Popovich asked. James nodded.

Kerr had appeared in five of a possible seventeen postseason con-tests and logged twelve minutes and fifty-seven seconds by the time Game 6 against the Mavericks arrived May 23 in Dallas. Counting the end of the regular season, he had sat out fifteen of the twenty-three latest outings, such an involuntary hibernation that Kerr be-gan calling himself Ted Williams, the baseball legend in cryogenic storage since dying nearly eleven months earlier. "I've been on ice," teammates heard him say. "I'm frozen. Just call me Ted." Realistic as ever, but also giving his coach cover, he offered the unnecessary reminder that "I'm 37. I'm slow. I'm not a very good defender." Dal-las pounced on Kerr, he admitted, by posting up six-foot-eight Walt Williams as soon as Kerr began defending Williams. "A lot of peo-ple don't know I was the MasterLock defender of the year in sixth grade," Kerr said. "Apparently the Mavericks weren't aware of that and they were going at me. There's a reason I don't play a whole lot, and I think we all know why that is. I'm not the greatest defender out there."

But with starting guard Parker sick, apparently food poisoning from room-service crème brûlée the night before, Popovich told Kerr to be ready. Kerr stayed with his pregame routine of shooting and one-on-one against assistant coach Mike Brown some ninety minutes before tip-off. Then he waited through most of three quar-ters for the chance that didn't come, even as Parker labored and the home team built a fifteen-point lead, prompting some Mavericks to already ponder a decisive Game 7 two days later. Popovich was finally desperate enough to call for Kerr with 3:44 remaining in the third quarter and the Spurs down 63–48 while befuddled by the Dallas zone defense. He had not made a basket in forty-three days, since the regular-season finale, and had attempted three shots all playoffs.

His first launch, a three-pointer from twenty-three feet with 1:40 left in the third, cut the Dallas lead to 65–56.

Watching as the Mavericks constantly double- and triple-teamed Duncan reminded Kerr of defenses sending the same mass cover-age at Jordan during the championship days as Bulls teammates.

Every time he looked inside, Kerr saw three opponents hanging on Duncan.

Kerr's second try, a three-pointer from twenty-five feet with 7:11 to play in the fourth quarter, got the Spurs a 71–71 tie.

Dallas stayed in zone and kept collapsing inside to drape Duncan in a way that created openings on the perimeter.

Kerr's third attempt, another three-pointer from twenty-five, with 6:28 remaining, put San Antonio up 74–71.

On the Spurs bench, Budenholzer was struck by a thought: *Thank God.* "We needed him so badly." On the Mavericks bench, assistant coach Paul Mokeski was melting into his chair with frustration. It was bad enough that 13 years earlier he had urged Cavaliers teammate Kerr to let the ball fly without concern, a pep talk Uncle Mo was suddenly paying dearly for. Worse, his instructions to Dallas defenders had been clear as soon as Kerr entered: the Mavs had to get in his face, before Kerr could set his feet, and force him to dribble to find an opening. Kerr couldn't create in his prime, and certainly not this late in his career. Before Mokeski knew it, though, he was staring at the nightmare of the catch-and-shoot specialist taking a stance and waiting for a pass.

The fourth shot, yet another three-pointer, a twenty-four-footer with 5:13 showing, extended San Antonio's lead to 79–71, en route to a 90–78 victory that sent the Spurs to the Finals against the New Jersey Nets. A fitting finish to his career, Popovich called the thirteen minutes, speaking of Kerr's retirement as a done deal while Steve continued to label it only a possibility. "The greatest feeling ever," Kerr said. "The greatest feeling ever." When Mokeski congratulated Kerr as they hugged on the court, his mind flashed back to what had become very bad advice as Cleveland teammates.

In the victorious locker room, awash in the exaltation of his latest surreal moment, his sarcastic side revving to Grant Park '97 levels, Kerr told Popovich they would need to talk contract extension for the Spurs to have any hope of him deigning to play in the championship series. Asked by TNT's Ernie Johnson to sum up the performance, Kerr thanked Ted Williams for allowing him to escape the cryogenic chamber where they had been "residing." When PR man James walked Kerr back to the court about ten minutes after the game for a live interview in front of the scorer's table with Don Harris of WOAI, the NBC affiliate in San Antonio, Kerr radiated with what Harris saw as the constant smile of "pure, innocent kid joy" of hitting a home run to win the Little League championship. "All I wanted was a moment," Kerr had told him off the air during a few minutes of waiting politely for the connection to the studio to blink on. "A chance for all the preparation to pay off."

When Harris glanced down before going live, he saw that the hairs on Kerr's arms were standing up. Harris looked at his guest's neck and noticed goose bumps there as well. Nothing changed when they went on the air. The goose bumps continued to pop and Kerr remained the Little League hero, making no attempt to play it cool and repeating the sentiment he shared before the interview. All he wanted was a chance. The night, he later described, was "a perfect culmination for me, a perfect way to go out. It confirmed what I've always believed, that keeping at something will pay off in the end." Kerr was still so excited even after the energy rush on the court, the hour flight to San Antonio, the drive home, and winding down at the end of the night that he climbed into bed and stared at the ceiling, unable to fall asleep.

In either the strangest of coincidences or the most fitting occurrences for someone whose road had become all about bad scenes turning into dream outcomes, the second-greatest night of Kerr's playing career had also been as the finish to a dreadful series. Nothing in uniform would match the reverberation of toppling the Jazz six years earlier and, he believed, changing the trajectory of his life, but resuscitating himself for the second half in Dallas would remain his showcase game. He was the superstar for an extended stretch, not a single shot. Even when Kerr returned to the usual 2002–2003 role of unused insurance policy as San Antonio claimed the title in six games, May 29 in Dallas was such a big moment in Spurs history that it would hold up as a symbolic walk off the stage.

He went out on top, as a champion for the fifth time, the career leader in three-point accuracy, one of the most-respected and best-liked players of the generation, and one of the underdog success stories of the league. By the time Kerr made official what had been obvious and announced his retirement on August 7, 2003, only one other 1988 draft pick, Rod Strickland, was still active. No guard in the class shot better and no one who played longer than one season came close to his 45.4 percent behind the arc. Among the ten players selected immediately before Kerr, five made fewer than twenty-five appearances. Among the ten chosen after him, six didn't even make the NBA.

"This is my 15th year in the league and it's probably 15 more than I should have had really, with the ability I was given," Kerr said in his final days. "But things have just completely gone my way throughout my career, even back to college, going to Arizona and getting to play for Lute Olson, and playing in the NBA for Lenny Wilkens and Phil Jackson, and even playing with great players like Michael Jordan and Tim Duncan. It's just amazing that I'm still here and I'm not even sure why that is. I know I've worked hard and I know I've gotten some breaks. But I've just ended up on the right team all the time." In personality, at least, he left as he entered—self-aware, humble, and appreciative. Everything else, though, had changed.

CHAPTER 10

Speeches and Shouting Matches

He immediately ruled out a comeback—"Let's put it this way: There's not a big market out there for 38-year-old, slow, white guards coming out of retirement." Instead, Kerr plunged into a series of dramatic life changes, with a fresh career path in broadcasting and a new family base after being convinced by former Arizona and Bulls teammate Jud Buechler to move to his hometown, San Diego. The kid who went body surfing and boogey boarding in the foam off Pacific Palisades bought a longboard soon after relocating to Southern California, 150 miles south of the home where Ann still lived, and fell in love with surfing. To satisfy the need for competition, Kerr threw himself into tennis, two-hour hard-court matches that hammered at his knees.

Moving into television was an obvious first professional step into retirement. Of all the jobs he would hold, none was so obviously destined for success as Kerr with a microphone, a destiny since his youth, of prank calls to talk-radio shows and delivering high school American history reports in the bombastic timbre of Howard Cosell. He was a natural with an unparalleled comfort level with the media and an ability to translate strategy into conversational language combined with a biting sense of humor. The only difference in the fall of 2003 was that he would be a paid Moth.

Kerr was just wrong about how he got there. His usual explanation—the prime spot was the ripple effect of hitting the shot for the Bulls in the 1997 Finals—was far down the list of reasons TNT hired him without previous experience. Fifteen seasons in the pros was all the résumé bosses needed for name recognition, and any TV executive would have recognized his personality as star quality. So many did, in fact, that Kerr would be hired by two networks, a full-time home calling NBA contests for TNT and later occasional college games for Fox Sports. If anything, referencing frozen Ted Williams in the TNT interview after beating the Mavericks clinched his hire by parent company Turner Sports, not bringing a title to Chicago six years earlier.

His résumé as a public speaker grew in 2004, near the end of his first season with TNT, to include the University of Arizona commencement address. The seventeen-year-old who got a backhanded invitation to Tucson had become the thirty-eight-year-old veteran asked to impart sage advice, an irony not lost on the speaker most of all. And the mood, not just the location, would be perfect, a serious message interspersed with the frivolity of the occasion that at UA included flinging tortillas as Frisbees. Some were messy after being picked off the ground and others hurt on impact if especially dry, and one year a projectile smacked school president Peter Likins in the face. Likins urged an end to the tradition and by the time Kerr was preparing his remarks, Likins had instituted robe searches for the Class of '04 in an attempt to confiscate unauthorized flatbread. The local legend returning to campus was no help. "I think it's great," Kerr said a few days before his speech. "I'll be ready for them. I'll have my queso ready, so I can have a little snack while I'm up there."

In the most fitting of developments, the entire school, not just the basketball program this time, invited Kerr only if the first choice fell through. Likins was waiting on George W. Bush's availability for May 15 and had a contingency plan to move the processional from the usual two ceremonies in the basketball arena to a single event in the football stadium to meet the projected level of interest. Even Steeeeeve Kerrrrr!!! back in Tucson and back in McKale Center, with his uniform number 25 in the rafters, could not compete with a presidential visit. When the White House declined—as Kevin Johnson, Reggie Miller, and other prospects had decades before—

Kerr again happily filled the fallback role in a commencement that remained airborne rowdy despite Likins's crackdown.

The consolation prize generated great interest anyway, the most since Secretary of State Madeleine Albright five years before. UA hoops fans and former Kerr classmates asked the school if they could attend as well, just to hear the address at the 9:30 A.M. commencement or the repeat at 1:00 P.M., before he flew to California to work the Lakers-Spurs playoff game for TNT that night. Those who did show just for the speaker were among the estimated 25,000 attendees including educator Ann Kerr, who flew in from Los Angeles, scheduled to hear her son and see 5,043 students receive undergraduate and graduate degrees.

"Many of you may know the story," Kerr said from the podium, "but Dr. Likins called me back in November and asked if I would give the commencement speech, and despite a few pangs of anxiety, I accepted his offer. But three weeks later, he called back and said, 'I'm terribly embarrassed about this, but it seems that the leader of the free world has requested the opportunity to give the address, only at this point, he's not sure if he'll be available. Would you be offended if we put you on hold until we get a definitive answer from him?' To which I responded, 'Dr. Likins, whatever Lute Olson wants to do is fine with me!'"

It was two sessions of being left open in Game 6 against the Jazz, speeches that pivoted from genuflecting before Olson to mocking himself, praising his parents, lampooning Rodman and touching on Middle East terrorism and *Brown v. Board of Education*. He even doubled back to Olson for a dig that played on the emotions of the Wildcats' loss in the first round of the NCAA tournament a month before. ("By the way, graduates, you can all call him 'Lute' now. As undergraduates it had to be 'Coach Olson.' Now it can be 'Lute' or whatever you want. I know I called him something else after the Seton Hall game last season, but that's another story.") Basketball player Steve Kerr never came close to the agility of speaker Steve Kerr in McKale.

"You know," he said, "when I was in my fourth season in the NBA, I played for the Cleveland Cavaliers, and thanks to an injury suffered by a teammate, I was forced into the starting lineup for a game in Chicago. Lenny Wilkens, my coach, told me before the game, 'You're guarding Michael Jordan.' Until today, that was the most nervous I'd ever been in my life. I knew I didn't belong on the floor with the greatest player of all time, and today I'm wondering if I should be here in McKale Center giving the commencement address to 5,000 distinguished University of Arizona graduates. That game did not go well. The Bulls beat us by 30, and I scored two points. Michael had 48. I can only hope today goes a little better."

Kerr was accurate in spirit if not exacting in detail. The Bulls won by twenty-eight points and Jordan scored forty-four, although certainly not all on Kerr in a game he started but played only fifteen minutes.

"I'd also like to thank Dr. Likins and the student body council for presenting me with this opportunity," he continued. "It's certainly one that I never could have imagined, and if you'd seen my first-semester grades back in 1983, I'm sure you wouldn't have either."

And: "My parents literally showed me a whole world that existed beyond typical American culture. They gave me an education in understanding people; in being compassionate and respectful. They taught me that though people may speak or dress differently, or have customs or beliefs that were foreign to me, it was important to take the time to not only understand those differences, but to embrace them as well. That came in handy years later when Dennis Rodman became my teammate with the Bulls."

Turning serious later in the speech, speaking slightly less than a mile from the Babcock dorm room where he learned the news that changed him forever, he offered that "We're in an age of severe cultural and religious differences around the world. We are in desperate need of cultural exchange and understanding. People everywhere have learned that lesson in tragic ways, losing loved ones to terrorism or to war. My family experienced that agony when I was a freshman here at the U of A. My father, Malcolm Kerr, who was the president of the American University in Beirut, was killed by extremist assassins who were angry at our country's military presence in Lebanon. That was 20 years ago, and as I read daily about the deaths of our brave servicemen and poor Iraqi civilians, about terrorism, about religious extremists and war-mongering politicians, I can't help but think how sad it is that cultural and political relations have gotten even worse in the 20 years since my dad was killed."

His Arizona past was looming even larger behind the scenes as Robert Sarver quietly maneuvered to buy the Suns. Sarver was an Olson family friend and had been especially generous when Bobbi Olson fell seriously ill in Hungary while her husband conducted coaching clinics in the summer of 1998, dispatching his Gulfstream to whisk Bobbi back to Tucson for treatment for advanced ovarian cancer. In 2004, when Sarver was interested in becoming an NBA owner, Lute Olson connected Sarver to Kerr as someone who could arrange an introduction to Commissioner David Stern, apparently unaware Stern was accessible by nature and especially to anyone with the desire and money to purchase a franchise. Stern would have pedaled from his Manhattan office to the desert to meet a potential buyer flashing the right bank account, with or without Kerr brokering a meeting. When Sarver finalized his $401 million purchase of the Suns in July, he gave Kerr a 1 percent ownership stake for laying the foundation with the league and because putting Steve Kerr on any masthead in Arizona was good business. It turned out that the real Kerr-Suns public-relations coupling was bringing him on as a consultant with zero responsibility, not drafting him in 1988.

Being hired the same 2004 off-season by Yahoo!Sports as an NBA columnist was the chance to indulge a lifelong passion. Just as Malcolm wrote or edited five books on the Middle East and kept in touch with family and friends in faraway lands through a torrent of letters, and Ann kept a diary, taught English, and penned an emotional book centered on her experiences in Lebanon, Steve was equally taken by the process. He jotted down stories from his playing days, insisting he was keeping a personal scrapbook of a special time and not preparing to publish, and as an adult loved to dissect the craft. He would speak with writers about narrative tension and foreshadowing. Kerr by nature was eternally inquisitive on a variety of topics and a prodigious reader with the same range, but sitting at a keyboard went beyond general interest.

Yahoo! signed him to a season-long contract in a marketing move similar to Cris Carter being hired to break down the NFL and Jack McDowell and Ryne Sandberg to analyze baseball, then it quickly learned it would be getting something different. While Carter's postings in particular were often ghostwritten by senior editor Joe Lago, and other marquee contributors were unreliable with deadlines and scheduled video appearances, Kerr from the first day had the approach and dependability of an experienced journalist. He emailed copy on time and free of mistakes and offered opinions in conversational tones from the lofty platform of a five-time champion, as the company obviously wanted. Though a side job to his TV work, the author typically filing twice a week was so invested he regularly asked which topics were generating the most traffic so he could tailor future ideas for maximum success.

"Before I even had to call him, he would already be reaching out to me about ideas," Lago said. "A story would break and before I could even pick up the phone, he would have already emailed me . . . or texted me, like, 'Hey, I'm running to the airport. I saw so-and-so, whatever signing or whatever. I really want to weigh in on this. Count on me for like eight hundred words or whatever and I'll write on the plane and I'll send it to you as soon as I get off my flight.' He was like a dream. Seriously. What other writer does that?"

"He is a unique talent, and I struggle trying to think of anyone in basketball history who can do the things he does," Kerr wrote of Dallas power forward Dirk Nowitzki that season. "Larry Bird comes to mind, but Nowitzki runs the floor much faster. Kiki Vandeweghe? Maybe. But Dirk is much bigger and a better ball handler. James Worthy? Didn't have the shooting range."

"The Warriors are not good," he noted in placing Golden State fourth from the bottom in his December 8, 2004, rankings. "I'll let you know when that changes." The Nets were only one spot better. "Help has arrived in the form of Jason Kidd. I can see it now: Kidd leading the fast break, [Richard] Jefferson on his right and . . . everybody else 40 feet behind them."

There was even a swipe to at least partially avenge an old wound, whether readers took it as analysis or, among the few who knew of his frustration over being traded by the Trail Blazers, an inside joke. Writing of Knicks personnel boss Isiah Thomas acquiring Jamal Crawford when New York already had Stephon Marbury dominating the shooting in the backcourt, "Isiah seems to be following the blueprint designed by Portland GM Bob Whitsitt several years ago—get the 12 most talented players you can find on one roster and let the coach sort it out. Ask Mike Dunleavy and Maurice Cheeks how they feel about that strategy." It was not lost on Kerr that the coach who would have to sort it out this time in New York was one of his favorites, Lenny Wilkens.

The 2006–2007 regular season closed with Kerr so emotionally invested in the Yahoo! work that he asked to file every day in the playoffs despite being paid a set rate for the campaign, not by the article. He would essentially be doing volunteer work to feed his writing fix. One of the days was spent calling Mavericks-Warriors in Oakland for TNT as Golden State completed a first-round upset and bedlam reigned with fans screaming themselves hoarse and threatening to blow the bolts off Oracle Arena. It was a hellacious, glorious noise that stayed with Kerr for years. The "best atmosphere I've ever felt in my life, as a broadcaster, even as a player," he called it in 2014, a weighty statement for someone who experienced five finals and a Final Four in an arena, not the emptiness of a converted football or baseball stadium. "I've never seen anything like that."

The Suns at the same time had gone from winning the Pacific Division with a 61-21 record and beating the Lakers in the first round to losing to the Spurs with Mike D'Antoni as coach and general manager. Kerr seemed content far behind the scenes with a sliver ownership stake and enjoyable work in broadcasting. He was aiming for a future in coaching but several years later, after his kids were out of the house. When Sarver pressed him in the summer of 2007 to replace D'Antoni in the front office, Kerr, whether wanting to protect his investment or guilted into accepting to repay Sarver for the ownership gift, relented. He was named GM on June 2.

Kerr immediately immersed himself in the front office in every way, not only attending basketball operations meetings but conferences on the business side as well. Just as he told new teams soon after joining as a player to reach out if he could help in any way, usually with the media, the rookie GM quickly sent the same message to various departments as one of the bosses. He would not hesitate to leverage his popularity in the state if it could help sell the Suns. Kerr, his top assistant David Griffin said, "was the best salesman the organization had."

Still, Kerr kept only a spartan condominium in Scottsdale, mostly a place to sleep and watch games and occasionally eat, while regularly jetting to San Diego to remain a constant in his family life. He knew from the days as a Trail Blazer, when owner Paul Allen and especially GM Bob Whitsitt were portrayed as visitors for living near Seattle and maintaining temporary housing in Portland, that optics mattered. It may have been different because Portland had an inferiority complex to big brother Seattle, and Whitsitt could have called anywhere home and been hailed a hero if the team won a title, but Kerr was well versed in appearances. Sending the message of being invested was important.

The actual work, not the visuals, was the problem. Under orders from Sarver to cut payroll, Kerr sold the twenty-fourth pick in the draft, Rudy Fernandez, to the Trail Blazers, allowing the Suns to dodge one guaranteed salary. Nine days later, they dumped another by trading key reserve Kurt Thomas and a pair of first-round choices to Seattle for essentially nothing, a second-round choice, as Sarver prioritized finances over title hopes. Kerr was allowed to sign free agent Grant Hill, but Phoenix turned down an extension for four-time All-Star Shawn Marion, leading to Kerr's first training camp as an executive beginning with Marion requesting a trade.

The regular season had barely started when Kerr, with a surprising lack of awareness for someone with his experience and feel for locker-room culture, approached D'Antoni after a loss with the suggestion the Suns call more post-up plays for Amar'e Stoudemire. D'Antoni, angry at being told how to coach, and in no mood to discuss it immediately after a defeat, struck back. The ensuing shouting match in the coach's office that ordinarily could have been explained away as an innocent misstep by an inexperienced general manager instead became a flashpoint with the backdrop of the Suns in a unique time. D'Antoni, in his sixth season of his NBA role with eight more in Italy, not only had to answer to a novice boss but one who had replaced him as head of basketball operations. D'Antoni was also well aware of Kerr's reputation around the league as a coaching star of the future, creating unavoidable speculation. Assistant coach Dan D'Antoni was in his brother's ear about Kerr as a threat. The fact that both the head coach and the general manager were among the best-liked people in the game and able to remain laid-back in a stressful business changed nothing.

D'Antoni and his backers refused to accept that Kerr was not interested in coaching until after his kids were out of the house and that he certainly didn't want the job by stepping over a man he liked personally and wanted on the sideline, as long as D'Antoni was open to adjustments. It didn't help perceptions that one of Kerr's biggest influences, Popovich, took a similar path to his first head coaching job by firing Bob Hill and naming himself the replacement. Kerr was also obviously a Sarver favorite, so the owner one day nudging Kerr to the sideline, just as seemed to happen with the front office, was a logical outcome. As much as he saw a future on the sideline, though, Kerr never would have volunteered for the job in 2007–2008 and likely would have resisted any pressure to take over.

With no additional scrapes after the November conflict, or at least none that became public, D'Antoni and Kerr were able to work together. Professionalism and similarly likable personalities prevailed long before Kerr had to face his own version of Jackson-Krause in Chicago. The relationship improved to where Kerr came to observe, "We've come a long way in terms of trusting each other.

I've always liked the guy and his demeanor. Not a lot really gets under his skin. I admire his background—all of his travels in Italy, his perseverance—and it doesn't hurt that our political beliefs are similar." The mending only went so far, though. Later in the season, asked whether Kerr questions him about how players are used in a game, D'Antoni laughed. "Not if he wants to live long," the coach said, turning noticeably testy. "That wouldn't work."

Trading Marion and Marcus Banks to Miami for Shaquille O'Neal was Kerr's move with D'Antoni on board, no matter how much O'Neal in his plodding years of post-Lakers decline was contrary to Phoenix's up-tempo offense and even though the Suns were 34-14. It was both the act of Kerr feeling he needed to do something after Marion asked to be traded and an organization reduced to trying anything to get past the Spurs. Playing fast hadn't worked, so it was time to mix in size. Kerr did the deal on February 6 and the next day caught an afternoon flight to San Diego, reached Nick's freshman basketball game by five o'clock, had dinner with the family, and slept in his own bed before turning back around to Phoenix the next morning.

The sight of the new acquisition sitting the first five games after the trade with hip and leg injuries, the same ailments that cost him time with the Heat before the deal, was the reminder that Kerr had acquired a thirty-five-year-old making $20 million who was also hurt. Then the Suns lost four of eight immediately after the swap. "The only way I win in this is if we win," he said. "We made the decision to do this, and I'm the guy whose name is on the line. It might become, 'Bring me the head of Steve Kerr,' but that's okay. I know what Shaq can bring to the court and to a team. And, besides all that, I just don't want to do things like everyone else does them." In typical Kerr fashion, the Moth had answers at the ready.

The blowback was worse than he imagined. Kerr was shocked at the cruelty the night of a loss to the 76ers and the fourth defeat in six games since the trade. One email arrived from dead@beirut.com and a sender identified as "Your Father." After chastising Kerr for trading Kurt Thomas, James Jones, and Marion and drafting Alando Tucker, the note concluded, "One last thing. PLO, PLO, ASU had it right." A second email contained a similar message, with the mention that, "Steve, you are an idiot and the ASU fans had it right. Beirut! Beirut! Beirut!"

"I knew this job would come with some stress, but I had no idea someone would do something like this," Kerr said after sharing the letters with Paul Rubin for a *Phoenix New Times* profile of the general manager under siege. "It's very hurtful, and beyond my comprehension." Rubin didn't even include the worst of it, agreeing to Kerr's request to not use the most searing of the language that referenced Malcolm getting what he deserved, for the sake of his family.

Not only had Kerr never faced such criticism, even at age forty-two and with decades in the public eye, he had rarely even been in position to be held so accountable. His senior season at Arizona was the only previous time, as the emotional leader and co-star of a title contender, but 1987–1988 was also with the Wildcats and their plucky everyman point guard as an inspirational tale. So much goodwill had been built up that he could have missed twice as many shots in the Final Four and still been a hero. The rest of the way was either a non-issue (Suns rookie, Magic Trail Blazers), an extra behind much bigger names (Cavaliers, Bulls, Spurs), or so good it was nearly impossible to criticize (TNT). At midseason 2007–2008, though, Kerr was suddenly standing in the middle of a busy intersection, the center of the commotion of the Suns in a tenuous place, the man who put his name to Sarver's tossing salaries overboard, the cause of a perceived rift with a likable coach who delivered results and funball, and now the boldest move of all by bringing in O'Neal.

Agreeing to dinner and a lengthy interview with Rubin posed the new risk of Kerr opening himself to greater public ridicule now that whatever public response he received would be chronicled in print. He voluntarily went anyway, although with the beneficial timing of a five-game winning streak by the time Rubin arranged a table near a TV and met Kerr downtown at the Half Moon Sports Grill to watch Suns-SuperSonics from Seattle. Kerr was recognized in the crowded spot, but left alone to eat, sip a beer, and take in the game, until his team made it six in a row and a group of young men sitting nearby began chanting "Steve Kerr! Steve Kerr! Steve Kerr!" It wasn't the drawn-out tribute call from McKale, but he approached the fans with a smile.

"Thanks a lot, you guys," Kerr said, before pausing for effect.

"But I'll bet you, two weeks ago, you weren't going 'Steve Kerr, Steve Kerr,' huh? It was more like, 'What the *fuck* is Steve Kerr doing?'" Anyone in hearing range broke up.

Accepting blame and deflecting credit, even in times that doubled as vindication, and maybe especially in difficult moments that turned triumphant, had already become classic Kerr. If he turned the greatest moment of his professional life into the punch line of needing to bail out timid Michael Jordan, if he sarcastically demanded an extension from the Spurs after a very brief triumph, refracting a sixth consecutive victory into a flashback of fans trashing him was nothing. He had the ultimate advantage of knowing he didn't work hard to get the Phoenix job in the first place, that he didn't want to keep it long, and that getting fired, the worst-case scenario for most, would simply mean sifting through all the offers to become a coach or return to broadcasting. "He'll feed his kids pancakes, work on his laptop, field a call about trading for Shaq, or something," his mother said. "He's such a devoted father, family man, husband. When people say the trade might cost him his job and he says, 'Good,' he really means it. If it doesn't turn out like he hoped, he'll move on."

More aware of his safety net than anyone, Kerr often joked about the San Diego life he would be having with Margot, fifteen-year-old Nick, thirteen-year-old Maddy, and ten-year-old Matthew. He could be playing tennis at the club or relaxing in a swank hotel room before a broadcast, Kerr would say, instead of jousting with agents, handling personnel decisions, and trying to build a sustainable relationship with the coach. People brought it up to him other times, asking rhetorically what the hell he was doing working for a living when he could be longboarding Pacific swells off San Diego County, or golfing, or never losing a game as a network analyst.

Kerr would respond with a smile of agreement and keep showing up the next day.

Feeling disconnected from the team was the worst of it, a job hazard he realized with regret that first season and never got over. Sometimes, it was the actual distance of being out of town scouting while the Suns were on the road and he remained in Phoenix or when he used the opening for a San Diego dash. More often, though, he felt the lack of involvement in daily on-court interactions or locker-room camaraderie he loved after so many experiences on teams awash in good chemistry. The Suns had plenty of that too, with historically good leaders Steve Nash and Grant Hill in 2007–2008 and the welcoming personalities of D'Antoni and the coaching staff. But having to watch longingly through holes in the fence proved to Kerr once and for all he needed to be on the court. He was a coach, not an executive.

Kerr realized as much even before the first season in Phoenix ended with more aggravation than the challenging start—a third playoff loss to the Spurs in four years despite O'Neal's solid contribution of 15.2 points, 9.2 rebounds, and 2.60 blocks in 30.2. By the time D'Antoni, still feeling unsupported by both his bosses, quit in an interview with *Sports Illustrated*'s Jack McCallum after the finale in San Antonio, not in conversation with Sarver or Kerr in a telling disregard, the rookie general manager had lived several seasons in one.

Not only was management forced to surrender to the reality that D'Antoni was anxious to leave a city where he was appreciated and a locker room where he was greatly respected, but Kerr for one of the few times in his life was the cause of conflict, maybe the only time in a basketball setting. Appearing overbearing, at least to D'Antoni, was the most unlikely of descriptions for the guy who got along with everyone. Even actual fights, with opponent Stacey King in the playoffs or teammate Michael Jordan in practice, passed quickly and successfully. Having to unexpectedly head a coaching search in the summer of 2008, after eleven months on the job, was a rare personal blow as well.

D'Antoni, in demand, needed only eleven days after the loss to the Spurs to reach an agreement with the Knicks. (D'Antoni would come to regret the career shift—"I shouldn't have gone to New York," he said in 2012. "I should have stuck in there and battled. You don't get to coach somebody like [Nash] too many times. It's pretty sacred and you need to take care of it. I didn't.") Kerr, meanwhile, gathered a familiar list of potential replacements before making Spurs assistant Mike Budenholzer, former San Antonio teammate Terry Porter, former Suns teammate Tyrone Corbin, and Houston assistant Elston Turner the finalists. Porter pushed to the front for Kerr as the only one among the four to have been a head coach.

It took only until January, less than halfway through the season, for Kerr to realize his mistake. Adding O'Neal the previous season was an odd fit for an offense predicated on speed, but at least it was a calculated gamble in search of new ways to counter the San Antonio menace. Porter's arrival, though, brought an entire change of direction with an increased emphasis on defense, as Kerr wanted from D'Antoni, but slowed the tempo so much that veterans used to running were in basketball straitjackets. The Suns, Nash said, had so lost their identity that players fell out of shape. With Phoenix at 28-23 at the All-Star break and on pace to miss the playoffs, Kerr fired his choice after eight and a half months on the calendar, three and a half months of regular season, and fifty-one games in the kind of devastating setback aging rosters cannot afford. "Probably the most difficult thing I've ever had to do was to relieve someone of his duties you like, respect, and admire so much," he said. "But it had to be done. I could feel it. We could feel it as an organization."

Gentry, a D'Antoni assistant who stayed on under Porter, was so obviously the successor, albeit as interim coach, that Kerr delivered the promotion with an apology. Kerr told Gentry that he should have hired him last summer, and that he made a mistake. Knowing Kerr well, from the days scouting Palisades, Gentry was not surprised at the unusual wording of the offer, but also didn't need the mea culpa to move forward. He could have been in New

York, absorbing continuous body blows with D'Antoni and the rest of the previous Suns staff that stayed together, but instead was in a city he enjoyed, working for a head of basketball operations he liked and respected, and excited for the upgrade when it did come. Gentry even considered the reasons for hiring Porter in the first place to be sound.

The change was immediate in the way many teams feel an energy surge after a coaching switch, but also startling. So relieved were the Suns to get back to the D'Antoni system under Gentry, they scored 140 points the first game back from the All-Star break, 142 the second, and another 140 the third. Even with the comedown of a six-game losing streak in March, Phoenix improved from a .549 winning percentage before the move to .581 after. Though Phoenix still missed the playoffs at 48-36, the closing kick was enough to rejuvenate the organization, send Kerr into summer in search of bold strikes and convince Sarver to remove Gentry's interim label,

The first was to trade O'Neal. While he would recall Kerr keeping him informed of the possibility by saying the Cavaliers had been asking for the thirty-seven-year-old center, the Suns were not disappointed to get away from the $20 million due in 2009–2010, whoever initiated the talks. "I was impressed," O'Neal wrote of the phone conversation with Kerr. "That's all any player wants—to be treated fairly and honestly. I told him, 'I appreciate it. Go ahead and do what you have to do.' He didn't have to call me. It was his right to do whatever he wanted, but he made the effort and I appreciated it. He was like that the whole time I was there. He'd say, 'Hey, I need you to do this' or 'We're going to sit you and rest you this game.' I'd say, 'Are you sure?' and he'd say, 'Yes, we think it would be good for you.' I would have done anything for Steve Kerr. All he had to do was ask." When Kerr called his former Orlando teammate June 24 to report Phoenix and Cleveland had an agreement on a deal that would mostly bring financial relief in return, O'Neal was equally understanding. In retirement, after playing for six franchises and interacting with countless executives, he would maintain that "Steve is one of the most honest GMs I've ever been around."

Preparing for the draft at the same time trade talks progressed, Kerr locked in on Davidson's Stephen Curry while aware that Curry would not last until Phoenix's selection at number fourteen. The Kings, picking fourth, might go point guard, the Timberwolves (fifth and sixth) were definitely thinking point guard, the Warriors (seventh) were enamored with Curry, and the Knicks (eighth) could see Curry as perfect for the D'Antoni offense on skates. The Curry camp wanted New York as well and sent clear signals to Sacramento, Minnesota, and Golden State to spend their choices elsewhere or end up with an unhappy rookie. The Warriors had fallen so hard for Curry, though, that they ranked him second on their draft board, behind only Oklahoma big man Blake Griffin. Coach Don Nelson, approaching heresy, said Curry reminded him of Nash in being able to shoot with range, find openings in the defense to score from other spots, and create for others.

Kerr's only chance would be to trade up. When discussions moved to a package centered on Amar'e Stoudemire and number fourteen for number seven, the Warriors, after years of futile attempts to find a dependable big man, were intrigued by the chance to land a power forward coming off an All-Star season in exchange for the uncertainty of a rookie. Plus, they already had a productive point guard, Monta Ellis. But Golden State loved Curry as much as Kerr did. General manager Larry Riley, an admirer since the NCAA tournament the previous season, scouted Davidson-Purdue in Indianapolis in December specifically to see if Curry caved against a physical Big Ten opponent, then left more impressed than ever when Curry handled the jarring defense and continued to make smart plays even on a poor shooting afternoon. Riley would also need a strong indication that Stoudemire was interested in Oakland as a long-term home, not just for 2009–2010 as the final year of his contract before sprinting to the exit as a free agent. Turning away from the potential of Curry was a risk Riley was willing to consider for six or eight seasons of Stoudemire shredding defenses, but not at the risk of getting Stoudemire for one.

When the draft began inside Madison Square Garden, the Suns

wrongly believed they had a deal with the Warriors, if Curry made it that far, to reroute him to Arizona. Golden State wasn't going to proceed without talking to Stoudemire about his future, and Riley hadn't even asked Kerr for the required permission to speak with a player under contract in Phoenix as the selections began. If Curry was on the board, the Warriors decided, they would take him to keep him. If not, they were open to trade talks and even wanting to deal rather than choose among several players they did not like. Kerr so thought he had an agreement with Riley that cheering could be heard coming from the Phoenix war room when the Timberwolves took point guards with the fifth and sixth choices, but not Curry.

Seven hundred miles away in Oakland, the Warriors gladly watched as Hasheem Thabeet, Jonny Flynn, and Tyreke Evans, players Riley didn't want, were picked. His dream outcome remained alive. Going in, Riley anticipated having to decide between James Harden and Curry, with Curry the likely winner, but the potential difficult decision was eliminated when Oklahoma City took Harden third. At the very moment the Suns were celebrating Minnesota's decision, Riley's best-case scenario had materialized. As Kerr learned later with great dismay, the Warriors took the top shooting prospect in the draft to keep him, leaving Phoenix to select Earl Clark at fourteen. All hope of Kerr riding what he was sure was the future greatness of Curry was gone.

Kerr knew that same summer that his relationship with Sarver was splintering, to the surprise of the general manager more than anyone. He was prepared all along, one friend said, for agents to grind him over contracts and playing time, and ready for travel away from the luxury life of the team charter to scout college games. He was even braced for the fallout from difficult decisions, albeit not to the level of demented emails, but he did not originally see a divide with his supervisor coming. Whether Sarver misled him about autonomy or changed directions would never become clear, only that the player who spent decades priding himself on staying ready had become the executive unprepared for a large obstacle. Even a season earlier, O'Neal sensed Kerr "had his own issues with the owner," suggesting Kerr was not the only one struggling to deal with Sarver as domineering and meddlesome without any basketball background.

"I think Steve had a challenge in terms of dealing with people in the organization, starting at the top, in terms of how to function in his role as general manager," said one person Kerr confided in. "That was an issue for him." Even the rush of four and a half months of intense action—firing Porter, hiring Gentry, the high-energy finish to the regular season, believing he had a trade to land Curry, dealing O'Neal—could not mask a growing dislike for the job.

"You can tell with Steve," one member of the organization said. "Steve's an exuberant, outgoing guy, a lot of fun to be around. Toward the end it just wasn't as much fun for him. You could see it."

The Suns' 14-3 start was an obvious help, the start to a season he would greatly enjoy on the court and also vindication for the roster and coaching decisions over the previous months. The close to 2008–2009 had not, it turned out, just been a meaningless spike in a lost campaign. Now playing amid some pressure, Phoenix reasserted itself as a factor in the conference as the signature Mach I offense fired away, with potent results, to offset the lack of defense and rebounding. That turned into a 54-28 finish to the regular season and a 2–1 series lead in the first round of the playoffs against the Trail Blazers as Senate Bill 1070 was signed into law in Arizona by Governor Jan Brewer. A game later, during the flight home from Portland, Sarver and Kerr discussed possible responses to the legislation, which directed law enforcement to question people about their immigration status and request documentation if they were suspected of being in the country illegally. How could the Suns signal their support for Arizona's large Latino community?

It was Sarver's idea after Phoenix eliminated the Trail Blazers to have players wear jerseys with Los Suns across the front for a home game against the Spurs in the second round. They used the same orange uniforms in two March wins as part of the league-wide Noche Latino marketing push, only this time the schedule broke perfectly for a public statement: the Suns would wear them again on May 5—Cinco de Mayo. President Barack Obama earlier in the day put an additional spotlight on the protest by noting during a Cinco de Mayo event in the Rose Garden, "I know that a lot of you would rather be watching tonight's game. The Spurs against Los Suns from Phoenix." NBA Commissioner David Stern called the team's actions appropriate, the players' union similarly supported politicizing Game 2, and Popovich said he only wished he'd had enough advance notice to order Los Spurs jerseys for San Antonio to wear. Among the dissenters, Phil Jackson, of all people, pulled back from social awareness inside the locker room with "I don't think teams should get involved in the political stuff," and, "Where we stand as basketball teams, we should let that kind of play out and let the political end of that go where it's going to go." Of the eighty-four letters to the editor the *Arizona Republic* received on the topic on May 5, seventy-nine were against the decision suggested by Sarver and approved by players.

Not merely backing his boss and his roster, Kerr went all the way to the historical perspective: "It's hard to imagine in this country that we have to produce papers. It rings up images of Nazi Germany. We understand that the intentions of the law are not for that to happen, but you have to be very, very careful. . . . It's important that everyone in our state and nation understands this is an issue that needs to be explored. So, we're trying to expose it."

It was the first time he had spoken out so forcefully on a political issue, even if the words soon faded as attention turned back to basketball. No future social commentary, though, would match the harshness of linking Arizona lawmakers to Nazis. The governor's spokesman termed the feedback "ugly" and "hateful" while noting he could not recall any member of the Suns speaking up during four months of public debate on the bill, only to jump in after the fact.

Attention in town quickly shifted back to basketball as the Suns won Game 2 amid the controversy and then Game 3 in San Antonio to move to the verge of finally beating the Spurs in a series and with the possibility of a sweep. As the clock ticked down in Game 4 and the climax neared, *Arizona Republic* beat writer Paul Coro on press row spotted Kerr standing in front of his seat among what remained of the spectators, arms reaching to the ceiling of AT&T Center in celebration of the instant and the big picture of what it meant for a franchise with so many scars from previous losses to San Antonio. It was his pinnacle as a general manager, and one reason he would remember 2009–2010 as a fun time from a basketball perspective. His roster decisions came through, the team was trending upward again, and he had a bond with players and coaches. Subsequently losing to the Lakers in the West final couldn't change that.

Nevertheless, Sarver approached him with two unattractive options: a one-year contract at the current salary or a three-year deal that would repeat Kerr's original deal along with a new bonus for reaching the third season, 2012–2013. No long-term job security while working for an owner who often ignored his advice or an immediate 10 percent pay cut to have his 2010–2011 wages match 2007–2008. Kerr didn't expect a raise amid reports of difficult financial times for the organization and knew all too well his decision put Sarver on the hook for the $2.5 million still owed Porter, but it was also easy to view the tepid offers as Sarver's lack of confidence in his general manager. Meanwhile, Griffin's deal was also expiring at the end of June, and Gentry had one season left and no sign of an extension.

When the Philadelphia 76ers hired Doug Collins as coach on May 21, creating an opening for a TNT analyst, Kerr had options of his own, beyond the obvious one of walking away and fielding offers while in San Diego in his one and only residence. Yet Kerr, though more convinced than ever that he belonged on the sideline and not in the front office, was appreciating what the Suns were building enough that he would have been able to swallow the pay cut. He cared that he was enjoying the moment and the people around him, not how the public slap would be perceived.

What he could not accept was Sarver letting Gentry go into 2010–2011 as a potential lame duck needing to sweat through every day to prove he was the man for the job. The Suns had finally climbed Mount Spurs, they had reached the conference finals, the arena was at 95.8 percent of capacity for the forty-one regular-season home games, better than the league average, and Kerr was following through with his plan to fold promising youth in with Nash, Hill, and Stoudemire. If the basketball staff wasn't going to be rewarded then, Kerr reasoned, they never would be.

The sides negotiated again on June 14 with Kerr still hoping and planning to return. On June 15, the Suns called a press conference to announce his abrupt departure to return to TNT, leaving Gentry to inherit some GM responsibilities during the search for Kerr's successor. "I wouldn't say it's a big surprise," Sarver said, spinning hard. "Television is what he did before he came on board. It's a change of plans from during the season. It boiled down to a number of things, including lifestyle and the [TV] opportunity. I was hoping to have him back." Kerr insisted his decision was not about money, and Sarver contradicted him on that too, noting that the salary issue was "a small part of it." Kerr may have been determined to take the high road to avoid unleashing another storm of criticism on Sarver, who, after all, had unnecessarily handed him the pot of gold of partial ownership for facilitating a meeting with Stern that needed no facilitating. Or it might have been semantics. Kerr might have been fine with the money, hit and all, but Gentry's arrangement prompted him to take a stand. That contract, not his own, was the breaking point.

"Steve knew he was fine for the rest of his life," David Griffin said. "Not being able to do the right thing for people was the end for him. At the end of the day, he's a human being more than anything. He wants to live his life to a certain standard as a man, and when he couldn't deliver upon that, he was done."

Collins leaving for the 76ers was fortunate timing that allowed the Suns to concoct the cover story of Kerr's own departure as being an opportunity to return to TV and family. In reality, Kerr likely would have walked away even without TNT as a soft landing. Sarver portrayed it as an amicable parting, and it never had been in Kerr's nature to publicly bury someone even when justified. He wouldn't do it now either in the only bad breakup of his professional life. OKP beyond the Chicago city limits as well, he publicly expressed little more than bewilderment over Krause's desire to break up the Bulls, despite an obvious allegiance to Phil Jackson, he vented to friends about being wronged by Whitsitt but never openly dinged Trail Blazers management, and so it would be with Sarver and Phoenix. Besides, Kerr still had a practical reason for wanting the Suns to appear a stable operation gliding to the future—he retained the ownership stake after returning to broadcasting.

The three seasons with the Suns, despite the mixed results and exasperating end, would prove beneficial in shaping the Kerr of later years. In that way, the 155-91 record in the regular season and 11-10 in the playoffs on his watch was an invaluable personal positive. The veteran of locker-room culture should have thought more carefully about time and place in suggesting change, but the conflict with D'Antoni would become a valuable lesson in relationship-building between a coach and general manager. The disagreements with Sarver amplified his belief from Chicago that the partnership needed to be among three people, with the owner synced with the two leaders of the on-court decisions. And the flop of the Porter hire warned him of how important it was for a new coach to shape his system to the existing personnel. All were events that sharpened the vision of what Kerr wanted when he stepped into coaching, a move that seemed inevitable in the summer of 2010 as he became a broadcaster and full-time San Diego resident again.

CHAPTER 11

In Demand

Former opponent Michael Cage, retired after a lengthy career, immediately noticed "a more relaxed, happy Steve Kerr" when they crossed paths and chatted at their daughters' tournaments in the girls' volleyball hotbeds of San Diego County and just north in Orange County. Kerr standing near a court with his arms folded and appearing fully at ease was the common sighting as fatherly angst from watching Nick in basketball and Maddy in volleyball became the only sports-related stress in his life and family time happily dominated his world again. Although he retained the small ownership slice in the Suns and rooted for Gentry among several favorites still in Phoenix, most notably Steve Nash and Grant Hill on the court, the world of executive decisions and ghastly emails moved to the background as 2010–2011 began.

Kerr was forty-four years old—in the greater issue, Nick was seventeen, Maddy fifteen, and Matthew twelve—and doing a lot more than pondering the future. City-hopping with TNT became Kerr's entrance into practices and shootarounds as well as an opportunity to quiz coaches in the private meetings teams were required to hold with national broadcasters before games. While he probably would have been welcomed to the workouts anyway, a common practice for friends within the game, even those aware of his interest in a future on the bench may not have known he was working toward that goal by stuffing notebooks with information he learned in the sessions. Opponents were aiding the learning curve that would lead to the commentator coming back to beat them.

He would have collected the plays even without teams holding the door open for him, just as scouts sitting courtside to prepare for an upcoming opponent leave with several detailed breakdowns, even the names of the plays called out. Similarly, Kerr appropriated ideas while watching games on his flat-screen at home, without benefit of VIP access. He spent years diagramming plays, watching LeBron James and, in a particularly valuable bit of forecasting, imagining himself preparing to face the immovable force in a playoff series. He analyzed potential assistants for his future staff and noted how coaches handled delicate moments. The chance to regularly volley ideas with future peers, to talk through situations on and off the court, would prove valuable as his personal file grew by the week. "He asked some questions that might not fit on a telecast, but that he could use down the line," TNT partner Marv Albert conceded, even if some responses were haphazardly recorded on the cardboard in his dress shirts when they came back from the dry cleaners.

Kerr already had a natural dedication for preparation—habitual in pregame routine as a player, habitual in wanting to be the most experienced first-time coach in history—when he attended a sports leadership conference at the Aspen Institute in Colorado in the summer of 2013 and visited with Jeff Van Gundy. Write down everything, the former Knicks and Rockets coach advised Kerr. What you want to emulate, what you want to change, what you have learned along the way. Develop a philosophy and organize your thoughts. Ramping up efforts while closing in on his new dream, Kerr created a Word file on his laptop to continuously log details for later consideration, all the way to ruminating over policies for families accompanying the team for road games to whether players who got little or no action in a game should be required to do cardio work afterward. A friend and high school coach would pull game clips Kerr spotted on TV and create another file with iMovie.

Phil Jackson had been talking privately since the days of Bulls backup shooting guard Steve Kerr about eventually hiring him as a head coach, needing only to fill in the location and year they would be reunited. Kerr, in Jackson's eyes, would not merely be a successful NBA coach. He would be a great one with an ideal combination of intelligence, work ethic, and communication skills, bound by a personality that connects with almost everyone in the game. A long playing career with five rings and mountainous basketball names Jordan, Duncan, Popovich, and Jackson atop the list of admirers would be helpful credibility if Kerr took a job without experience as at least an assistant coach. Jackson's insistent behind-the-scenes predictions were so convincing they prompted his friend Sam Smith, the *Chicago Tribune* writer, to urge the Washington Wizards in June 2003 to take the risk of hiring Kerr upon retirement in an unorthodox move of going directly from playing to the number-one spot on the bench.

Jackson's early certainty soon grew into a strong sense in several front offices that Kerr, though unproven as a coach and with mixed results in the lone stint in management, was a rising star in either role. The Trail Blazers, one of Kerr's former teams, were so enamored that President Larry Miller made him a primary target in the search for a general manager in May 2011, got turned down, then made another run eleven months later when the job reopened, only to be politely turned down again. Miller could offer a city Kerr enjoyed, the support of an aggressive owner with very deep pockets, Microsoft cofounder Paul Allen, and a location two and a half hours from San Diego by plane and still got nowhere.

Even long friendships made no difference. When Orlando fired Stan Van Gundy as head of basketball operations a month after Kerr spurned the Trail Blazers, Alex Martins, having through the years climbed from director of public relations to president, put Kerr at the top of his wish list. "I think he thought about it for half a second," Martins said, an answer so definitive there was no reason to forward the top candidate to owner Rich DeVos for further consideration.

There were likewise feelers from four or five teams to gauge interest in coaching, with the same diplomatic response. The high school player ignored by most every school in the country, the college player passed over forty-nine times in the draft, the NBA player who in the summer of 1993 had to pursue teams, not the other way around, had by the early 2010s crossed into an alternate world where he was an object of affection. He had multiple choices not only on where to work but in which of two premium roles. Coaching was the clear preference, but at the right time, after Nick, Maddy, and Matthew were older.

He was admired on so many levels, in fact, that interest from potential employers reached the surreal: White House conversations to deputize Kerr as emissary to North Korea. Though highly unconventional, the suggestion made sense to economist Marcus Noland as President Barack Obama sought advice from experts in mid-2012 on how to deal with new leader Kim Jong-un. When U.S. secretary of state Madeleine Albright brought a basketball signed by Michael Jordan as a gift for Kim's father and predecessor, Kim Jong Il, on a visit to Pyongyang in 2000, the present was so treasured it would be displayed in a glass case in the International Friendship Exhibition Hall north of the capital, a hallowed venue where visitors were required to pass through an air-blowing machine to enter and wear shoe covers.

Get Kerr, Noland proposed to Obama in the Roosevelt Room. The CIA a few years earlier had weighed recruiting Dennis Rodman as it became apparent Kim Jong-un was being groomed to replace his father, but the idea never gained traction. Now that the son was in charge and Obama called the meeting to solicit input on how to deal with the young leader, Noland encouraged the president who took office after living in Chicago and serving as a senator from Illinois to leverage the Bulls angle. It didn't have to be the undependable, erratic Rodman. Kerr met the basketball requirement of living the Jordan years, including the 1997 Paris exhibition games with Swiss student Pak Un in attendance, and had spent time among different cultures while growing up and watching his father navigate delicate international situations. At the very least, Kerr could handle a game of H-O-R-S-E with Kim while U.S. officials observed in hopes of finding diplomatic clues.

Sitting across the table from Obama, Noland could see the blood drain from the faces of the two advisers on each side of the president, both from the National Security Council, at the suggestion to send a basketball player on a diplomatic mission with such high stakes. "They literally were turning white." Noland realized his proposal was the definition of unconventional and understood the reaction of the NSC specialists on the region, but he pressed forward with the premise that traditional negotiations had not worked either. Maybe it was time to try something different, and the veteran of three trips to North Korea saw Kerr as the best of the different after Jordan and Pippen declined previous overtures with warp speed. It was strictly coincidental that Noland knew fellow Swarthmore student John Kerr in the 1980s. In the end, Obama never appeared interested and the idea was quickly dismissed without serious consideration.

The chance to partner with Jackson seemed to emerge in 2013, after the Kings were sold to a group that would move the team to Seattle and, it was expected, hire Jackson to run the front office, followed by Jackson hiring Kerr. The plan fell apart when NBA owners voted to keep the team in Sacramento, ending the sale. Even then, the relationship had only strengthened by the time Jackson became president of basketball operations for the Knicks in March 2014, their unequal teacher-student alliance in the Bulls' traveling circus of the 1990s having morphed into equal footing. Kerr still leaned on Jackson for advice and prized his friendship, only now Jackson likewise sought input from his former pupil. Kerr had grown into an adviser. It was as if three decades of professional respect and personal admiration had built into the perfect, unimaginable timing of Jackson taking over his first team at the same moment Kerr finally felt comfortable being away from home for weeks in a row.

Kerr going to New York was an instant and, understandably, logical speculation. The *New York Post* asked Olson and was told, "I think he can handle New York, and being with Phil makes him much more secure in what he's doing." SiriusXM asked Kukoc, who replied that Kerr "knows everything about basketball. I am just concerned about his willingness to be a coach, travel, spend that time in the hotels, the locker rooms, the games. . . . If he's ready to do that, I don't see any problem with Steve being a good basketball coach." The second half of April and the first weeks of May, Kerr's relocation to Madison Square Garden was commonly spoken of as a done deal.

Kukoc, while correct about the grind, had missed the point with his Bulls teammate. Time around a team—the hotels, the locker rooms, the games—was exactly what Kerr missed and why he had become anxious, not just willing, to trade the velvet life of a broadcaster for the pressure of the sideline. Spending a lot more time away from the family was a drawback, to be sure. But the chatter on the bus after a practice in some random city, the camaraderie, the feeling of a close win after executing a game plan in the fourth quarter were the lures, not the concerns. "It's where his joy for the game comes from," David Griffin said. "It's the locker room. It's the guys. The big picture part, while intellectually he was made for that, spiritually he's made for [coaching]." Nick and Maddy were in college, and Matthew was a high school senior. It was time.

Golden State was in the first round of the playoffs and in no position to court replacements as the disconnect with its coach grew so canyonesque that management had all but decided to fire Mark Jackson even if the underdog Warriors beat the Clippers. The acrimony between Jackson and bosses who considered him distant and combative had reached the point of blotting out the positives, including the contradiction of a good relationship with many players, most notably franchise cornerstone Stephen Curry. Beyond the personality clash, the front office wanted an offense with more ball movement, as opposed to Jackson's designs that favored isolation basketball to spotlight the growing greatness of the Curry–Klay Thompson backcourt.

One more win, in Game 7 on the road, probably would not have saved Jackson, but it might have changed history by extending the season and ending the Kerr relationship before it started. Needing to wait at least ten days, and possibly weeks, might have been a tipping point as Kerr aimed for a quick resolution to avoid stalling his mentor in New York. Another Golden State favorite, Stan Van

Gundy, moved toward accepting an offer from the Pistons to become coach and general manager, a dual role the Warriors would
not consider with Myers quickly on his own path to a bright future.

All the while, Kerr was playing out the many drawbacks of the
New York situation, most obviously the distance to San Diego and
the poor records and worse management under owner James Dolan.
Three seasons with Sarver was supposedly enough to teach Kerr
about the importance of cohesion among the top decision-makers,
yet here he was just four years later, knowingly walking into a situation more dysfunctional than the Suns of the early 2000s. Kerr
knew the very public rap sheet on Knicks ownership—a loss in a
sexual harassment lawsuit, regular turnover in coaching and the
front office, negative publicity from every direction—but he went
to close ally Albert anyway for an insider's perspective based on
Albert's thirty-seven years as Knicks play-by-play man before being
fired in 2004. "Steve reads everything," he said. "This was not something he didn't know. But he wanted to get deeper into it."

In other moments of deliberation, Kerr envisioned being alone
in a hotel room in Manhattan as the latest blizzard growled outside, game planning for an incapable team, and feeling lonely, 2,500
miles from San Diego. Phoenix was hard enough emotionally while
the team was winning at a decent rate and he was close enough to
jet home for dinner. New York would mean losing and loneliness.

That he continued toward the Knicks anyway was testament to
both his admiration for Jackson and his appreciation of Jackson's
part in jump-starting Kerr's career. To one confidant who listened
through Kerr's depressing projection of a hotel future in wintertime
New York as defeats mounted, "It was obligation, from his view. He
felt he owed Phil. Phil didn't say, 'You owe me.'" Kerr's emotions
were being stretched from one coast to the other. "The point was,
he was thinking, 'Yeah, it's great to work with Phil, yeah, I would
love to do it. It would be like a repayment of mine that I could feel
good moving forward that I could repay him for all he did for me."
Kerr saw all the signs that he was walking into a colossal career
mistake, yet pressed on rather than disappoint Jackson.

Resolving one layer of uncertainty, the Warriors' 2013–2014 ended with a loss in Los Angeles in Game 7 on May 3, a disappointing result but also, as it would turn out, one of the best outcomes in team history. Kerr was nearing a decision as Golden State closed the season twenty miles from Pacific Palisades soon after no less an informed observer than Lute Olson said Kerr would "more than likely" take the New York job, an assessment reinforced by Olson's weekly conversations with his former point guard. Finally, Phil Jackson said Kerr on May 5 committed to become the next coach of the Knicks.

Resolving the next layer, the Warriors fired Mark Jackson on May 6 and faced the predictable blowback for dumping the coach who played a major role in a franchise with a recent woeful history reaching fifty-one wins, in Curry's fast track to stardom, and in shaping a top-five defense. Management, especially hands-on owner Joe Lacob and general manager Bob Myers, had prioritized mood outside the locker room over devalued results, exactly the opposite of the 1990s Bulls, for whom thick tension was the norm and also acceptable as long as victories flowed. Worse, Lacob and Myers made the move minus a clear path to the future, with no successor lined up to replace the guy who delivered results.

The initial approach to one of their top candidates could not have been more discouraging. Kerr replied to their overture that he was far down the road with the Knicks, that he wanted to let that possibility play out as the sides worked toward a financial agreement and that, in essence, in the most gracious terms, they should look elsewhere. If you change your mind, Lacob and Myers told him when there was nothing else to say, we'd still like to talk. New York increased its offer to four years and $17.6 million, a contract Kerr considered "very fair," but he had yet to address a major concern. He had yet to speak with Dolan.

Kerr was on the road nineteen consecutive days by his count, calling a game about every other night, which made it difficult to visit Knicks brass at Madison Square Garden in Manhattan or the training facility in suburban Westchester. But not impossible—he and Albert worked the Raptors-Nets playoff contest in Brooklyn on April 27 and did not have another assignment until Wizards-Bulls two days later in Chicago. Whether Dolan made himself unavailable for as little as a phone conversation or Jackson and top lieutenant Steve Mills kept Dolan away over concerns that a conversation with the owner would send Kerr running the other way, the candidate never got the chance to ease his fears over the Garden as a place of never-ending turmoil. He had a dinner with Jackson, but nothing else. For his part, trusted friend or not, Jackson never hustled himself onto a plane bound for whatever TNT game Kerr was working, contract in hand to turn on the charm and close the deal. Jackson would regret that inaction for the rest of his life.

Golden State brass—Lacob, Myers, and assistant general managers Travis Schlenk and Kirk Lacob—flew to Orlando to meet with Van Gundy, aware he was nearing an agreement with the Pistons. The process to replace Mark Jackson had barely started and the Warriors were already playing catch-up, with two favorites essentially off the board. They jetted across the country anyway, to Van Gundy's adopted hometown, leaving open the slim possibility he would get excited enough about the promising young roster to turn away from the Pistons for a lesser role in Oakland.

Myers's cell phone rang during the meeting in a hotel. It was Mike Tannenbaum, Kerr's agent. Myers stepped out to take the call. Kerr is not locked into the Knicks, Tannenbaum told him.

Joe Lacob's cell phone rang. Kerr's caller ID flashed on the screen. It was Lacob's turn to step into the hallway. New York isn't a done deal, Kerr confided.

The Warriors' world had turned so dramatically in an instant that Kerr was now pursuing them after telling Jackson he was going to New York, and in the middle of a meeting with a candidate on the other side of the wall. Joe Lacob immediately realized "there was an opening, which we weren't sure there was ever going to be. I know it was a possibility because that deal wasn't done. But certainly you had to presume that he was going to go in another direction. So when we got that call, that was an opening. And usually when there's an opening, Bob Myers and I run through the door. We make it happen." Plus, unlike the ooze of Dolan's history, Golden State offered the familiarity of prior firsthand connections with Lacob, former agent Myers, and team president Rick Welts, a friend since their shared time in Phoenix management. The Warriors suddenly, inexplicably, had a chance.

Both sides proceeded with urgency as the Golden State contingent headed from Orlando to Oklahoma City, where Kerr was calling a playoff game, the day after the Van Gundy meeting to press their case in a way the Knicks never did. As excited as the Warriors were for the opportunity, it was Kerr who attacked the opening and turned a job interview into a crescendo that Joe Lacob called a "tour de force," three hours of Kerr's analytical mind, advanced communications skills, confidence, and preparation trumpeting at once as he finally took his notes out of idle. Rather than play it cool and make it seem only a colossal financial package combined with an emperor's power could lure him from the basketball easy chair of network color analyst, he titled one of his earliest PowerPoint slides, "Why I'm Ready to Be a Head Coach."

There was little need for gentle diplomacy inside the conference room at the Oklahoma City airport, not since he was the one who had reached out to the Warriors, on his own and in directing Tannenbaum to also get proactive to turn away from New York. Kerr clearly liked the Golden State possibilities, assuming they were thinking along the same lines financially, and so this was no time to be delicate or disorganized. He was neither. The candidate was soon grilling the employers, specifically wanting to know why there was an opening after obvious gains under Jackson, because a change after fifty-one victories and nearly winning a Game 7 on the road while short-handed could be an indictment of the front office more than the coach. Satisfied with the frank explanation that the atmosphere had turned toxic between coach and too many parts of the organization, Kerr became more convinced his future was in Oakland.

He was friendly yet assertive, detailed while also keeping the conversation moving across several topics, and self-assured but vulnerable enough to admit he would need the help of experienced assistant coaches. Kerr broke down the kind of staff he would hire, including his targets for assistant coaches, recognizable names that would be mentioned as potential replacements as soon as the novice stumbled, a detail the front-office leaders took as a welcome sense of security in direct contrast to their perception of Mark Jackson. David Blatt, a Massachusetts native who became a coaching star in Europe, and well-respected NBA hands Alvin Gentry and Ron Adams topped the wish list. Kerr owned the room while dissecting proposed changes on offense and defense, embracing analytics, breaking down the roster, and even suggesting sleep plans and diet routines he believed would pay off in the standings. The Warriors in attendance swooned.

Kerr left the meeting believing Golden State would be the owner-general manager-coach relationship he prioritized after the years in the fractured Suns hierarchy, just as he knew the same bond would not exist with Dolan in New York. The disparity was as obvious with the rosters—Golden State had twenty-six-year-old Curry and twenty-four-year-old Thompson and the top seven players in minutes from a playoff club returning, while New York offered twenty-nine-year-old Carmelo Anthony and the likelihood of multiple seasons of rebuilding. The Warriors offered a superior contract as well, five years and $25 million. And location, of course, with Maddy in neighboring Berkeley as a Cal freshman and Oakland an hour flight up the coast from San Diego as Matthew entered his senior year of high school and Nick headed into his junior year at the University of San Diego. The Bay Area even had Tolbert, recast in retirement as a broadcaster. The chance to work for Phil Jackson was a massive plus for New York, but it was also one against the many.

Kerr-Warriors was such an obvious match that the sides needed all of one day to go from meeting to negotiating the pact to announcing the agreement on May 14. Kerr, continuing in organized fashion, had already spoken to Curry by phone. Golden State had

gone from a desperate spot, with Van Gundy and Kerr ticketed elsewhere, to a dream result in about forty-eight hours from the calls in
Orlando to a deal. It became an especially happy outcome for Kerr
when Phil Jackson accepted the news from his presumed protégé
with grace and sent Kerr on his way without a guilt trip. Ultimately,
Kerr reasoned his change as, "I told Phil I was going to come as long
as we could work a contract out. And we didn't ever work a contract
out. I was going to go assuming they made a fair offer—which they
ultimately did—but during that span when we started to negotiate,
the Warriors' job opened up. So I felt horrible because Phil means
so much to me." Jackson additionally softened the blow by telling
Kerr that coming to New York and later regretting it would have
been the worst thing for both of them.

Kerr had unknowingly built a case that he was looking for an
escape from the Knicks no matter what, or at the very least that he
was heading to New York despite recognizing the mistake. He pur-
sued the Warriors after telling Jackson he would come. He said he
needed fair financial terms from Dolan, got an offer he considered
fair, and declined it anyway. He had already been second-guessing
himself—the losing, the distance, the ownership—before signaling
his strong interest in Golden State in mid-meeting with Van Gundy.

Even the family was surprised at the whiplash of events. "We
all thought he was going to take [the Knicks] job, and we weren't
trying to influence his decision or anything," Maddy said. The deal
with the Warriors came together so fast that she didn't even know
Golden State was an option until her dad texted the news just as she
was about to take a final exam at Cal, five miles from Oracle Arena.
"He's a total California person—I don't think he would have done
well in New York with the weather and being alone," she said. "He
needs my mom." (Steve would later tweak Maddy that accepting
the Warriors job came with realizing that the "two biggest factors
were my daughter being at Berkeley and Steph Curry being on the
team. And as I told my daughter, it was 90 percent Steph and 10
percent her.")

The Warriors went to work constructing credibility that did not exist. Unable to tout his experience on the job at the introductory press conference, they moved the success of the people Kerr had played for, the closest thing he had to a coaching record, into the spotlight. Olson sat in the front row as a video display showed "Kerr's Legendary Coaches," with shots of Jackson, Popovich, Wilkens, Fitzsimmons, and Olson. Kerr had a list of references and many believers around the league, but no tangible background, only the promise of being "willing to put in the work and put the right people around me."

"Look," Lacob said, "at the end of the day I know he knows a lot about basketball. We're taking a little bit of a risk on his coaching ability, but we did that with Mark and it worked. So it's just about finding the right fit for the organization and a guy who has extremely high potential, is a hard worker, and is very prepared. That's what we have got."

That Kerr's preparation was the exact opposite of his strongest coaching influences when they got high-level jobs went unsaid. Olson worked at five high schools and a junior college before reaching a Division I program. Fitzsimmons, Kerr's first NBA mentor, began as a JC coach for nine seasons. His second, Wilkens, was player-coach for the SuperSonics and Trail Blazers and then became a full-time coach. Jackson's proving ground included five seasons in the minor leagues, the Continental Basketball Association, even driving the team van for the Albany Patroons, work in Puerto Rico, and time as an assistant with the Nets and Bulls. Only then did he, ironically, turn down the top spot in New York to choose Chicago. Popovich had eight years as head coach at Pomona-Pitzer, a small university in Southern California, and runs as an assistant at Air Force, Kansas, Golden State, and San Antonio. Kerr had instincts and a Word doc.

Still, Popovich said early in Kerr's first regular season, before any real results were in, "Steve was a no-brainer. There are certain guys on your team that you know have an intuitive feel for the game.

They're also natural leaders and good people. They communicate well, have great work ethics, and high intelligence. He had all that stuff. It was pretty easy to see."

The risk was almost entirely on the Warriors, of course—they would suffer a setback, possibly severe, if Kerr failed, while he would have lifetime financial security from a deal signed in his forties and multiple invitations to return to network broadcasting. Given his reputation around the league as a coaching star in the making, he would undoubtedly have future opportunities there as well, even if the outcome in Oakland was bad. As it was, he got a superior roster and more money in a preferred location with an organization pumping positive energy. It could not have turned out better.

CHAPTER 12

Strength in Words

The Qantas beast, flight 94, a double-decker Airbus A380 super-heavy, pushed back from the gate at Los Angeles International Airport at 10:40 P.M. on June 11, 2014, roared into the night sky, and began a southwesterly course over the Pacific Ocean with Steve Kerr in 22J in business class. He left on Wednesday, crossed the International Dateline, and landed in Melbourne, Australia, on Friday after sixteen hours and twenty minutes of flight time, reaching the gate at 9:00 A.M. Kerr had just one full day in Melbourne and one in Sydney, whether his sleep cycle cooperated or not, before returning to California on the sixteenth with another A380 ride in business class that eased back from the terminal at 1:18 P.M. on Monday in Sydney, crossed the Dateline the other way, and parked in L.A. at 9:36 A.M. on Monday.

Communicating with players, not surprisingly, was a Kerr priority, his chance to talk through his vision for the team and the player. Communicating in person was even better. Andrew Bogut was in his native Australia, so 16,000 air miles and $13,213.60 in airfare for a brief visit it would be. Beyond the obvious purpose of the extravagant gesture as an attempt to build a relationship with an important locker-room voice, jetting to a different hemisphere sent the immediate message that the new coach dealt as directly as possible. It became a larger statement of Kerr's methods once the roster convened and saw the Australia hop as an act of genuine desire, not a showy moment that lacked follow-through.

Kerr went to Miami to visit Harrison Barnes, who was spending part of the off-season working out near his agent. He reached out to Draymond Green and Green's Michigan State coach, Tom Izzo, for additional insight into what Kerr knew would be particularly challenging bonding with the most emotional Warrior. ("He's an incredible guy, but he's different," Izzo remembers telling Kerr.) He spoke with Klay Thompson by phone after Thompson's father, former NBA veteran Mychal Thompson, assured Klay that Kerr's history playing for Jackson and Popovich meant the Warriors were in for a smooth transition. He knows what he's doing, Mychal told his son. In conversation with Curry, Kerr laid out the Popovich credo that stars are held to a higher standard, to set the tone for the rest of the roster. Kerr did not hesitate to say that he would get in the face of the franchise player, with the expectation Curry would be able to take it.

In May and June of 2014, Kerr swung his confidence like a heavy club in ways that startled even some Warriors. It was, strikingly, unlike anything from his days as a player, a level of self-assurance that didn't exist until his thirties, after high school and college and well into the fourth NBA stop. So certain was he about the positive direction, he told Barnes on the phone as they watched Spurs-Thunder in the Western Conference finals on television on opposite coasts, that he thought Golden State could be there, in the same round, next season. Barnes was incredulous. "I'm like, 'Dude, we just lost in the first round in Game 7, you know what I'm saying? You're saying that real confidently. You've never coached.'" To Andre Iguodala, the Warriors merely needed to find their weaknesses and correct them, as if it would be that simple. "If we stay sharp," the coach told him, "we can get a six-, seven-year run out of this thing."

The Warriors had won a single playoff series the previous seven years, and suddenly the new guy was gushing about being annual contenders into the next decade. It was no different from any coach taking the helm of any team by declaring it the start of a new era and setting championship goals, except Kerr was pointing to the heavens while suggesting the process would take months, not years. He had gone from a playing career of realistic expectations, leaving for

Tucson figuring he had little chance to play for a bad team and later heading to the pros hoping he could squeeze out a couple seasons to brash predictions with minimal supporting evidence. The Warriors obviously had promise, but they had also just finished sixth in the conference. The Thunder could point to a roster with Kevin Durant and Russell Westbrook, the Trail Blazers had Damian Lillard, C. J. McCollum, and LaMarcus Aldridge, and the Clippers offered a foundation of Chris Paul, Blake Griffin, and DeAndre Jordan. Golden State hardly had a monopoly on potential.

Being able to drop five rings on a table in a waterfall of diamonds gave him instant credibility as more than just another smooth talker. After all, he did know as well as anyone in the league what a championship-caliber roster looked like, even if he didn't know anything about it from a coach's vantage point. Kerr then boosted his standing by frequently praising Mark Jackson in private conversation with players and also in public comments, a sign to players that he didn't envision himself as the cocky genius with all the answers. Kerr, not one for acting superior anyway, was intent on sending the message that, as he later put it, "We're the lucky ones. We get to come in and coach you guys and you won 51 games last year." Never was his humility more important than the summer of 2014 as he built connections with an awareness he needed to lead like never before.

The first task was to construct a staff. Following through on the campaign promise made during the job interview in Oklahoma City, Kerr targeted experience for his top assistants. He knew David Blatt by reputation only, but they shared an agent, Tannenbaum, and an offensive philosophy based on ball movement and playing fast. Tannenbaum arranged a meeting at Los Angeles International Airport in June that led to Kerr offering a job and Blatt accepting. Kerr had similar success with two of his other preferred candidates, Ron Adams with twenty years on NBA benches with six teams and Alvin Gentry, his former hire as Suns head coach. Golden State did get turned down trying to pry Chip Engelland from the Spurs, a rejection that would eventually cost the Warriors, but another virtual Kerr lifer, former Arizona teammate and Phoenix scout Bruce Fraser, signed on.

Luke Walton wanted in. He offered very little in the way of bench experience, with one season as a player-development coach for the Lakers' minor league affiliate and a brief turn as a University of Memphis assistant to stay busy during the 2011 lockout, but that was part of the appeal for Kerr. The new coach wanted youth on the bench as well, figuring a former NBA veteran closer in age to the current generation would help keep the staff connected with players. Walton at thirty-four years old and one season removed from a ten-year career, fit the description, as did thirty-five-year-old former pro Jarron Collins as another hire. Plus, Walton had the ultimate references: he played for Lute Olson at Arizona, arriving eleven years after Kerr departed, and for Phil Jackson with the Lakers, and earned the same praise both attached to Kerr as a smart, mature, valuable team-first contributor on clubs with bigger stars.

Walton did not, however, know Kerr well, despite the common background and living twenty-five miles from Walton's hometown in San Diego County. Walton approached Kerr indirectly, through his closer relationship with Fraser. Fraser took the verbal application to Kerr. "We knew each other, so there's a relationship there," Walton said. "One, obviously, that helps. But two, playing for Phil Jackson, playing for Lute Olson, I knew that we were probably similar in the way we saw the game. The time I had spent with him, I thought he was an incredible person. He was fun to be around, he was interesting to talk with. I just thought I could learn a lot being on his team, being on his staff."

Kerr offered the same bravado to Blatt that he had with the players. The Warriors were going to be good in a way that would showcase assistants for head-coaching jobs around the league as soon as one year later, Kerr told him, and certainly after two seasons. Kerr could not have known he was underselling his optimism—Griffin and the Cavaliers asked to interview Blatt before the Golden State deal had been finalized. Kerr, able to understand sliding out from under a verbal commitment better than anybody, gave Blatt his blessing to back out of the move to Oakland to become a head coach. Cleveland hired Blatt on June 20, Kerr's updated staff was announced on July 3, with Walton the number-three assistant, and LeBron James announced July 11 he was signing with the Cavaliers as a free agent, setting a course neither coach could have imagined in the L.A. meeting. With the security of Gentry and Adams watching his back, the youthful energy of Walton and Collins, plus the comfort level of Fraser, Kerr had close to an ideal staff, even with the loss of Blatt, and therefore an ideal start.

Actual coaching began in early July with Kerr strangely but tellingly running the summer league team in Las Vegas, a job that ordinarily fell to junior members of staffs while the head coach watched from on high in the stands. Kerr wanted the experience, even with a roster dominated by players who weren't good enough to so much as be invited to training camp with the real Warriors in two and a half months. More than that, he was certain he needed it. Kerr so quickly felt his inexperience being exposed that, after concluding he was wasting valuable seconds diagramming plays in time-outs, he took a grease board to his suite at the Bellagio after a game and spent one of his first nights drawing plays high above the neon demolition derby of the Strip. Scribbling hoops shorthand, dry-erase marker to white background, needed to come faster. The player who prided himself on preparation had become the coach who wanted to simulate a time-out with four seconds to go on the road and Golden State down one as bedlam crashed around him.

Later in the off-season, in Kerr's office at team headquarters, he and top assistant Gentry would debate the best way to diagram Xs and Os. Label players by initials? By position? Position number? Nothing would be left to chance. "He's not a guy that was just going to jump into this without preparation," Gentry said. "It's something that he had been preparing for. He wanted to be a coach. We talked about that when he was the GM in Phoenix. Obviously the leadership comes natural to him." For all Kerr's image as a chill, fun-loving smart-ass, more aging surfer dude than cutthroat competitor, down to the Vans deck shoes and purposely tousled blond hair, he remained the overthinker of his youth. He even spent a month considering an internal slogan before deciding on "Strength in Numbers" as a match for his vision of roster depth and inclusivity. The motto was so well received the Warriors' marketing arm appropriated it for external use as well.

Interested in learning more about coaching philosophies, he flew north to attend two days of Seattle Seahawks practices, meet with coach Pete Carroll, and attend staff meetings. As workouts convulsed with loud music and traditional practice plans were halted for impromptu competitions, both intended to keep sessions lively and players engaged, Kerr couldn't help but think he was at the circus. But he would also come to view the trip as critical to his success and liberally stole ideas from the NFL coach, just as he had with future NBA peers during the TNT days.

"Give me one of your core values," Carroll told him during one of their conversations.

Kerr thought for a moment. "Joy."

"Okay, joy," Carroll said. "That has to be reflected in your practices every day."

Kerr, his coaching library still growing, returned to implement several Carroll approaches to inject joy into the drudgery of yet another practice. He would also continue to emphasize the four core values—competition, compassion, mindfulness, and joy—and occasionally write the words as a reminder. Putting together an introductory video to show players the night before camp opened, he asked friend Marv Albert to lend his distinctively emphatic voice as narrator, from a script sent by Kerr that made a point of injecting humor. When Warriors coaches convened in September for a three-day retreat in Northern California's Wine Country as final prep for training camp, the gathering included four film sessions a day at three to four hours each, along with strategy conversations, but also swimming, tennis, vino, and croquet. ("I'm the greatest black croquet player ever!" Gentry proclaimed in victory.) While there may have been doubt on the eve of the season regarding the capabilities of the unproven coach, there was the certainty the Golden State atmosphere would be in his style.

Most of his former college and NBA coaches, along with Carroll from the NFL, were close at heart as Kerr moved to establish his own identity while embracing the past. From Olson, he took the lesson that a team will play the way it practices. Still remembering his rookie season in Phoenix with vibrant Cotton Fitzsimmons and how "he had us laughing all the time, and that was a pretty powerful thing," Kerr sought to immediately establish this approach with the Albert voiceover. He liked that Wilkens ran a simple offense during their three and a half seasons together in Cleveland, emphasizing execution of a basic system over a bulging playbook. "Cotton Fitzsimmons and Lenny Wilkens couldn't be more different, personality wise," Kerr said. "But they were both great coaches because they were themselves. And that's what all my mentors have told me: 'Just be yourself, be true to yourself, stick to your principles, and it'll work.'" Jackson and Popovich, of course, had the largest influences as leaders who invited the real world into the locker room and, Jackson in particular, as a strong proponent of ball movement over one-on-one play, even with historically good individual talent on their side. That was reinforced as Kerr prepared for his debut by rewatching San Antonio's Finals victory over Miami several times in the summer as a reminder of what an offense in sync looks like and what he wanted the Warriors to become.

Four seasons of college ball spread over five years, fifteen years playing in the NBA, three as a general manager and eight more in two stints as a network broadcaster, finally converged as the Warriors opened practice in their facility on the fifth floor of the Marriott in downtown Oakland, seven miles up Interstate 880 from their game-night home at Oracle Arena. He arrived packing the same message as the face-to-face and phone conversations soon after being hired, only now with everyone together, the real team, not the Las Vegas version. The Warriors will pass more, Kerr emphasized before going into greater detail on the court in the weeks ahead, and the Warriors will have fun, he said, even if some allies couldn't

believe the personal touches that included blasting music in practices would work. "This is a fucking circus," Adams told Kerr early
in the 2014–2015 playlist. "It'll never work." But Kerr held firm.

Using technology unavailable during his playing career, Kerr
knew Golden State had finished last in the league in total passes the
season before at 243.8 per game, management's primary on-court
issue with Mark Jackson. The goal heading into 2014–2015 was to
break 300. Never trying to portray himself as an innovator to reach
the standard, Kerr hid nothing about being a collector as a strategist. He planned to borrow aspects of Tex Winter's triangle from
the Bulls days, instill the mindset of Popovich's unselfish Spurs, and
as he told former Sacramento guard Doug Christie, copy parts of
Christie's Kings of the early 2000s and their success running the
offense through two excellent passing big men, Vlade Divac and
Chris Webber. Whether the Warriors could adapt was unknown,
but Kerr at least had the starting point that his own bigs, center
Bogut and power forwards David Lee and Green, were excellent
passers for their positions.

Watching early practices and the eight exhibition games led Kerr
to decide Barnes, not the incumbent Iguodala, would start at small
forward, a decision fraught with potential negative consequences
given Iguodala's standing as a prominent locker-room voice. Beyond making a lineup change, Kerr exposed himself to the chance
of an internal rift with an unhappy veteran before even reaching
opening night. Several conversations between coach and player
during camp could not erase Iguodala's concern that he was being
eased out, that it was a demotion no matter how Kerr framed it and
the beginning of the end for him in the NBA.

When Iguodala accepted the move without public dissent,
though, the Warriors had a lot more than a lineup for October 29
at Sacramento and the at-last official debut of coach Steve Kerr.
Iguodala dialing down any possible tension by taking a reserve role
after working from the starting lineup his first ten seasons saved a
quick attack on Kerr's credibility, both from the outside with skep-
tics ready to pounce in the wake of the controversial Jackson fir-

ing and more important, within the locker room. Just as critically, the move became an important step forward for the Warriors as a whole in ways no one could have realized in the infant days of 2014–2015. "I thought it set a tone for our team from the beginning," Kerr would say months later, "a sacrifice."

The new lineup didn't even make it to the regular season before David Lee's strained left hamstring late in training camp forced another major adjustment. Promoting Draymond Green to the starting power forward was neither a surprise nor an original idea, coming months after Mark Jackson made the same move in the final four games of the playoffs against the Clippers, but it was not Kerr's preference. Then it turned from a temporary patch job into a serious roster concern when Lee missed the first three games and aggravated the injury in the fourth contest, November 5, as he returned in a reserve role to regain his timing and stamina. He would not play again until December 22.

The 5-0 start that would have been encouraging against any background was especially valuable for a coach in need of actual credibility, not merely a standing built entirely on his past. Even more notably, the Warriors were doing it short-handed and amid a flurry of turnovers Kerr termed "plays of insanity" that were more senseless mistakes early in possessions than overpassing in the new mandate for ball movement. By the time Lee returned to action December 22, the Warriors were 22-3, Curry's defense had gone from a source of derision to credible, and the lineup Kerr didn't want in October had become an accidental success. Adams even turned pro-circus. "This is an interesting stew you've cooked up," he told Kerr, "but it works."

It went unnoticed in such a happy place that Gentry would occasionally, if discreetly, serve as head coach, telling Kerr when to call time-out and sometimes even handing Kerr the whiteboard with a play already drawn up to be shared in the huddle. "But let me tell you," Gentry said, "he was prepared. He was prepared to be a head coach. He coached that team to a championship. Ron and I were along for the ride. We contributed, but that was his team, and he

coached that team, and he won that championship. I'm telling you."
Outsiders would have seen Kerr as needing a ventriloquist in the
heat of the moment and seized on the scene as evidence he could
handle slogans and conversations but was unprepared for the practical side of the job. The vindicated front office, though watching
wins pile up, took Kerr's willingness to encourage input from all
as a sign of strength. The Kerr personality was to not care about
perception either way.

All Kerr knew was that the new life was everything he once
dreamed. He would return to the Bay Area after road games gushing to Margot about his joy coaching this team. After practice in
Oakland on quiet afternoons, he could leave the office by 3:30, run
errands, and be hitting a bucket of balls at the driving range at 4:00,
loving the alone time. Other days he would walk the hills near his
home in Berkeley or do yoga. "He was just giddy," Margot said. "He
was on Cloud Nine. Because he knew how special this team was
and how rare it was to get this kind of group together."

It didn't take the reminder of two trips to New York at midseason
for Kerr to appreciate his good fortune. The Warriors rolling into
Madison Square Garden with a 39-9 record, on the other hand, was
the worst possible visual for Jackson in what had already devolved
into the latest debacle of a Knicks season in much the same way
his first try running basketball operations had become a wincing
contrast to the coaching success in Chicago and Los Angeles. The
spotlight naturally lasered onto the visiting coach and what could
have been, against the contrast of the Knicks at 10-40 under fallback
hire Derek Fisher. Golden State won by fourteen.

Returning to Manhattan for the All-Star game eight days later led
to a new round of questions, now from the worldwide media, about
snubbing his mentor. The second came with an official stamp of
success, after all, of Kerr coaching the West, since the Warriors had
the best record in the conference. Kerr handled February in New
York with typical diplomacy while hoping the entire line of conversation would go away to save Jackson further embarrassment.

Heading into the first round at 67-15 came with the exact statistical reads Kerr had hoped for the day he took the job, that the Warriors played at a faster pace than any team and, especially, that they averaged 306.6 passes per game. The goal for the new coach and the front office that wanted more ball movement from any hire had been such a success that they jumped from thirtieth and last in the league to ninth. No team made more baskets, only one made more three-pointers, no one had a better percentage behind the arc, and, maintaining the strides under Mark Jackson, they also had the best defensive rating and the best shooting defense. Golden State won so often and by so much that Kerr was able to routinely rest his starters in the fourth quarter, leading to the enviable outcome of the Warriors winning sixteen more games than the season before despite Bogut, Curry, and Thompson playing fewer minutes. Curry reduced his workload and still won the MVP award.

The Warriors' momentum carried into the playoffs with a 4–0 sweep of New Orleans in the first round and a fifteen-point victory over Memphis to start the conference semifinals. When the Grizzlies won the next two, though, Kerr was confronted by the biggest test of his young tenure. He had lucked into the unwanted lineup change of Lee's injury that allowed Draymond Green to develop into a defensive force, he had benefited from Iguodala accepting a demotion in favor of Harrison Barnes rather than challenge a coach on the job a few months, and he had Gentry and Adams as guiding hands, but the Warriors were suddenly down in a series and on the road. Plus, he appeared bothered by a perceived Twitter dig from Phil Jackson; whether intended for Kerr's Warriors in a 2–1 hole or every playoff participant, Jackson seemed to question the success of teams relying heavily on three-pointers. A sideswipe from Jackson of all people.

Trying to ease the concern he assumed Kerr must have been feeling at the first sign of adversity in the win-loss column all season, Myers told him in the quiet visitors' locker room after Game 3 that coaches aren't supposed to win the championship on the first try anyway. As much as Kerr realized Myers was handing him a release valve and not the early draft of a concession speech, he also appreciated that the attempted psychological ploy was exactly the right thing to say in the moment. The response from all the War- riors was to win the next three to eliminate Memphis and then the first three against the Rockets in the Western Conference finals to take instant control in an eventual 4–1 victory.

Facing the Cavaliers for the championship was a reminder of how far his life, not just his career, had come. Cleveland was where Kerr proved he could have an NBA career, where his first child, Nick, had been born, and where he made friendships that remained strong as the finals opened in Oakland. Blatt, the assistant coach he came so close to hiring a year before, was coaching the opponent. For real oddity, the games in Ohio were played forty miles north of the Ak- ron hospital where LeBron James and Stephen Curry had been born a little more than three years apart.

Away from the reminiscing, though, Kerr's team was again down 2–1, just as they had been in the Memphis series, and again on the road, this time while trying to contend with James and searching for a way to increase the pace from the Cavaliers' preferred stroll. Still able to keep the public mood light, he was asked how much pressure the Warriors were under on a scale of one to ten and re- plied, "The pressure is like a 5.13," and even smiled. Also, "I don't anticipate making changes in the lineup, no."

The potential solution to increasing the tempo came to Nick U'Ren as he watched clips of the San Antonio–Miami 2014 Finals in his Cleveland hotel room late the night before Game 4, the same series Kerr had months before pored over in admiration of the Spurs' offense. That a twenty-eight-year-old would be the man to change NBA history was the definition of improbable as U'Ren watched James with the Heat in the previous championship series and was struck by the realization that the Warriors should switch to a smaller lineup.

U'Ren having a voice at all was also telling. He met Kerr early in the Phoenix GM days while job hunting, kept in touch through emails and was brought on as a Suns intern by Kerr. One of Kerr's final acts before quitting was to make sure U'Ren was hired full-time, and one of Kerr's early moves with Golden State was to bring in U'Ren to handle everything from breaking down videos to keeping the coach's schedule to helping arrange the practice tunes that had become the norm. Now, with the season close to being on the line, U'Ren emerged as the embodiment of the Kerr mantra to keep everyone involved, even the special assistant-slash-music director.

The suggestion to shrink the lineup to turn more fleet and mobile went up the chain from U'Ren to Walton and from Walton to Kerr in a 3:00 A.M. text. Kerr saw it when he woke hours later, discussed the move with his staff at a morning meeting, and moved ahead with plans to sit Bogut and return forward Iguodala to a starting role. Kerr also recalled the positive results from Popovich making a similar adjustment in the middle of the 2014 Western Conference final by benching Tiago Splitter and starting Matt Bonner. If it worked, Kerr told U'Ren as the game approached, smart-ass as ever despite the stakes, Kerr would take credit. If it didn't, it would be U'Ren's fault.

Kerr at his most optimistic could not have imagined what happened next. The chain of events that would last years began with the Warriors' 103–82 victory to tie the series, thanks to the coach and the coach alone. ("Well," Kerr said the next afternoon, staying in character, "as I told Nick today, he's gotten way too much credit now. It's gone totally overboard. So enough about Nick.") The strategy to force the pace from the deliberate style the Cavaliers wanted to the up-tempo style the Warriors used as oxygen led to better ball movement and more efficiency on offense as Golden State went from ninety-three and ninety-one points the previous two outings to the familiar territory of triple digits. Staying in small-ball mode in Game 5—Green, Barnes, Iguodala, Thompson, and Curry started again—led to 104 points and a 3–2 advantage.

Winning the championship two nights later in Cleveland was vindication for the front office that gambled by firing a successful coach without a successor lined up and increased the risk by choosing a replacement with zero experience. Golden State turned out to be exactly as Kerr brashly insisted in private summer conversations with players and potential staff hires. He was correct about lineup decisions at the start of the season and the conclusion, recruited the right assistants, showed commanding leadership without muting his inclusive personality, and he was right about the offense. The Warriors, Jerry West said, "looked like San Antonio in many, many ways, except he wanted to play faster," praise hard to top in the Kerr world. Kerr also found special satisfaction in Iguodala being named Finals MVP, seeing it as payback for Iguodala's early sacrifice and a fitting definition of "Strength in Numbers."

The locker room was "chaos," Kerr said. "Pure joy. The thing about the NBA playoffs, and I've been through this as a player and going all the way to the Finals five times as a player, but it had been 12 years since I'd been there. My last year with the Spurs. I almost forgot just how grueling the stretch is. I mean, two straight months of emotional stress and physical stress. Just the roller-coaster ride that you're on. There are days when you think, boy, I don't know if this is going to happen. Then there are days that go better. As soon as you win a game, you celebrate for a few minutes and your stomach ties up in knots thinking about the next game. So you go through this for two months. Yeah, there's a lot of pentup energy and relief more than anything in that locker room."

Kerr may have worked a season for the moment, but he waited years for the chance. He had been thinking about coaching since high school and by late in college, after the passing thought of becoming an athletic director, was convinced that his future would be on the sideline. Building a fan club of front offices around the league had given him the luxury of waiting for Nick, Maddy, and Matthew to grow up rather than needing to jump at an opportunity, and the Warriors of 2014–2015 provided the perfect place for him to break in. Kerr's sixth championship was easily one of the most meaningful.

Not only that, but the Game 4 adjustment dramatically changed more than the direction of the finals. Launching Curry, Thompson, Iguodala, Barnes, and Green turned out to be the first meaningful look at the small-ball alignment that would so torture opponents for years that it became known as the Death Lineup, even if they didn't start together. Encouraging input from all directions, a Kerr cornerstone from the start, had paid off in tangible and amazing ways. He had joy, at least for the moment.

CHAPTER 13

Agony

Steve Kerr was so unconcerned about the tweak in his back during Game 5 at Oracle Arena that he played golf and beach volleyball in the early days of his first off-season as a championship coach. He had hugged Margot and the kids without difficulty on the court following Game 6 in Cleveland as the Warriors celebrated their new title, his sixth, just as he appeared to sit comfortably in the backseat of the open convertible slowly rolling through Oakland in the victory parade. His relaxing summer began with no pressing concern beyond staff adjustments after Alvin Gentry's departure to become head coach in New Orleans. Kerr even planned to ease up at summer league and move from the sidelines to the traditional boss's role of spectator.

By the time he arrived in Las Vegas a couple weeks later, though, getting from his hotel room to the car required constant rest stops, sometimes every twenty yards, to sit in a swivel chair at a bank of slot machines. Once he eased into a seat at the games, Kerr appeared fine to most who stopped to visit. To others, he confided he was barely functioning, an especially alarming statement from someone never known to complain. He was, he said, in agony.

Kerr had finally become a coach and then immediately a champion coach, he had what by all indications was a family life surrounded by the same love and support he had been raised with, and he got the chance to ride the Curry wave after all, years removed from the draft-night letdown in 2009, yet hurt was everywhere. What should have been days of ecstasy in a life that had fallen into place were instead almost a constant endurance test of how much torment his body could withstand. Surgery to repair a ruptured disc on July 28, enough time to recover before training camp two months later, resulted in leaking spinal fluid and an unimaginable physical misery that surpassed the searing pain of summer league. Migraine headaches invaded almost daily, nausea and dizziness were common, and there were days he saw spots and needed to steady himself by leaning on a wall or grabbing a chair to avoid falling. The disc wasn't the problem anymore.

With Kerr's body at war with itself, he underwent a second surgery, a corrective procedure, on September 4. Eight days later, Bob Myers learned his thirty-three-year-old brother-in-law was killed by falling boulders during a Mount Kilimanjaro climb. The off-season in the wake of the title was turning horrific with increasing velocity, the only good news being that Nick Kerr transferred to Cal for his final season of eligibility.

His father did make it back for the start of camp at the end of the month, as planned, but for only two days before admitting he could not push through the pain and discomfort. He needed an indefinite leave of absence. That the target date for a return was kept open-ended—"We don't anticipate the recovery process will be long term, but as of today we don't know the exact timeframe," Myers said—signaled how little handle the team and its coach had on the situation, which was turning desperate. Adding to the uncertainty, the Warriors faced the possibility of opening the regular season in a few weeks with Walton still the interim coach and still an inexperienced thirty-five-year-old handed a championship roster. Even if Walton did have a lengthy history on the bench compared to the guy on the job the year before, Kerr also had the cushion of taking over a team that could win a round or two in the playoffs if everything broke right. Walton went from the fourth assistant, before Blatt left for Cleveland and Gentry for New Orleans, to game planning for the title favorite in about sixteen months. Kerr also had months to prepare for his first day on the job. Walton had hours.

Walton also had the unwanted insight of dealing with severe back problems, as did his father, Bill Walton, and Phil Jackson.

Jackson needed to have his spine fused after a 1968 injury and was unable to walk fluidly by his late forties as he coached Kerr in Chicago, about the same time June Jackson was predicting her husband would soon walk with a cane. Luke Walton had seen his dad driven to the brink of suicide in part by the misery of agonizing pain in retirement. And when the son missed fifty games while playing for Jackson's Lakers in 2009–2010, Bill Walton was near tears as his soft blue eyes welled up and his commanding voice choked to a halt in wishing Luke would retire rather than deal with the same suffering later in life. "I don't want to see him in pain," Bill said. "I don't want to see the ramifications." Luke recovered to play parts of three more seasons, and by 2015 was talking to Kerr about their shared plight at the same time Walton was thrust into the unexpected role in Oakland.

Just as the good start to 2014–2015 was prized credibility for the rookie coach, the Warriors' break from the gate a year later was especially valuable to Walton, and to Kerr by extension for selecting Walton over the more experienced Adams. It took only until December, one full month into the season, for the Warriors to grow into something more than a formidable defending champion. The usual interest surrounding Curry, Thompson, and Green had been joined by the unique story line of Kerr's plight and the Warriors getting off to the best start in NBA history at 16-0. Eight more victories followed, six on the road, before the team bus rolled into downtown Milwaukee at 3:00 A.M. on December 12 with the temperature around zero. A couple hundred bundled fans waited undeterred outside the hotel.

Comparisons to the Bulls of 1995–1996 and the Lakers of the 1980s had already started, early but understandably with Golden State, on a seventy-nine-win pace heading into the Christmas Day rematch against the Cavaliers. Chicago had the single-season record of seventy-two victories, with Kerr as a key contributor. Warriors-Lakers was more the image of California teams with pyrotechnic offenses as the starting point to many connections—Klay Thompson's father Mychal on the Los Angeles roster part of the run, Kerr in high school in Southern California in the early '80s, Jerry West in Golden State management and a minority owner after building the Showtime era as general manager, and L.A. forward Bob McAdoo a distant cousin of Warriors reserve James Michael McAdoo. West had done broadcasting before becoming a coach for the first time. Bob Myers was a Bay Area native who attended UCLA. Co-owner Peter Guber was a Los Angeles resident who had a stake in the Dodgers—with Magic Johnson. Kareem Abdul-Jabbar looked to Oakland in 2015 and decided he saw "certain similarities between the Warriors and Showtime Lakers in their embrace of teamwork. Teamwork is what really makes this game function and they are consummate team players." Golden State, he continued, is "exciting. They just seemed to come out of nowhere. But they make you smile and make you want to dance."

At home near San Diego, as pain stabbed away at his head and neck with such severity that the most ordinary tasks turned agonizing, historical debates meant nothing to Kerr. Weeks with little relief turned into months, and months turned into a half-season away from the team in addition to missing most of training camp and the exhibition schedule, until he finally began to confront the decision that would drag him even lower: without mentioning it publicly, he weighed quitting. So difficult was it for the notorious overthinker to contemplate walking away from his dream job, and aware that staying positive was part of the stated recovery plan, that he tried to resist the debate. But Kerr felt nearly out of options after two surgeries, countless grasps at lesser remedies, and Margot's endless internet searches on leaking spinal fluid. He would text Myers one day hinting at a return, then send another message the next morning saying, "Bob, I just don't know if I'm going to get better."

The same Steve Kerr who through the years spoke openly about many personal topics offered only general medical updates as the crisis continued, a personal policy that never wavered. Signs of recovery and an imminent return did begin to appear in January, minus the reasons for the improvements, as he became a regular in the Golden State traveling party and seemed the Kerr of old while still staying off the bench. In Portland, an Uber driver taking the staff to dinner, recognizing Walton but apparently not Kerr, took off on the injustice of the Warriors' wins being credited to Kerr in absentia. Yeah, the invisible Kerr said from the backseat, the real head coach is an asshole. It was the signal for everyone to jump in. The guy even called the league office to make sure he got awarded the victories, Walton chimed in. Kerr sounds like a real jerk, the driver announced in conclusion.

An off night in Chicago nearly two weeks later brought the added encouragement of the group heading to the Second City comedy club, a favorite of Steve and Margot's since the Bulls days. He was enough of a regular by 2016, whenever the schedule allowed, that calling ahead for tickets got the party seated in the Rail, the VIP section in the full house of three hundred spectators. The box office could also alert the producer and the producer could then have the stage manager approach Kerr about taking the stage during the improv portion of the show. Saying yes under ordinary circumstances would be normal for him. Excitedly agreeing amid lights and noise in the delicate days of the comeback was practically a medical update.

The Golden State contingent was invited backstage to meet the cast during the fifteen-minute intermission between the second and final acts, exchanging friendly small talk with the cast and taking pictures before returning to the Rail. Kerr waited until one of the performers, Jamison Webb, introduced the special guest two hours into the show, a little after 10:00 P.M. Webb hailed him as a Chicago sports legend and one of the greatest shooters in NBA history.

The crowd erupted in a way Webb rarely, if ever, saw in two years at Second City. The warm response most celebrities received in Kerr's case was a massive cheer seventeen and a half years after his last game as a Bull and a standing ovation from fifteen or twenty customers, fifteen or twenty more than VIPs typically got in the small theater. He spent time onstage with Webb and the five other performers, mostly shoulder to shoulder facing the audience, in a collaborative improvisational routine that required the amateur to keep up with trained comedians with quick responses whenever singled out by a conductor. The switch to another participant sometimes came midsentence. The amateur appeared confident and comfortable, loving the moment and not just going along. The crowd was "laughing and cheering because it's a funny, smart, likable person onstage who's being charismatic and being charismatic in a very kind of natural, modest way," Webb said. "And I saw that. I saw people thrilled to see Steve Kerr, and then I think the joy that comes with 'Oh, good. He's funny and smart and nice too.' There's that thing of, 'Cool, he's comfortable and confident,' and, yeah, he is that guy who wasn't afraid to take the big shot and all of that. He has that comfort and that confidence without it coming across as cocky or that kind of thing. I definitely saw that with the crowd that night."

Kerr was ready. On January 22, the man who went 39-4 without stepping on a sideline during a game told the Warriors at the morning shootaround he would return that night against the Pacers at Oracle Arena, igniting a celebration by players. Kerr was clearly far from healed, a reality he never denied, but he was in a place where he could manage the symptoms that showed in head twists to loosen neck muscles or by rubbing his temples or forehead. What had become just as obvious was that he needed to coach again—"I needed the job to distract me and engage me." Instead of wanting to get healthy to return to work, he returned to work to get healthy. To Kerr in a world gone fragile, the mounting basketball stakes of the second half of 2015–2016 and the playoffs that would follow were welcome distractions capable of pulling him through the darkness.

It was hardly the first time. Kerr was "incredibly shy" as a boy before morphing into a music-video star and award-winning Moth who took the stage at Second City because "I needed basketball to bring it out of me, being interviewed by the media, getting more confident with myself, becoming a better player. I wasn't a very confident kid growing up. But I was a good writer and read a lot so I had a lot of that communication inside of me." In college, hoops kept him moving forward after his father's death, and four and a half years later, just after Arizona, the Olympic trials forced Kerr to get past the Final Four crash landing. The medical plight in his fifties tightened his bond with basketball, to where it shaped his personality and helped carry him through emotional and now physical trauma. Few in NBA history would find the sport more of a life preserver.

Chasing reserve guard Steve Kerr and the Bulls of twenty years earlier for the single-season record of seventy-two wins was exactly the kind of welcome distraction coach Steve Kerr coveted as he returned with the Warriors on pace for seventy-four victories. The traditional champion's visit to the White House the night after Curry diced up the Wizards for fifty-one points a few miles away was another, this time with the bonus of being saluted by noted basketball fan and transplanted Chicagoan Barack Obama.

"Now, it is rare to be in the presence of guys from the greatest team in NBA history," the president said in the East Room with three rows of Golden State players, coaches, and executives on risers behind him. "So we're pretty lucky today, because we've got one of those players in the house—Steve Kerr from the 1995–1996 Chicago Bulls! It's good to see you back." Turning his attention to Curry, a golfing partner the summer before, Obama noted the reigning MVP was "clowning" the Wizards the previous night. When offered the chance to speak, Kerr moved to the podium in Second City mode.

"Thank you. I'm a little thirsty. Is that my water or yours?"

"It is," Obama replied. "Go for it."

"I thought maybe it was yours," Kerr said. "I'm guessing it's yours. I want to say thank you. I also want to say congratulations for becoming the first president in our nation's great history to use the term 'clowning.' Although maybe Teddy Roosevelt used it somewhere in there, I don't know. But we want to thank you. Our organization is so honored to be here, to meet you, to tour the White House and to celebrate our championship with you here. Our general manager, Bob Myers, who you met earlier, also mentioned to me that you're going to be a free agent at the end of this year. So we don't know if you have anything lined up yet, but—"

"I'm ready to go," Obama said.

The ensuing months provided additional ways for Kerr to take his mind off health concerns. Kevin Durant, in Oakland with the Thunder on February 6, seemed unusually interested in the progress of the Warriors' new arena in San Francisco, and before the game accepted an invitation to talk with a senior Golden State executive to hear more about Chase Center under construction. When the teams met again in Oklahoma City near the end of February, Kerr and Green had a halftime shouting match that could be heard in the hallway. On April 16, the Warriors beat the Grizzlies for win number seventy-three and the record, a mark players wanted as further evidence, along with the championship topper they were sure was coming, of being the greatest team in history. Ten days after that, Kerr, receiving credit for the system he put in place, was voted Coach of the Year despite missing 53 percent of the regular-season games. He made sure Walton posed with him in pictures.

Even that left little room for celebration. While still providing few details about the struggle and usually making health queries off-limits to the media, Kerr at the same time made no attempt at a public front that he had recovered as people around the team whispered concern. "I wouldn't equate my health with anything that's happened basketball wise," he said early in the playoffs, typically frank in discussing at least the big-picture personal implications while skipping the details. "I'll put it this way. Under normal circumstances if I hadn't had this health issue this would have been one of the great years of my life. But instead it was, honestly, one of the worst. Probably the worst." Also, he added, "I don't think I would have anyway, but there's no way this job will stress me out to the point where it's 'Oh, my God, I can't do this.' Because I know it's a game and it's a job. And it's a really fun job and a great job, but it's not one that anybody should work themselves up over to the point where they lose perspective. Health is everything. It's no longer a cliché for me."

After little resistance from the Rockets in the opening round or the Trail Blazers in the second, Golden State lost three of the first four against the Thunder in the Western Conference final. That was concerning enough, but the Warriors couldn't even stay close in games, let alone the series, as Marcus Thompson II of the Athletic entered the visitors' locker room in Oklahoma City to assess the mood of the team. Green mapped out how the Warriors would win the next game in Oakland and the one after that back in OKC just because, and that nobody was going to beat them in a Game 7 at home after that. His tone clearly revealed concern, though, with the usual Green bravado replaced by playing the underdog card of a team that would accept the challenge of proving the world, and the odds, wrong. Curry was calm to the point of mocking Thompson for so much as wondering if Golden State should be concerned about the very steep climb of a 3–1 deficit. He asked Thompson if he had ever watched the Warriors play.

The Warriors did have the confidence of history after climbing out of a 2–1 hole against both the Grizzlies in the second round and the Cavaliers in the Finals the year before. And both of those were with a road game up next. At least this time they were going back to Oracle to fuel up on energy.

Thompson finally caught Kerr just as the coach, long after his official media availability, was leaving the locker room, armed not only with the indicators from Green and Curry but also the intel of how much Kerr disliked Russell Westbrook's game. Kerr had privately shared the same insight with many reporters through the years, just as he believed the Thunder was undependable late in a season of too many blown leads, and now Kerr was believing it all the way to the certainty that Golden State repeat hopes were very much alive.

In contrast to Green's change of tone and Curry poking at Thompson for daring to doubt, Kerr was matter-of-fact as he and Thompson left the locker room and strolled a hallway, one bound for the team bus and a flight to California and the other for the media work area to write. Well, Kerr told Thompson, you know Westbrook's going to give us a game, and you know the Thunder will fall apart down the stretch one of the next three. "It was like he was counting them out," Thompson said, unable to avoid noticing the backward reality of the coach trailing 3–1 bluntly dismissing the team that needed only one win in three tries. Kerr was that entrenched in his confidence that, given relatively equal talent, ball movement, and a team approach would always win over the unreliable, me-first style he saw in Westbrook.

These were lessons learned at every stop Kerr had made since the 1980s, from Jerry Marvin at Palisades as a John Wooden disciple to Gregg Popovich and a roster dotted by future Hall of Famers. Even Phil Jackson with Michael Jordan, before and after Kerr's arrival, and arguably especially Phil Jackson. Jackson could have justifiably scribbled together an offense with a dozen versions of getting the ball to his unstoppable star and having the four other Bulls run the other direction, yet he stayed with Tex Winter's equal-opportunity triangle until Jordan finally bought into trusting teammates and titles rained down. Kerr in the locker room in Oklahoma City had the advantage of an unselfish and playoff-tested group as he walked with Thompson, but he was mostly falling back on decades of basketball schooling in laying out how good would triumph over evil. Team play would triumph over one-on-one attack mode.

Winning Game 5 in Oakland two nights later was a start. When the Warriors won Game 6 in Oklahoma City two days later, it was Kerr's vision come to life—the Thunder went from leading 83–75 at the start of the fourth quarter to losing 108–101, with Durant missing six of seven shots the final twelve minutes, Westbrook five of seven, and no OKC player managing more than one assist. As Westbrook committed three late turnovers in sixty-four seconds, Thompson instantly flashed back to Kerr's called shot. The Thunder, and Westbrook in particular, had fallen apart, just as predicted, followed by the Game 7 loss that completed the collapse.

Volleying jokes with the president in the East Room, winning Coach of the Year, beating Oklahoma City with a bold prediction—Kerr was riding the wave of a magical four months at a time he needed it most, in the hardest season of his life despite the optics. "I can't believe all this," Margot said as her husband's improbable journey through the decades continued in gloriously strange ways. "I don't even know how all this happened; I really don't. I have no idea. It is a lot of luck, but he's really a smart guy." Even the bad news of Luke Walton leaving the Warriors was tempered by Kerr's personal excitement that a friend and close professional ally had been hired as Lakers coach at age thirty-six.

The force of the swing the other way was more sudden and more impactful. Kerr's life, not just his basketball realm, began to change the morning of June 1 when a UCLA student shot and killed an engineering professor, left a note, and turned the gun on himself—about a half-mile from Ann Kerr's office as coordinator of the Fulbright scholarship program. The murder and two-hour campus lockdown the day before the Warriors and Cavaliers opened the championship series sent her to January 18, 1984, in Beirut. Eleven days after the UCLA tragedy, a man parked his van outside the Pulse nightclub in Orlando, Florida, entered with an assault rifle, a handgun, and extra ammunition and started blasting. The initial assault alone was fifteen seconds of *pop-pop-pop* before the siege continued for nearly three and a half hours as the killer searched room to room to create more carnage and made 911 calls to pledge allegiance to the Islamic State. Victims begged for their lives, screaming at the murderer for mercy, and called or texted loved ones amid the 180 rounds from police. By the time the gunman was killed at 5:15 in a shoot-out with law enforcement, forty-nine people were lost and fifty-three wounded.

With a 3–1 series lead and on the verge of another title, Kerr took the perspective that "for lack of a better way of putting it, this"—he pointed toward the court—"is all bullshit. It's so much fun, and it's rewarding to be part of a team, and to have a quest and to try and win a championship. It's great thinking we've established this legacy and hung a banner, and all of that is very important in terms of bringing joy to the fans' lives—that's where the true importance of what we do lies—but in the grand scheme of things, it's still bullshit.

I've found that out." A continent away from Orlando the next night, with Ann Kerr and several other family members in attendance, the Warriors held a moment of silence prior to Game 5. Steve, minutes before trying to win a second title in as many years of coaching, bowed his head and thought of Malcolm. "It's very personal, because you've gone through it," he said. "You understand how much they are suffering, just like how our family went through that suffering. When you think of it, all of these statistics have names and these names have faces. They are people who are now lost." Remaining standing for the national anthem, Kerr found himself trying to count the number of times the Warriors held an on-court quiet reflection before a game.

A Cavaliers win followed, and then another in Game 6 in Cleveland to even the series. Little attention was paid to the next major event on the Quicken Loans Arena calendar—the Republican National Convention, where Donald Trump would be selected as the Republican nominee for president. Back in Oakland three nights later for Game 7, Kerr's world changed again when the Cavaliers claimed a shocking championship.

Everything had been reversed. The coach who marshaled a comeback from a 3–1 deficit the series before walked off as the coach of the first club to blow a 3–1 Finals lead. The Warriors clinched in Cleveland in 2015, and the Cavaliers won in Oracle Arena in 2016. The season that opened with twenty-four consecutive victories ended with three straight defeats and the team that led the league in shooting and offensive rating went scoreless the final 4:38. Hailed for the lineup adjustments a year earlier, Kerr was loudly criticized for giving unproductive minutes to big men Festus Ezeli and Anderson Varejao in Game 7 in an attempt to replace the injured Andrew Bogut. Inserting Ezeli for Barnes midway through the fourth quarter broke an offensive momentum that never returned.

It took four days before Kerr gave in and watched the tape, admitting upon review that the Warriors had suffered from tactical errors as well as poor execution. "Sometimes it works out and everybody says, 'Oh, what a great move,'" he said. "And then sometimes it doesn't work out, and you feel like an idiot. It's just the way it goes. You do your best. You make a decision for a good reason and then it either works or it doesn't. And there were a couple of them in this series that didn't, and I will lament." Kerr handled the implosion with the outlook of someone who had downplayed the importance of the outcome even when Golden State appeared comfortably ahead and he pointed to the court and put basketball in perspective. Kerr handled it so well in fact that he later asked for the nets to be cut down, a traditional part of a champion's celebration, and shipped to the Cavaliers as a souvenir they had earned but not claimed.

Kerr could also appreciate more than anyone on the losing side that Charlotte Hornets owner Michael Jordan provided the harshest takedown at a dinner in New York with Joe Lacob and four other owners. Amid drinks and frivolity, Jordan, delivering to Lacob in words some of what he long before gave Kerr in fists, zeroed in on his Golden State counterpart for breaking the Chicago record for wins in the regular season but failing to close the deal in June. "You know," Jordan told Lacob, "seventy-three don't mean shit." ("He's fantastic, and I'm not going to cross him," Lacob would eventually say. "But that kind of hurt, you know?")

At the same time, Kerr was crossing a line that would forever change his image. Under scrutiny for the first time as a coach for the Game 7 decisions that contributed to the historical collapse, he answered all basketball questions, yet wanted to move into a new phase of his life in the June of guns, nightmare flashbacks for his mother on a college campus, and the Trump campaign that followed the NBA into Cleveland. Like a man reminded by a health scare to seize every day, while also coming to understand how far his voice carried from the tall podium built by the grand success of his new career, Kerr went from being willing to speak out on issues to wanting to create a collision.

Kerr all but announced his new direction while recording *The TK Show* podcast with Bay Area News Group columnist Tim Kawakami on June 24. The conversation bounced from deconstructing Game 7 to Golden State's mindset with the start of free agency approaching to their mutual enjoyment of *Game of Thrones* to Kerr's latest book recommendation (*The Nightingale*) for thirty minutes and thirty seconds, until Kawakami shifted into his wrap-up. Beginning to thank his guest for coming on, setting the stage for an easy Kerr exit, the coach interrupted.

"Hey," Kerr said. "Can I mention one more thing?"

"Sure, sure," Kawakami said. He could see Kerr had a piece of paper, but he didn't know what was written on it and didn't know where Kerr was about to go. Maybe, Kawakami figured, Kerr wanted to interject an uplifting end-of-season message to fans or publicly thank Lacob and the organization for unwavering support in a difficult season.

"I know as a basketball coach I don't often get political," Kerr began. He briefly looked at the paper before appearing to speak extemporaneously. "But if you don't mind, I just want to say when 90 percent of our country wants background checks on gun purchases and we've got our Senate and our House not only voting it down but using the Bill of Rights as a reason for people to have rights to carry these automatic weapons and we're getting people murdered every day at an alarming rate, these mass—I just have to get this off my chest. Our government is insane."

The moment struck Kawakami as one in which Kerr had felt moved to speak up. The number of dead and injured from gun violence was rising at a grotesque rate, one incident too close to home had sent his mother to a painful place, the two most recent mass casualties were both in cities where he once lived, he was not sleeping much or eating well, he couldn't stay focused long enough to dive into deep books—Kerr was overflowing with frustration and anger until, finally, something had to be said. Feeling enough urgency to stop Kawakami from signing off, Kerr was suddenly proactive in using his platform to initiate debate. Even if it involved the highest levels of government.

CHAPTER 14

The Fury of a Patient Man

Klay Thompson arrived in the Hamptons on June 29 after tending to USA Basketball business in New York City in advance of the Olympics later in the summer of 2016, claimed the best bedroom, hit the beach, and assumed the role of lord of the manor while awaiting the arrival of the rest of the Golden State galaxy the next day. He went bike riding, kicked a soccer ball around, apparently with a gardener, and likewise rustled up a new acquaintance to play tennis on a grass court for the first time in his long love affair with the sport. The flight from the Bay Area delivered Steve Kerr, Stephen Curry, Joe Lacob, Kirk Lacob, Bob Myers, and Andre Iguodala on June 30 before the group was driven to the home of a Joe Lacob friend that would be base camp, while Draymond Green arrived separately. At least something went according to plan in June.

Kevin Durant, a Maryland native who went to college in Texas and spent the previous nine seasons in Seattle and Oklahoma City, rented a home in tony East Hampton to allow agent Rich Kleiman constant in-person contact while still being near his family before he and Kleiman headed to Asia on a Nike promotional tour. The team trying to keep Durant, the Thunder, and the four wanting to pry him away would make their pitches on the neutral territory of 189 Further Lane. More specifically, at a 7,400-square-foot property a block from the beach on eastern Long Island with a winding driveway, a pool, and a lush garden setting, 3.2 acres of seclusion at $100,000 for ten days. The Warriors had the convenience of Thompson Manor close by. They also had the knowledge they could lose out on the top free agent of the summer and probably still return in October as title favorites, with the core of the roster that won seventy-three games intact and thirsting for redemption.

When the Warriors motored from their lodging to the Durant uber-rental on July 1 as the first meeting on the first day of free agency, even their transportation was intended as a message: four players, three executives, and one coach together, in a minibus, hoping Durant would be scouting the arrival to see camaraderie rolling toward the house. He noticed with the exact intended effect as the contingent disembarked to the smell of sea air and the sound of waves. "Everybody was in the same car," Durant said. "Joe, Steve, Bob, Draymond, Klay, Steph, Andre, Kirk Lacob. I was like, man, this already looks like a family. I want to be part of it. I was excited about that."

Kerr brought a presentation of twenty quick offensive clips to show how he would use Durant in a system built on ball movement and the teamwork Kerr didn't believe the Thunder had with Westbrook. Kerr, sensing basketball junkie Durant enjoyed the chance to talk strategy, wanted to show how Durant would remain a scoring sensation even sharing the court with Curry and Thompson. More than anything, though, Kerr and the front office quickly read the room, based on questions from Durant, Kleiman, Durant's father, and other advisers and realized Durant most needed a connection with potential teammates, a bond noticeably absent in Oklahoma City. It became obvious that no matter how many people were there, the meeting came down to the five players, four of them Warriors, and especially to Durant wanting confirmation from Curry they could coexist with one ball.

Kerr, a gifted communicator, articulate, warm, and network trained in delivery, made his biggest contribution by instinctively realizing he should say little. He presented the video breakdown and got out of the way. Kerr came to view his contribution to the crucial moment in franchise history as, "Bob and I each said one or two things and that was about it. It was all players, really," while Lacob caught the same vibe and turned uncharacteristically subdued. "He's just so cool, so plain Jane," Iguodala said of Kerr. "You could sit through an entire dinner where he was at the table and never notice him. But he's always paying attention, always noticing details. And he knows when to talk and when to listen." The four Warriors and the host stepped into the backyard to talk alone and connected in a way that, in retrospect, closed the deal, although Durant also later noted, "I was already sold when they walked in." In fact, Green later revealed Durant had committed to the move as the two exchanged texts before Green had even left the locker room following Game 7 against the Cavaliers.

Durant offered no such hint on July 1 and in the following days listened to pitches from the Celtics, Heat, Spurs, and Clippers before giving Oklahoma City the final word, leaving the Warriors to wonder. Myers's gut was that "We're not getting him. He's quiet. He's doesn't say much. I had no history with him. Didn't know him. His group, his representatives, asked good questions, but I had no idea where we stood. It's just maybe my personality, but I did not leave thinking anything more than, well, we tried the best we could. That's all. I did not feel positive about it. That's the truth." When he saw news reports Boston brought Tom Brady to the house for its presentation, Myers jokingly wondered if Golden State should have included Joe Montana.

Waiting for a Durant decision, Kerr left for a Hawaii vacation and Myers went to South Lake Tahoe for family time but spent endless hours attached to his phone in the early days of free agency. Myers was in front of his in-laws' home when he got the good news from Durant and Kleiman in a call Fourth of July morning in California, fifty feet from where he received word in 2013 free agent Iguodala would join the Warriors and a few miles from where Cavaliers reserve Steve Kerr took the 1989 casino joyride with teammates and reporters. Kerr found out when Margot shook him awake in the hotel room at 5:00 A.M. after seeing the news on Twitter. At the press conference three days later in Oakland to officially introduce his latest All-Star, Kerr joked, "Well, I haven't made the decision yet, but he might start."

Beyond the usual sarcasm, Kerr had stepped back into a pressure setting as the person charged with devising a game plan to keep three major scoring threats—Curry, Thompson, and Durant—happy. He at least had the credibility of a title and clear command of the locker room, unlike the newcomer needing to prove himself two years before, except this time was also in the wake of the Finals collapse and while still greatly impacted by the first back surgery. Kerr in private conversation could be so precise detailing the continuing agony that, as one person he confided in said, "It was really hard to hear." Searching for any solution, he had through many months of unceasing pain tried marijuana as a suppository, painkillers, meditation, yoga, and acupuncture.

Kerr's basketball problems increased when Durant arrived at camp "skittish" and "nervous," in the words of Golden State coaches, and, in Durant's own description, worried that "I'm going to have to play perfect," a state of mind that would slow the transition to a new system. Kerr saw a starting small forward whose "head was spinning the first couple of months." The adjustment was just as choppy for Curry, who knew coming in he would have to alter his game but struggled with the unexpected mental tweak of incorporating a potential scoring champion: "you can get kind of paralyzed by your own talent because you have so many options and you tend to overthink things." He was speaking Kerr's language. The dilemma came to a head; even though the Warriors were still winning at a high rate, Curry took only eleven shots in the Christmas game at Cleveland, prompting a team meeting that cleared the air and led to better cohesion.

Donald Trump was inaugurated three weeks later. It took Kerr nine days to speak out against the new president, criticizing an executive order to suspend immigration from several predominantly Muslim countries, a directive the White House said would combat terrorism. The grandson of a couple who met helping refugees and the son of a couple who preached inclusiveness and promoted the positives of the Arab world, speaking as a victim of terrorism himself, was appalled. It didn't help Kerr's mood that his relationship with Green, eternally an exposed electrical wire, had turned particularly contentious. Just when the Curry issue seemed to get resolved, Green grew ungrounded and emotional—"Pissed at the world, pissed at me," Kerr called it—until finally Kerr played Green twenty-three minutes and kept him on the bench the final 10:25 at home against the Nets. Only after Kerr handed Green a letter a day later, a note, that opened with the embracing language of how much his coach loved and respected him and that could tell one of his favorite people was hurting, did the strain begin to ease. The next concern was all of forty-eight hours away, when Durant suffered a sprained knee ligament that would sideline him five weeks and also scuttled an attempt at team unity the next day as he and others skipped the planned trip to the National Museum of African American History and Culture in Washington.

"Yes, I should be having the time of my life," Kerr said as the professional and personal challenges mounted, "but between not feeling great physically and the political climate, it doesn't feel as happy and carefree as it did two years ago when I first took the job. My back was healthy, it was all new, Obama was president, and the world seemed kind of normal. This has been a weird year for sure."

The sentiment became more accurate when Iguodala was fined $10,000 by the league for reacting to Kerr resting him March 10 at Minnesota with, "I do what master say," and using the N-word three times. The response was an inside joke, Iguodala later clarified, not a swing at the coach. Kerr backed both points—the coach and player were so close that some around the organization referred to Iguodala as Steve's Pet—with the similar dismissal that "he has a very cryptic sense of humor. Only thing I would say is there's certain humorous things you should say in the sanctity of the locker room and certain humorous things you might want to keep from the media, and that was one them, and he knows that." Also, he said to reporters the next day, "You got Andre'd."

It was hardly the first time he put the locker room above all. Pippen quit on the Bulls at the end of a playoff game and was arrested for having a loaded pistol in his car, yet Kerr offered only constant praise of Pippen as a Chicago and Portland teammate, even sympathizing with Pippen after he refused to play the final 1.8 seconds of a playoff game in 1994. "It was a devastating thing. Scottie never could have judged the magnitude of his actions. I felt so badly for him." In retirement, it got no worse than Kerr writing in a 2004 Yahoo! story that sitting was "the biggest mistake of Pippen's career, and unfortunately it will be part of his legacy." The Trail Blazers in Kerr's one season had a roster whose misdeeds drove away a loyal fan base, yet he always spoke of the good times with the group.

When the Iguodala issue passed without damage beyond the fine, the Warriors took off on a fourteen-game winning streak that included Durant returning for the last victory. They were, by all appearances, positioned perfectly, with momentum and good health just in time for the playoffs. Behind the scenes was a different matter. Kerr's physical problems, previously manageable enough that he worked the final sixty-three games the previous season and the first eighty-four of 2016–2017, suddenly flared, for reasons he could not explain. Walking with Kerr to lunch in Oakland and then during the meal, Chris Ballard of *Sports Illustrated* noted Kerr rubbing his forehead and opening and closing his jaw in the way a passenger tries to adjust to a pressure change on a plane. "For years, Kerr looked as if he'd forever just returned from the beach—blonde hair, trim, crinkles at the eyes," Ballard wrote. "Now there was something hard about him; he was all edges, angles and creases." Jerry West, hurting for a man he admired, empathetically said, "Oh my God," on several occasions as he watched a coach drenched in pain try to will himself through another day, and management considered ordering Kerr on sabbatical. He made the call himself and took another leave of absence with the Warriors leading the first round against the Trail Blazers 2–0.

Replacement Mike Brown had the advantage in April 2017 Luke Walton did not eighteen months before, the extensive experience of two stops as a head coach and three as an assistant, including a pair of seasons with Kerr in San Antonio. Brown did not, however, have the calendar on his side. While Walton took over in training camp and initially worked with the cushion that a losing streak early in the season would not cut too deep, a playoff disruption could be fatal to a group already trying to live down the finals collapse of the previous year. Offering an encouraging response, the Warriors finished the sweep against Portland and dismissed Utah with the same 4–0 statement in the second round.

The sight of their coach back at practice the day before the conference finals opened was the latest in gaining speed, followed by Kerr delivering a halftime speech in Game 1 with the Warriors down twenty. Focus on getting stops, he urged, and "settle in, and we'll be all right." It led to a 113–111 victory and the Spurs going from sixty-two points before the break to forty-nine after, with the obvious assistance of San Antonio playing most of the final two quarters without injured star Kawhi Leonard. When Kerr next accompanied the team to San Antonio in a similar role behind the scenes, a complete return seemed imminent as Golden State added a third consecutive 4–0 series victory and then an easy win against the Cavaliers to begin the championship series and extend the winning streak to fifteen.

Even with as few as three games and no more than six remaining, Kerr waited until he was confident he could make a permanent return. The worst development in his mind, however short-term, would be the stop-and-start of coming back only to be driven away after a game or two, to get so close to the sport he needed for a full recovery and then be robbed all over again.

Kerr thought June 3 he would be on the sideline in front of the home crowd the next night after missing eleven games and forty-seven days as full-time leader, but wanted to see how he felt in the morning to be sure. He woke up ready to return, gave the news to friend and former TNT colleague David Aldridge for a pregame interview, and walked into the media room to answer questions from the press corps with a mix of humor that quickly defused the pressure of the Finals.

"Apparently it was not a distraction," he said of his absence. "I don't know. We have not lost, so that's a good indication that it was not a distraction. And what's our record now without me?

Like 812–6 or something?" (It was 46–4.) Asked what he would tell the team before the Warriors took the court, he replied, "I'm going to pull out the Win One for the Gipper speech. What's the movie? 'Knute Rockne, All American'? Yeah, probably show that. Maybe get a little teary-eyed. Implore them to win it for me because it's not important for them to win it for themselves." His assessment of Brown's job in the interim role was "I just think the numbers are totally deceiving. You can talk like 15–0 or whatever he did, but the team was just falling apart at the seams, and so I just had to get back to make sure we righted the ship," before turning serious and offering extensive praise for the temp.

As the Warriors celebrated the championship four games later inside Oracle Arena, with Kerr on the job each time to complete a 16-1 postseason, he embraced Myers with tears in his eyes as yellow and blue confetti fluttered down around them. He shared a hug with Iguodala as Iguodala told him no one had taught him the game the way Kerr had. "Winning is fantastic," Kerr said. "I've been so lucky to be part of so many championship teams as a player and now as a coach and it never gets old. But tonight was a little different, just based on the things I've had to go through during this time." He would remember the combination of two-way talent, the hunt for revenge after the previous Finals, and Durant going for his first title as the best Golden State roster in at least Kerr's first five seasons. The unnecessary perspective of what could have been came when the Knicks fired Phil Jackson sixteen days later.

Kerr through the early weeks of the off-season remained open to the possibility of another White House visit despite an obvious dislike for the administration. Thinking decisions through as always, he was at the very least considering a pitch to the players that keeping the traditional appointment would be a statement on rising above political differences. Maybe sports could provide a unifying moment, he figured, and just maybe it would be the rare chance for the Warriors to share their viewpoints in direct conversation with Trump. "I, like many of our players, am very offended by some of Trump's words and actions," Kerr said. "On the other hand, I do

think there's something to respecting the office, respecting our in-
stitutions, our government. And I think it can make a statement in
a time when there is so much divide and everybody seems to be
angry with each other. It might be a good statement for us to go
and to show, 'Hey, let's put this aside, put all this partisan stuff aside,
and personal stuff aside, respect the institution, and maybe even if
one of you players wants to voice your concerns over what's happening, what better opportunity to do so.' That may be incredibly
idealistic, but I would want to at least bring that up with our players as an option rather than just coming out and saying, 'No way,
I'm not going.'" Commissioner Adam Silver went further, saying
he wanted the Warriors to make the ceremonial stop during the off
day in Washington carved out on the schedule for the defending
champion every year. Players weighed the idea of going in hopes of
a conversation with the president, only without the usual photo op
that would bring him attention.

The deadly clash August 12 in Charlottesville, Virginia, followed
three days later by Trump's description of "very fine people" on
both sides of the violence, even though white supremacists were on
one of the sides, became the breaking point for Kerr. "Fuck that," he
told at least one person in shredding the original attempt at compromise. "No fuckin' way." The plugged-in Monte Poole from Comcast
Sports Bay Area reported Kerr decided before the season against a
visit, only kept it quiet to not appear to be assuming another title.
Wanting the team to make the decision, Kerr didn't take his new
position public, but what little doubt remained that the coach was
aligned with the players ended when Curry said at media day on the
eve of training camp he would not go to the White House. Trump,
trying to play catch-up, incorrectly spun his response on Twitter
into Curry hesitating. "Here it is," Margot said in waking her husband up the next morning, as if they had been expecting the retort
via social media. Trump withdrew the invitation the Warriors had
already turned down.

Kerr was moved to compose another first-person piece for *Sports
Illustrated,* as told to Ballard. "Would we have gone?" Kerr wrote.

"Probably not. The truth is we all struggled with spending time with a man who has offended us with his words and actions time and again. But I can tell you one thing: it wouldn't have been for the traditional ceremony, to shake hands and smile for cameras. Internally, we'd discussed whether it'd be possible to just go and meet as private citizens and have a serious, poignant discussion about some of the issues we're concerned about. But he's made it hard for any of us to actually enter the White House, because what's going on is not normal. It's childish stuff: belittling people and calling them names. So to expect to go in and have a civil, serious discourse? Yeah, that's probably not going to happen." Kerr likewise tagged Trump as immature ("It's a basic adult thing that you learn as you grow up: People aren't always going to agree with you"), directly accused him of shaming the presidency ("In his Tweet to Steph, Trump talked about honoring the White House but, really, isn't it *you* who must honor the White House, Mr. President?"), and putting a wedge through the country ("You represent all of us. Don't divide us"). Kerr also said among the 950 words in one of the most recognizable outlets in the country, "There's no need to get into a war of words."

Becoming more politically outspoken had grown into going head-to-head with a White House that relished verbal combat, with Kerr among the many counterpunchers in sports but one of the few who would initiate contact. It was a confrontation. It was how Margot had come to describe her fun-loving, friendly husband with the buried fuse that burns bright and fast once lit: "Beware the fury of a patient man," a line from the seventeenth-century English poet John Dryden she learned from reading a book on former tennis star Arthur Ashe. Both Kerrs would reference the description and readied people new to Steve's world to be prepared to find cover as soon as smoke was spotted coming from the coach.

He broke clipboards on the sideline. Once, he took offense to an innocent question from Kawakami that Kerr wrongly viewed as the columnist trying to embarrass him and the next day loudly cussed out Kawakami on the court at shootaround—You motherfucker, you asked me that fuckin' question about being goddamned out-coached, you're fucking thinking I'm being out-coached. "Tolbert told me about that when he was hired," Kawakami said. "'Steve is the most competitive guy I've ever known, and he's the fastest to get mad I've ever known. It's fast. It's not there's a little lead-up, he's getting mad, he's getting mad. No. It's from green light to burning red light faster than anybody.' Tolbert told me that. As Steve and I are going at it, I am thinking about that. Like, 'This is what Tolbert said, and that's one of his best friends, so it's all true.'" The next time Kerr and Kawakami saw each other, the coach, having vented, made a point to say they were back on good terms.

By the summer of 2017 and into the new season, Trump more than anyone pushed Kerr to the fiery place. "I think some people probably think I spend all my time studying politics, and I don't," he said. "I spend most of my time watching basketball and planning practice for the next day and thinking about the game. That's my true passion. But I do read a lot about politics and I follow what's going on, and I'm worried. I'm worried about our country. That's really the gist of my feeling comfortable about speaking out." He again advocated for stronger gun-control laws after a sniper on the thirty-second floor of a Las Vegas hotel killed fifty-eight people at a music festival on the ground. He backed Colin Kaepernick as the controversy over NFL players kneeling during the national anthem became another White House talking point.

"I really wasn't that outspoken 10 years ago, maybe because nobody asked me," Kerr said. "And it seemed like the country was more comfortable and there wasn't this divide. I haven't seen this kind of divide in my lifetime. I'm sure it existed during Vietnam, but I was five years old and six years old when that came to a head. And the fact that there's so much media now means that I'm getting asked about [the] current political divide." He began getting questions unrelated to basketball "all the time. But I feel comfortable talking about it because I feel like it's important. I feel really strongly about the issues that are going on right now. It's scary. It's a very scary time right now for our country. And I think it's important for everybody to speak their mind. I just happen to have a very big platform." The concession to the darkening mood was reducing his Twitter use in an attempt to become less angry.

On the court, Kerr noticed Durant more comfortable in his surroundings and confident in his role as 2017–2018 began, in contrast to the same time the year before and maybe, with the burden of winning a title gone, better than the superstar showing in the Finals. He was fluid and certain even while the Warriors started slow—4-3 and then 15-6—with the feel of a team paying for the draining preseason trip to China more than complacency. Wanting to send a message to the roster to take ownership, Kerr had players run some time-outs against the Suns in February. Later that month, Durant had the personal satisfaction of including forty students from his hometown of Seat Pleasant, Maryland, when the Warriors toured the National Museum of African American History and Culture in Washington in place of the traditional White House visit. Durant's presence alone was a contrast to the somber mood of the 2017 tour he missed the morning after the knee injury against the Wizards. In 2018, it felt more joyful, with the entire team in attendance along with the kids from Seat Pleasant and ten more from the Tragedy Assistance Program for Survivors, a group that helps children who lost loved ones in the military.

Despite a general dislike of museums, preferring the action of Broadway shows or other performances, Kerr was among the most engaged people in the group during the three hours. He was, said Damion Thomas, a curator who led the tour, "as excited to be there as the players. That's one thing that stood out to me." The party moved among several exhibits on the five floors below ground and five above, through galleries spotlighting slavery to segregation to the role of African Americans in sports history, with Kerr asking questions and making comments along the way. With the Warriors making a point to keep the visit apolitical, wanting the attention to be on the museum and the chance to learn, Thomas took note of how much the coach embraced the walk through history. Kerr, sticking to the plan, passed up every chance to poke Trump, declining to even say the next day whether he missed the White House stop. "You're not going to get me to go down that path, sorry," was as far as he would go.

He did not stay in neutral long. Becoming more outspoken led Kerr to taking a prominent role in a town hall–style meeting at Newark High School in the Bay Area two weeks later for a conversation on gun violence that included two congressmen and the older brother of two students who hid in closets during the killing spree at a Parkland, Florida, high school the month before. Standing before an audience of high school students in Northern California, inspired by the activism of teenagers, he felt momentum in the fight that had long been personal but only within the last year had become an especially public stand. Twelve days later, Kerr participated in March for Our Lives in Oakland.

He began getting questions on social issues or the president before games, after games, and on practice days, sometimes answering in detail, and other times politely declining, as he had the day after the Washington museum tour. It was easy to anticipate fielding more such questions as Golden State traveled seventy-five miles to play the Kings in a tip-off hours after a rally in downtown Sacramento to protest the fatal shooting of Stephon Clark by two police officers. The Warriors did not attend the protest, Kerr explained, because "we're kind of busy today," before continuing with fifty-five uninterrupted seconds of support for the Clark family and the community.

Tyler Tynes from the website SB Nation found that answer lacking. "You don't think there's a contradiction there when you talk a lot about race or an issue like that? But then there's a march and somebody gets killed and you don't actually show up?"

Kerr grinned, as if he couldn't believe the line of questioning was continuing. "You're serious?" he responded.

"Yeah, I am," Tynes said.

Kerr had always enjoyed healthy debate, loved the back-and-forth to help him think through ideas, and was always open to hearing points he might have missed, but he would not accept being framed as hypocritical a week after the March for Our Lives and nineteen days after taking a public stand at Newark High. Tynes doubting Kerr's commitment to curb gun violence seemed to cross a line, especially when it came from a reporter several others in the media scrum thought was intent on instigating something. Sounding agitated but without raising his voice, the coach delivered a forty-two-second reply of how "I'm very confident and comfortable in my own skin and our players' lives," that "I'm also very serious about my job," and, "you can be accusatory if you'd like." Kerr was taken aback for one of the few times in decades of skillfully dealing with the media.

Kerr at the same time had the actual problem of a roster laboring through extended stretches of the second half and, of greater concern, listless when it should have been getting locked into playoff mode. The Warriors "had a bad vibe around the team," Curry said, while Kerr, though not realizing the long-term implications, noticed early signs of the Draymond Green–Kevin Durant conflict that would spray into public view the next season. The group "was starting to drift a little bit," Kerr said, adding, "We were losing some of that connection."

Phil Jackson wasn't watching much basketball in retirement, but he saw enough at home in Montana to detect a tired group. The Warriors "showed the wear and tear of those past years," he said. "They've been going at this for four years, and the injuries are starting to become more frequent, and age is starting to tell." As late as April 5, with five days remaining in the regular season, Kerr berated the Warriors so badly in the locker room and then publicly to the media after a twenty-point loss at Indiana that his assistant coaches told the boss he went too far. Kerr, stewing through too many nights of nonexistent effort and sloppy execution, was worried for one of the few times in the first five years of the new career. Then, in the final game of playoff prep, they were flat from the start at Utah, Green questioned the heart of some teammates, especially Durant, while screaming at the bench, and Golden State lost by forty.

Facing the Spurs in the first round at least brought comic relief of San Antonio intern Nick Kerr among the opposition—"We pat him down every day after work," Popovich said earlier in the season—but also sadness at the death of Popovich's wife Erin the day before Game 3 following a lengthy illness. Between Durant's growing emotional disconnect, becoming a national target for rage, the maddening end to the regular season, and the passing of Erin Popovich, 2017–2018 had become a great challenge. At least Kerr was improved physically, with difficult days, but never difficult enough to miss a game. He remained so optimistic about the direction of the team that all it took was beating the Spurs in the opener to convince him the Golden State defense was locked in. "That's when I knew we could do this," he said. It didn't matter that the read came against a team missing its best player, the injured Kawhi Leonard, whose rise to stardom was tied to work with Chip Engelland. The Warriors finished off San Antonio in five games and dispatched New Orleans with the same convincing 4–1 performance to advance to the West finals against Houston.

The concerns late in the regular season were so far gone that Kerr was undeterred by a 3–2 deficit to the Rockets and coach Mike D'Antoni to the point of growing cocky while on the brink of elimination. Unlike predicting the comeback against the Thunder two years earlier in straightforward tones, calling his shot in Houston to Marcus Thompson II and Ethan Strauss of the Athletic felt like Kerr riding the emotions of a new discovery. The last two reporters in the nearly empty locker room were a couple steps away as Kerr, aware of their presence, approached the few remaining players individually before the flight to Oakland with the message, "We're gonna win this," practically on a loop. With Draymond Green, it came with a hug. Kerr's words were infused with more emotion than his analytical breakdown of Oklahoma City '16, an energy he hoped to transfer to the entire roster, even if the group didn't lack confidence in the first place.

"Look," Kerr told Thompson and Strauss, "we're winning the next two."

In fact, he said, the Warriors would win the next six—finishing off the Rockets and then needing only the minimum of four games to beat East representative Cleveland or Boston in the Finals to claim another championship. The all-time good guy was also incredibly brazen. All Kerr asked Thompson and Strauss, media members he trusted, was to keep the prediction off the record until it became reality, which he was sure it would. Not wanting to risk a very good relationship or walk away from the rarity of unique content during a series being chronicled by hundreds, and knowing they couldn't get beat on the story while working for the same outlet, the reporters agreed and held to the verbal pact.

Kerr "just saw something" in Game 5, "and I thought, 'Yeah, we got this.' Now there's a lot of chance that can happen. Somebody sprains an ankle, or the ball bounces the wrong way, whatever, but I felt like as long as nothing happened injury wise, we were going to win that series." He was certain to the point of joking on national television while trailing 3–2 in the series and ahead only seven points entering the fourth quarter. When TNT sideline reporter David Aldridge asked during the between-period interview about the Warriors' lack of experience in elimination games, Kerr responded, "We have seen elimination. We have. We saw it in OKC. Do your homework, David. C'mon." Though he turned and walked a few feet back to the bench so quickly that he appeared angry, Kerr was anything but, and later called Aldridge to apologize in case his former colleague took heat from viewers who misread playful banter between friends.

When Golden State dominated the final quarter to win by twenty-nine and then won Game 7 on the road as the Rockets missed twenty-seven consecutive three-pointers, Kerr took a big step toward being proven right. Both his boast and his team received a scare when the championship series opened with the Warriors needing overtime to beat the Cavaliers at home, but that was followed by a nineteen-point victory in Oakland and back-to-back wins in Cleveland, the last by twenty-three. Kerr had called everything except the scores. Drenched in champagne and heading to another parade, he couldn't help but remind Strauss, "You thought

I was crazy but I told you, I felt good after Game 5 in the Houston series."

Kerr did not bring up his other reason for celebration: he had worked a full schedule, 103 games including the playoffs, for the first time since his debut campaign of 2014–2015. "I've learned how to manage my symptoms," he said late in the regular season. "I've learned kind of how to get through the pain. So I'm doing better with it in terms of managing it. Like I said, I love coaching, love what I'm doing, and that's carrying me through a lot of this." The third championship moved him into sixth place on the all-time coaching list with the knowledge that the five ahead of him were either in the Hall of Fame (Phil Jackson, Red Auerbach, John Kundla, and Pat Riley) or would be as soon as he was prepared to deal with the hated spotlight (Popovich). Kerr was far from being eligible, needing twenty-five years as a full-time head coach or assistant or be four years into retirement, yet he had rocketed to the verge of enshrinement in just four seasons and before his first contract had expired.

It led into one of the most pleasurable summers in years, without so much as having to weigh a White House invitation that was not coming and would not have been accepted. When he arrived at Warriors headquarters in Oakland for the draft, mostly as an observer, thirteen days after finishing the finals sweep, Kerr had already taken a surfing vacation in Mexico and started on a beard, before showing up wearing flip-flops and a vintage Cubs cap. "First of all," he said, "I have nothing to do with tonight. I have zero influence, which is exactly how I want it." He signed a contract extension one season before the original deal would expire. The family traveled in Europe for a couple weeks and watched U.S. Open tennis in New York. He went to Springfield, Massachusetts, for the Hall of Fame induction ceremonies for the Class of 2018 that included Kerr favorites Rick Welts, Steve Nash, and Grant Hill. The Warriors hired Nick Kerr as assistant video coordinator. Returning to the golf course for a few rounds in San Diego in late summer made the off-season complete. "So I am doing better," Kerr said. "And man, what a long haul. I work every day. I do a lot of stuff to make sure I'm staying on the improving path. But man, getting old, it sucks." Three years after the dual surgeries and after turning fifty-three just before the start of training camp, he was finally able to say the worst was behind him.

Taking on the long-term commitment of joining Popovich's Team USA staff for the World Cup in the summer of 2019 and the Olympics in 2020 was the strongest public sign of Kerr's confidence in his recovery. Whether he would be offered the role was never in doubt—he was one of only five or six NBA coaches considered when Popovich and USA Basketball managing director Jerry Colangelo began to assemble the staff, the Popovich who considered Kerr a close friend and the same Colangelo who drafted Kerr as the Phoenix general manager in 1988 and had remained an admirer. Knowing they wanted to include a college coach, they immediately decided on Villanova's Jay Wright. They agreed on Kerr with similar ease, appreciating not only his basketball acumen but because they had firsthand knowledge his personality would blend well with players and executives alike. Nate McMillan was named the third assistant, before later being replaced by Lloyd Pierce.

Kerr feeling good enough to give away part of his recovery time each of the next two summers was the latest sign of his improving health as the Warriors reconvened for 2018–2019 with the core of the championship team intact. While aware he needed to give the roster room to make mistakes on tired legs that again played into June, Kerr was also so determined to avoid complacency that he was concerned about the return of the same coaching staff. No prominent assistant left for another job and no one deserved to be replaced, stability but also a missed opportunity for the infusion of new energy he wanted.

Kerr did have the benefit of an eventual lineup adjustment with the arrival of the free agent center DeMarcus Cousins, plus the challenge corralling the emotions of the tempestuous newcomer at center. Cousins was also an ideal style fit as a talented and willing passer, although he wouldn't play for months while recovering from a torn Achilles' tendon. The search for ways to keep the Warriors from going stale instead turned to considering having players lead shootarounds and again run selected time-outs in games, along with a favorite Kerr tactic, passed down from Jackson, of inserting humorous clips into film sessions.

The Bulls saw scenes from *Apocalypse Now, The Wizard of Oz, Pulp Fiction*, the Three Stooges, *What About Bob?*, and others chosen to deliver a point as well as stay alert during the monotony of constant winning streaks with few challengers on the horizon. (When Jackson chose *The Devil's Advocate*, with Al Pacino as the title character searching for additions to his fiery below, players were asked if the coach was messaging Krause more than the roster. "Don't go there," Buechler said. "Don't even go there." Dickey Simpkins said he would wait to sign his next contract before answering.) "One of the things I learned from Phil was how important it was being funny watching game film, editing stuff in from movies," Kerr said. "Nobody I had ever played for had ever done that, and, to me, that was such an effective way of getting a message across. When you could tie together the point you're trying to make on the basketball floor with a humorous message coming from a movie—when the message is clear and it carries over to what you're trying to teach—you're not having to either kiss up to the player or criticize them. You're just telling them something, but you're using humor. I thought that was part of Phil's genius, and it's something that we try to employ all the time."

Kerr, with the benefit of better video technology and a much larger staff, continued the tradition and considered it an especially valuable tool as 2018–2019 opened with the concern that years of success might turn the Warriors content. Anything to avoid a team lulling itself into playing on autopilot. The unwanted cure for drowsy play was Green turning incendiary in an argument with Durant that started on the bench late in the fourteenth game and carried into the locker room after the road loss to the Clippers, shouting that included Green emphatically telling Durant he was not needed on the team and should leave as a free agent at the end of the season. Kerr saw it as the two players ready to fight and took a lead role in Green being suspended for one game. Later in the season, during a home loss to the 15-52 Suns, Kerr told Mike Brown on the sideline during an especially frustrating stretch, "I'm so fucking tired of Draymond."

While tensions between Kerr and Durant were just as apparent, they were also more severe in the absence of the mutual respect and personal bond Kerr and Green shared, the connection that carried them through prickly moments. Kerr and Durant were more business acquaintances with a common goal, especially in the second half of 2018–2019 as Durant distanced himself from most of the organization. Kerr with months left on the schedule began to appear to several people resigned to Durant leaving as a free agent, exactly as Green had encouraged on the bench against the Clippers, and was just trying to make the best of a difficult situation. By the time the Warriors lost to the Celtics in March and Kerr explained Golden State did not play with enough passion or anger, Durant was barely trying to hide the strain. "I thought we move off joy," he said when asked about the assessment, tapping into a favored Kerr mantra. "Now anger?" Durant later insisted he was not mocking his coach, but Kerr knew otherwise.

A similar awareness prompted him to encourage players, staffers, and even fans to appreciate the moment, a Kerr mindset since at least his college years, but especially prominent during 2017–2018. It was as if he knew the potent might not last. In other times, his advice to be grateful for all they had was purposely unrelated to basketball in the mold of mentors Jackson with his tribal room and Popovich reminding someone looking glum that people in third-world countries were having a worse day. Kerr would likewise reference a humanitarian crisis, a natural disaster, or a national tragedy to make certain the Warriors appreciated their good fortune of grand wages and making a living playing sports. On the court, he wanted the group aiming for a fourth title in five years to savor each moment. He called it their best chance to win a title, "an incredible opportunity that may never come again. That's something that's important for everybody to realize—fans, management, players. It is lightning in a bottle. You can do everything perfectly and you still may not get to where you think you might be."

Curry called it the hardest regular season of their championship era. Once they reached the playoffs, though, the locker room noticeably came together for 4–2 wins over the Clippers and the Rockets in a particularly enjoyable second round for Kerr. Not only did Golden State eliminate Houston, and not only did that come while privately deriding Rockets star James Harden through the years as an undependable me-first individual talent in the Westbrook mold, but also with a clinching Game 6 that for years after would stand to Kerr as the epitome of selfless approach. "Holy shit," he said, remembering the night with a special glow. "This defines our team. This game defines what our guys are about." In one possession in particular with the added symbolism that it involved four players at the foundation all along, Curry passed to Green, Green passed to Iguodala, and Iguodala passed to Thompson for a three-pointer with thirty-six seconds remaining and an insurmountable lead. It was a primary reason May 10, 2019, inside the Toyota Center—not a night that ended with a champagne shower, nor a triumphant return to the sideline—would be Kerr's favorite game in five seasons as a coach.

The momentum carried into a 4–0 sweep of the Trail Blazers in a conference final that began with the Warriors' arrival in Portland the day a distraught seventeen-year-old walked into a high school classroom there wearing a black trench coat and carrying a shotgun. The assailant was subdued by football coach and security guard Keanon Lowe before doing any harm, more than enough of an opening for Kerr to be asked to comment before Game 3 the next night. He praised the heroism of Lowe, a former San Francisco 49ers and Philadelphia Eagles assistant coach, and condemned that school shootings had practically become routine for kids. A gunman killing twelve in Virginia Beach, Virginia, two weeks later, on an off day after Game 1 of the Finals against the Raptors, drove Kerr to a new level of action.

Brandishing the spotlight more boldly than ever, he walked into Toronto's ScotiaBank Arena before Game 2 wearing a T-shirt that proclaimed VOTE FOR OUR LIVES across the chest in support of the gun-control group March for Our Lives urging change through the ballot box. Keeping the black shirt with white lettering on during the mandatory pregame press conference for both coaches about ninety minutes before tip-off, knowing he would likely be asked about the wardrobe choice, was Kerr moving from accepting questions beyond basketball to wanting them. The carnage of Virginia Beach pushed him to practically beg for the conversation on the league's biggest stage.

"The insanity of it all," he said ten days later in Oakland as part of finger wagging in conversation with Sean Gregory of *Time* magazine that touched on global warming, the economy, California wildfires, and, naturally, Trump and the Republican Senate. Before the biggest night of the season for the Warriors, Game 6 while staring over the ledge of elimination far below or a 3–3 tie and new life against the Raptors, Kerr invited Gregory into his office at Oracle Arena with an openness to discuss the world, not merely pressing basketball business. A 2003 letter from John Wooden in the precise cursive that stayed with Wooden late in life hung on the wall: "It has always pleased me to see the game played without excessive showmanship and exemplary conduct both on and off the court. And you are in that same category along with David Robinson, Tim Duncan, John Stockton, Jerry West and, of course many others." The season could end the next night, Golden State had no counter to Toronto's Kawhi Leonard, but things needed to be said and he wouldn't bother responding to fans who thought he should use the Kerr megaphone only for sports. "I don't have one," he said. "I don't care."

Kerr was additionally struggling to process Durant rupturing his right Achilles' tendon in the same Game 5 the Warriors won to avoid elimination. "I just told the team I didn't know what to say because on the one hand I'm so proud of them, just the amazing heart and grit that they showed, and on the other I'm just devastated for Kevin," he said. The wide range of conflicted emotions in the locker room was "bizarre." As if Leonard and the Raptors weren't causing enough problems, fate was turning against Kerr's championship era. Klay Thompson tearing a knee ligament in Game 6 in Oakland made it official. Golden State lost another critical player and the series.

Almost as soon as Toronto claimed the title in a smoldering outcome for the Warriors, Kerr seemed to grasp the end of something larger than a season, understanding even in the disappointing instant the group that had accomplished so much would never be the same again. Thompson would likely miss at least the first half of the next season, and Durant, expected to leave as a free agent anyway, probably would be out all 2019–2020. Kerr, the ultimate realist, knew the payback he avoided in Chicago was coming.

Not wanting the assistant coaches and the video team to disperse into the Oakland night without taking time to embrace all that had come before, hoping, as always, that they would value their good fortune, Kerr gathered the group in his office and offered a favorite beer, Modelo Especial. He went around the room, Fraser said, "and connected with our staff, talking about his appreciation for each of us, which he'd never done like that before. Not trying to make us feel better. Just letting us know he cared."

The suddenness of it all, dropping three of the first four in the Finals and Thompson and Durant suffering serious injuries within three days, was staggering to the point of disbelief. "I don't know how to explain anything in the last two weeks," Myers said. The Warriors were taken down by a wicked streak of health problems and in part by Kerr's own inner circle. It was Engelland, after all, whose tutoring helped turn Spurs defensive standout Leonard into an offensive threat as well, before Leonard was traded to Toronto and became the difference-maker who averaged 28.5 points in the six games of the championship series. Ground to the bone by five campaigns in a row of playing into June, with 105 playoff games alone, another one and a quarter seasons, Kerr asked Commissioner Adam Silver when Silver came to the locker room after Game 6 if the Warriors could skip 2019–2020 as a sabbatical. "Maybe go to Italy, ride bikes and sip wine," Kerr said. "Take the year off." He was trying to be funny, not prophetic.

CHAPTER 15

Tremendous Forces at Play

Three years after the receiving line at the swanky beach digs, Kevin Durant broke up with the Warriors with such determination that he announced his decision on the earliest possible date without so much as talking to interested teams on the phone. Even the victorious Brooklyn Nets seemed taken aback when Durant named them his latest true love despite not visiting club headquarters or talking with team officials, among them coach Kenny Atkinson, whose reaction included, "It feels unfair, in a way. Can you do a better job than Steve Kerr has?" Just as he learned of Durant choosing Golden State in 2016 while vacationing in Hawaii, Kerr got the 2019 word there as well, this time on a beach from overhearing a stranger scream the news thirty feet away.

While Kerr would have welcomed the presence of an incandescent offensive talent in the lineup, to those who know him he was not disappointed nor, like most everyone else with Golden State, surprised Durant opted for a new direction. The departure allowed the Warriors to get to the future sooner, without having to idle as Durant likely missed all 2019–2020, and provided Kerr the shakeup he wanted a year earlier. Kerr had the major lineup adjustments of incorporating a new small forward to replace Durant, D'Angelo Russell arriving as part of the sign-and-trade with the Nets and the expectation Thompson would miss at least the first half of the season recovering from the knee injury. Russell would replace Thompson at shooting guard in the meantime. The season might be uncomfortable in the standings, but Kerr was energized by the challenge that came complete with the symbolism of the Warriors starting another new life with the move into shiny Chase Center.

Plus, there was the enthusiasm of finally getting on the court with Team USA in August, nine months after the announcement that he had been chosen as a Popovich assistant and thirty-three years after playing for his country in his star-crossed world championships in Spain. The American squad met in Las Vegas for the same mini-camp USA Basketball often held to prepare for international competitions, only now with the head coach and a high-profile assistant jousting with the White House and heading into the delicate diplomatic waters of China for the tournament.

Officials said nothing to Kerr, however, before Las Vegas or once players and staff gathered. "Not to him specifically," Colangelo said. "I did it in a different manner. To the group I said, 'We want to go about our business. We're here to represent the United States, we're here to play the games, we're here to do all of that. This is not about politics. This is not the platform for that.' I wanted a separation. People were entitled to their own opinions on anything in life, and you know that Steve has been outspoken about the things that he believes in. But I think there's a time and a place, that's all." Popovich delivered a similar message when he hosted players and coaches for a meeting at the Wynn, that, as he summarized the next day, "We can't fix the divisiveness in our country. But what we can do is be a great example of how people can come together for a common goal and achieve it. It's our responsibility to not only become the best team we can be, but it's the way we conduct ourselves with USA on our shirts. We're representing a lot of people." It was left to others to remind Popovich that he had previously labeled Trump "a soulless coward" who is "unfit intellectually, emotionally, and psychologically" to be president and who "brings out the dark side of human beings," among other critiques.

Kerr in recent weeks had used Twitter to share videos and articles critical of Trump and to push for stricter gun control in the wake of shootings in Texas and Ohio. He referenced "gutless leadership" in Washington and shortly after arriving for the minicamp said, "Somebody could walk in the door in the gym right now and start spraying us with an AR-15. They could. It might happen because we're all vulnerable, whether we go to a concert, a church, the mall or go to the movie theater or a school." As part of Team USA, though, "I'm proud to represent my country and do it with this group in a positive, classy way. We have a chance to do something that's very unifying."

The five-week official commitment, beyond planning meetings and conversations ahead of Las Vegas, began with the minicamp and scrimmage against young NBA players considered leading candidates for future Team USA squads. The travel that followed took the Americans to Anaheim, about halfway between Pacific Palisades and San Diego, for an exhibition against Spain, then Melbourne and Sydney for final tune-ups against Australia and Canada. On arrival in China, they opened the World Cup in Shanghai with wins over the Czech Republic, Turkey, and Japan. Moving south along the East China Sea for the next round, the favorite for the gold medal improved to 5-0 by defeating Greece and Brazil.

Along the way, Team USA forward Harrison Barnes, the former Warriors starter, saw a different Kerr than he had during their previous time together. The summer 2019 version of Kerr was an assistant coach away from the primary pressure, far from the weight of the NBA outcomes that would determine his coaching legacy. And, he was with Popovich, Chip Engelland, and former Spurs assistant Ime Udoka, part of the support staff. "One, just the team we had," Barnes said. "But two, he'd been around those guys forever. He's around Chip Engelland. He's around Ime. He's around Pop. He's around guys he's had a lot of respect for. They had their own time of just kind of being around each other. I think it was more of a reunion for them." Kerr traveling from Las Vegas and Anaheim to Australia and China appeared to bounce with a joy to match the portable glow of his debut coaching season in 2014–2015, when he practically could not believe his good fortune. "For sure," Barnes said. "He was definitely in his element. Absolutely."

"It was wonderful," Popovich said. "Not just because of the

friendship. That was pretty easy. Just being there with he and Lloyd and Jay. It was like a clinic every day. I learned a lot. We worked hard, had a lot of fun, had a great group. It was a long deal. It was like fifty days or so, but it was a wonderful experience. I really enjoyed everything."

Not even the bad outcome of the United States losing the next two in Dongguan, against France and Serbia, before beating Poland in Beijing to salvage a disappointing seventh place could deter Popovich and Kerr from boasting of the summer as a positive experience. For Kerr, the chance to work closely with one of his mentors, different in his eyes than four seasons of playing for Popovich, was a highlight of his coaching career, with the additional excitement that the staff was projected to remain in place for the Tokyo Games.

Kerr returned to the United States in mid-September as arguably the leading candidate to succeed Popovich as coach of the national team, albeit possibly many years down the line considering Popovich was beginning his first Olympic cycle and predecessor Mike Krzyzewski had the role for three. Of far greater concern in the moment Kerr would be going back to his full-time job with easily the briefest rest of his Golden State tenure and would have only weeks to lock into the challenge of the Warriors minus Durant and, for at least several months, without Thompson.

"Well, I'm excited about it," Kerr said the day before the team took the court for the first time. "It's different. It's a very different season. Every year is a challenge, and the circumstances are unique. This is such a dramatic change from where we've been over the last four years that I think it allows for more change, more internal evaluation, what can we do better. You know, the new building is almost a metaphor for how we can approach the season. We've got a chance to reset some things, anything we feel like could improve our team. It's a great opportunity to start fresh on some things." In more practical terms, "I would say we will have to work much harder than we have had to the last four seasons because of the number of new players. We've got a lot of work to do."

He was fifty-four years old with three titles in his current job alone, yet still describing himself as a young coach with much to learn, the same vulnerability and honesty that helped convince a band of team executives stopping in Oklahoma City for an interview to hire unproven Kerr in 2014. Only weeks before, he was stealing plays while watching international action in China, this time without the dry cleaners' cardboard as scrap paper at the TNT table courtside, and he was likewise invigorated as 2019–2020 approached with the ground opening beneath him. Though a different feel for the modern Warriors of sixty-seven, seventy-three, sixty-seven, fifty-eight, and fifty-seven victories their first five seasons together, it was all too familiar for the Kerr dismissed in college recruiting, part of the pack heading into the NBA, taking over Golden State with zero experience and suddenly the coach of a typical roster. Of all the problems ahead, handling adversity would not be one of them.

It was no different when the critique veered all the way to the highest reaches of politics. Kerr ducking the chance to support human rights protesters in China as the NBA collectively avoided criticizing the country where it had billions invested renewed the verbal war with Trump. This time the White House was on the offense after Kerr offered "no comment" on the fallout from the controversy that threatened the league's relationship with the most populous country in the world: "It's a really bizarre international story. A lot of us don't know what to make of it. It's something I'm reading about like everyone else is, but I'm not gonna comment further."

Trump pounced. "I watched this guy, Steve Kerr, and he was like a little boy who was so scared to be even answering the question," Trump said of one of his vocal adversaries who likewise knew how to leverage the media. "He couldn't answer the question. He was shaking. 'Oh, I don't know. I don't know.' He didn't know how to answer the question. And yet he'll talk about the United States very badly. I watched Popovich. Sort of the same thing, but he didn't look quite as scared actually. But they talk badly about the United States, but when it talks about China, they don't want to say anything bad. I thought it was pretty sad actually. It'll be very interesting." Kerr and

Air Force Academy graduate Popovich, he added, were pandering to China. "And yet to our own country, they don't—it's like they don't respect it. I said, 'What a difference.' Isn't it sad?" Moving to revoke future invitations that had not been issued and almost certainly would not have been accepted, Trump reaffirmed he did not want Kerr at the White House.

Trump seemed unconcerned by the fact that Kerr had never spoken ill of the country, only some elected officials and policies, or that Kerr was not shaking. Kerr in one of the countless media scrums of his life occasionally shifted while sitting in a director's chair on the practice court but did not move any more than usual, especially if he was having a bad health day. The credible attack point the White House had but chose not to use was Kerr hiding behind the claim of lacking knowledge when in fact he was always well read on most major news topics and brother-in-law Hans van de Ven was a professor of modern Chinese history at Cambridge. Leaning on "It's a really bizarre international story" and "A lot of us don't know what to make of it," was a botched attempt to protect NBA financial interests more than Kerr being scared, as he would acknowledge the next summer. "Obviously," he conceded within days, "there are tremendous financial forces at play here too. So how you reconcile all that, I don't know."

Either way, it was an issue as vice president of communications Raymond Ridder texted Kerr with the alert that developments had reached a national scale, just before many others called and typed at him. Kerr had traded punches with the White House before, but as part of a group in 2015 while considering the traditional champion's visit. There had also been the imaging of one of Trump's least favorite public figures, Kerr, joining the Warriors in visiting another of Trump's least favorite public figures, Barack Obama, in Washington instead of stopping at 1600 Pennsylvania Avenue on the off day built into the Golden State schedule to celebrate the 2018 crown. This, though, was directly Kerr vs. Trump for the first time and the administration spin machine flexing at a basketball coach whose biggest transgression was what some viewed as a weak answer.

Kerr reported for the mandatory media availability ahead of the October 10 preseason game against Minnesota, the night after Trump's inaccurate criticism, and responded with a mix of somber tones and humor. "Raymond and I were just talking about it and if we were thinking about it earlier I was going to ride in on a tricycle with one of those beanies with a propeller it in because he called me a little boy," he said. "Just ride in and see if you guys got the joke, but we didn't think of it early enough. It was really surprising, mainly just because it was me. Then you stop and think that this is just every day, this is just another day. I was the shiny object yesterday, there was another one today, and there will be a new one tomorrow, and the circus will go on. It was just strange, but it happened." He went on to talk about living a privileged life that included meeting five previous presidents, starting with Reagan in the Oval Office visit with Ann in 1984 to thank the family for Malcolm's service. He spoke of what he saw as the dramatic change from the dignity and respect Kerr knew from leaders of both parties. Also, he wondered, "Does anyone want to talk about pick-and-roll coverage tonight?"

Mostly, he said later in the session, "It's hard for me to make a comment about something that impacts so many people, different countries, different governments. Not really feeling comfortable being in the midst of it, I think it makes more sense to lay low"—he paused two seconds for effect—"and be a scared little boy." The media sitting before him broke up. The exchange ended after several lengthy responses on the controversy at hand, Kerr interjecting thoughts on gun control, and even a closing query that poked at his baseball team being eliminated from the playoffs the day before. "Wow," he said. "That sounded like a shot. Tough day for me. The president goes at me and my Dodgers lose."

Jousting with the White House passed, as Kerr predicted, in enough time before the regular season for him to focus entirely on his actual problem of a roster in mid-crumble, and a transition to life among basketball commoners that came complete with a $78 parking ticket in his new San Francisco neighborhood soon after moving. He had transitioned from Chicago Stadium to the United

Center as a Bull in 1994, and from the Alamodome to the AT&T Center with the Spurs in 2002, but under winning circumstances, even with Michael Jordan in retirement. Relocating across the Bay Bridge was with nine of the fourteen players new and eight age twenty-three or younger. The opener was a nineteen-point loss to the Clippers, the second game an eighteen-point setback at Oklahoma City. The Warriors were down twenty-nine to the Suns in the third quarter on October 30 when Curry fractured his left hand, an injury that cost him fifty-eight games.

By the time Charlotte came to town November 2, Curry, Thompson, Green, Kevon Looney, and new arrival Russell were among seven players on the inactive list, $125.9 million in combined salary sidelined compared to $12.5 million for the active roster. Tickets for seats with a face value of $950 were already, in the fourth game, being offered for $400. It took only until the eleventh game for the coach to publicly acknowledge the Warriors were aiming for next season, hoping to turn 2019–2020 into a chance to develop players who would ordinarily not have received such a big opportunity. Shootarounds went from the flyby of twenty minutes in the championship years to about sixty minutes, some intense enough to be compared to previous training camps, while practices typically jumped from an hour to ninety minutes to allow more teaching.

"There would be nights I would love to take someone out based on a mistake they made," Kerr said before the first month had ended. "But I can't take them out. We don't even have that hammer as a coaching staff to be able to reward guys with playing time or penalizing them with taking playing time away." Realistic as ever, he admitted on another occasion that life as a punching bag "stinks." Just as he had implored the Warriors the season before to appreciate the time they had spent walking on rainbows, he said now, "This is more the reality of the NBA. The last five years we've been living in a world that isn't supposed to exist. Five years basically, record-wise the best stretch anybody has had over five years. This is reality."

The payback he missed in 1999 by joining the Spurs as opponents took special joy in beating the remnants of the championship Bulls was unavoidable as a Warrior in 2019–2020. Kerr this time was mostly left to absorb it on his own, with Thompson injured the entire season, Curry most of it, and Green a large portion, while newcomers and anonymous returnees garnered the most minutes. Five seasons of parades, a cocky owner, and Golden State cool that came to be perceived as smugness put the rest of the league in revenge mode no matter who was wearing the jersey. "I do believe in karma," one rival executive said as the losses stacked up in San Francisco. "In some respects, they're getting what they deserve." Decades of popularity had at least earned the coach some leniency. "Kerr always did things right," a member of another front office said. "Besides, they are like a wounded deer on the side of the road right now. No need to torture them; just put them out of their misery each game."

Watching from Los Angeles after his split from the Warriors in 2017, Jerry West grew concerned the tension of a season going downhill at a screaming rate would trigger a relapse of Kerr's physical problems. It did not. Kerr had bad days, yet continued to manage his ailments and still had not missed a game since returning in the 2017 finals. Similarly wondering about a setback, former Cavaliers teammate Craig Ehlo, having overcome an addiction to painkillers that started after multiple back surgeries, had previously reached out to encourage Kerr to be careful with medications. But "Steve is not stressed out about this," Stacey King, his Final Four opponent, combatant in Bulls-Cavaliers playoff scuffles, and Chicago teammate, reported after seeing Kerr in San Francisco. Kerr tried to view it as an opportunity to develop players who could contribute once Golden State was whole again, a perspective partly to be positive and partly from the sad, painful reality that there was nothing else to salvage in a 2019–2020 with a woefully overmatched roster. "He's a grown man," Popovich said. "He understands that circumstances often time send things in a different direction for a while. That's just the way life is. It's the same way with every single one of us standing here. Everything doesn't always go your way and if you think it should, you got a problem."

Others went more out of their way to show public support, from Walton, the former assistant who had become coach of the Kings, offering, "I think he's doing a great job," to Dallas's Rick Carlisle practically injuring himself with "Steve has done a great job and they are very difficult to play." The Warriors "are a scary team," Carlisle added, and "From a developmental standpoint it's been a masterpiece so far." He said it with Golden State at 9-32.

Kerr had the benefit, of course, of knowing the bruising was temporary, not his permanent life. On the worst nights, he could still look ahead to the reassuring image of a 2020–2021 lineup with Curry, Thompson, and Green, along with one of the top rookies if the Warriors kept their draft pick. Most of all, Kerr had the perspective that basketball was not close to the most important thing in the world. Despite everything, he said in early January 2020, the season had been "fun" and "a different challenge. But I've enjoyed it. These guys are great to work with and I love my staff. I enjoy coming to work every day."

The perspective of where Golden State's woes fit among the real issues was never more necessary than when the calendar turned and 2019–2020 developed into the worst season in pro basketball history. Retired Commissioner David Stern, the driving force in turning the league into an international conglomerate, died on New Year's Day. Kobe Bryant was killed in a helicopter crash twenty-five days later. The coronavirus pandemic halted business in March and protests against racism and police brutality later in the spring were felt in every big city. Lute Olson died in August, during the playoffs that resumed with every participating team locked down in a restricted environment near Orlando. As Kerr would be the first to note, needing just fifty-four games to clinch a losing record was a microscopic concern.

The Warriors were 15-50—on pace for 19-63 in a typical schedule—when their season ended early in a fitting final statement on the lost 2019–2020. Curry had five appearances, Green forty-three, Thompson zero, and Wiggins twelve. With little fan support, the new building felt hollow, and there were questions for the first time in the Kerr era about the sustainability of a roster whose best player, Curry, would turn thirty-three the next season. Steve Kerr once again found himself with something to prove.

Acknowledgments

Bob Myers could have ended this project early, and earned lifetime appreciation from the subject, if he had run me over when he had the chance. It would have been my fault. I was carelessly looking in the wrong direction while walking the perimeter of Chase Center to spot the media entrance on my first game at the new arena and crossed a parking lot entrance after Myers had already started to turn in his black SUV. As general manager of the Warriors, he wouldn't have been convicted in a Bay Area court anyway, but Myers, the attentive driver who stopped feet away from making me a hood ornament is still the first of many people to thank for the book being completed.

Steve Kerr would have preferred it didn't. He had been approached several times to tell his own story, especially in recent years as ramming heads with Donald Trump raised his mainstream profile, and he always declined with the same explanation: Gregg Popovich, his coach during two stints with the Spurs and later a mentor, said it was a bad idea, that any coach, even one with championship credentials, risks losing the roster as soon as players see him reveling in the spotlight. It did not matter to Kerr that Phil Jackson, his other major NBA influence, had such a dramatically different stance that Jackson wrote books during seasons and kept diaries for publication.

As Kerr explained in casual conversation after an interview a few years ago, long before I had interest in chronicling his life, an autobiography or even a biography handled by someone else might be viewed within the delicate emotional balance of the professional locker room as a glory grab. I would counter that his main players are smart enough to know the difference between the coach turning self-promoter and a project without direct involvement. Stephen Curry was previously the subject of a biography, as was Kevin Durant in his Warriors days, while Draymond Green knows media workings, and Klay Thompson grew up with his father in broadcasting. They would have understood Kerr's non-involvement, if they cared at all in the first place. But he was not going to risk it.

Aware of the position, I informed him of my intentions in the early summer of 2019 while emphasizing I was not asking for his involvement, only the usual access. Kerr responded with a polite but firm no. He would not do one-on-one interviews. Though disappointed, I took it as a business decision and nothing personal after decades of a cordial relationship, a belief confirmed when I asked questions in group settings and he responded with expansive answers and professionalism. Kerr was, and still is, one of the nicest and most accommodating people I have covered. He remains a Moth in good standing.

The entire Golden State organization fell in line and declared itself off-limits to anything beyond the access available to all. If predecessor Mark Jackson had the same issue, management would have whispered he was difficult and groaned about needlessly focusing on details beyond his control. But if Kerr, after the Monopoly money he has helped generate, declared the earth flat, the front office would turn into nodding bobbleheads. The Warriors are to be commended for taking a firm stand against positive publicity.

The responses from people who know Kerr well were mixed. Some turned down or did not respond to interview requests, some were fine with talking, and some were fine on the condition they not be named. (A few requested, and were given, anonymity for unrelated reasons.) Among those who did talk, many called the Popovich theory on avoiding attention an easy out for simply wanting to dodge a concentrated spotlight. But even the decision by those who declined provided helpful insight into the Kerr personality. Most nonparticipants were not concerned about angering him and being banished to his enemies list. They just didn't want to disappoint him. Making good-hearted Steve Kerr sad was worse than making him mad.

That unique reasoning was likewise telling, though not surprising. In forty years around professional and college sports, I have never heard people talk about someone the way they talk about Kerr. "Steve made me want to be a better human being," David Griffin, his top assistant in the Phoenix front office, said. "Forget basketball. And he does that for everybody he's with." A friend from Pacific Palisades confided, "Even if he were not a famous guy and an accomplished guy, just the way he goes about his business and how he treats people is something to this day I still think about and try to emulate as best I can."

Blair Kerkhoff of the *Kansas City Star* told the story of going to Oakland to cover Royals-A's baseball in 2016 and adding a basketball night for a feature on K.C. product Brandon Rush, a Golden State reserve. Fate conspired against Kerkhoff when the NBA schedule and the baseball slate unavoidably put him inside Oracle Arena as the Warriors went for the single-season win record, terrible timing, as Kerkhoff knew, to pursue a feature on a player on the fringe of the rotation. He awkwardly inserted a Rush question during the coach's pregame availability anyway, got a flowing answer on Rush's season and the projected role in the upcoming playoffs, and left the interview room happy. After the game, just after the Warriors had clinched the greatest regular season in league history, Kerr spotted him in a hallway and stopped the passing reporter he didn't know. He wanted to make sure Kerkhoff had everything he needed. Dozens of others have similar stories of Kerr treating people far from his inner circle with similar warmth, of visiting with arena workers as he walked the concourse in Phoenix hours before tip-off in his GM days or making ushers light up by remembering their names and some family details on his way to the court for pregame shooting as a player.

I do not think Kerr went out of his way to build roadblocks to protect his own future book, as some suggested. There is a good chance he will write one—he enjoys writing, has topics to address, and is becoming more proactive in using the megaphone that comes with being a celebrity in 2021 America—but it would more likely be thoughts on gun control, voting, racial divides, and other societal issues. Perhaps he will layer in the experiences of a full life to build his case or because a publisher will want Michael Jordan and Stephen Curry sprinkled among the position papers. It would be a surprise, though, if he pens a traditional life story. The only thing worse to Kerr than an outsider talking about him for a few hundred pages is doing it himself.

His efforts to hinder this project turned out to be little more than a minor setback. I have spent hundreds of days around his Warriors and previously conducted more hours of interviews within his orbit than I could count, including numerous individual conversations with the subject himself and the Golden State operation on lockdown. The attempt to put a unique career and remarkable life in context still included approximately 125 interviews, almost all one-on-one and about 90 percent new in addition to conversations from past years relevant to the book. The research beyond that included university archives, court records, presidential libraries, government oral histories, and airline logs among the many atypical digs for a sports biography.

I was greatly aided by the work of talented writers and broadcasters at every Kerr stop, from college to the present. That would have included high school as well, except he received amazingly little coverage for someone bound for a fifteen-year NBA career as the Southern California media, with dozens of better players to spotlight, mostly looked through him with the same indifference as college recruiters. Three websites were also particularly valuable beyond the local coverage: basketball-reference.com for statistics, YouTube.com to revisit games, and newspapers.com for stories from every year and every location.

The interview subjects who stepped into a time machine or offered perspective on a modern event informed and energized me with their willingness to help. I have been fortunate to know some of the 100-plus for years and hope I made new friends among the conversations in arenas, on practice courts, and by phone, many in an especially challenging time for all of us in early 2020 when a book on a sports figure mattered less than usual. They were unceasingly friendly and helpful. Some offered their own materials, others volunteered to lobby on my behalf to hesitant subjects, and many talked for more than an hour as I annoyingly pressed for details. (Was he standing to your left or right? Was the beer in bottles or cans? What color ink was the writing on the paper?) While that level of cooperation was obviously driven by the enjoyment of telling positive stories about a positive guy, the real reason was that I was dealing with good people.

Whatever success this book has will be due to my agent, Tim Hays, and my editors at William Morrow, Mauro DiPreta and Nick Amphlett. Tim and I were ready in May 2019 to roll out a proposal on the improbable rise of the Warriors to four titles in five years and needed only to wait a couple weeks for Golden State to beat Toronto for the latest. Kawhi Leonard, the Raptors, and the injury gods apparently did not like the topic. When the Warriors lost, a deep dive on the greatness of an operation that lost in the Finals and would be losing a lot the next season made no sense, and I began formulating a Kerr magazine piece that would hold up, the story of a guy who had spent his basketball life proving doubters wrong and was about to embark on the latest steep climb. When Hays suggested Kerr as a book, I was not enthusiastic. Tim not only convinced me why Kerr and why now, he championed the project the entire way and offered invaluable support far beyond negotiating the deal. I soon went from seeing that we did in fact have a book to wondering how it could have taken this long for someone to write it.

It was clear from the first conversation that DiPreta shared our vision that the story be about a man who had an interesting career but a fascinating life, that those experiences, not basketball, made Kerr a compelling subject. Writing about Kerr through a sports lens would have been a mistake. Amphlett then took on a leading role in shaping the content with important insights, especially in keeping a wide-ranging story focused. Beyond their professional expertise, Mauro, Nick, and assistant editor Vedika Khanna were invested partners, just as I was grateful for the support at HarperCollins from publisher Liate Stehlik, associate publisher Ben Steinberg, and managing editor Pam Barricklow.

Bryant Johnson at the U.S. District Court in Washington and Lisa Nehus Saxon were especially helpful in obtaining research. The students of Palisades High and Santa Monica City College are lucky to have Lisa as a teacher and I am fortunate to call her a friend. Several current college sports information directors went out of their way to help as I searched for someone no longer connected to the school. Only Raymond Ridder and the superb Golden State PR team could be told to help as little as possible within league policy, carry out the order with loyalty to the organization, and still be professional and welcoming. Raymond is the Steve Kerr of his field, a superstar liked by all.

I am hesitant to name the people who provided encouragement and direction along the way, some without realizing it, because the list would be book-length on its own and I am grateful to all the friends and colleagues who pushed this along. But for starters, thanks, Skip Nicholson, Ron Rapoport, Mark Heisler, Fran Blinebury, Roland Lazenby, and Seth Davis. I am fortunate to be surrounded by so many people of generous spirit. We lost one of my favorite people, not just favorite NBA writers, with the passing of Martin McNeal late in the writing process. I hope these pages show I picked up some of his sharp basketball eye and candor.

Most of all, there is the home team. Taylor, Jordan, and Nora constantly inspire me, encourage me, teach me, and put up with me under normal circumstances, but deserve extra praise for doing it in the most abnormal of times. They were the biggest part of the process even in the earliest days. Near the end, though, I was often pushing to the finish as a high school student, a middle school student, and their mother turned professor navigated remote math, science, and more. They are the main people to thank for the book being completed.

Notes

Prologue

1   *ask if the Warriors:* Tim Kawakami, "Sadness, Exhaustion, Pride, and the Possible Inevitable End of the Warriors Dynasty," The Athletic, June 14, 2019, https://theathletic.com/1027479/2019/06/14/kawakami-sadness-exhaustion-pride-and-the-possible-inevitable-end-of-the-warriors-dynasty/.

2   *"and connected with":* Chris Ballard, "Inside the Warriors' New Reality and Their Uncertain Future," *Sports Illustrated,* June 15, 2019, https://www.si.com/nba/2019/06/15/golden-state-warriors-steve-kerr-kevin-durant-klay-thompson-stephen-curry-nba-finals-uncertain-future-free-agency-rumors.

2   *"I can't tell you":* Steve Kerr, postgame press conference comments, June 13, 2019, "NBA Finals: Warriors v Raptors," *ASAP Sports,* http://www.asapsports.com/show_interview.php?id=151021.

3   *"I've been one of":* Dan Knapp, "Fighting Back from Injury and Personal Tragedy, Steve Kerr Leads Arizona to the Top of the Heap," *People,* February 8, 1988, https://people.com/archive/fighting-back-from-injury-and-personal-tragedy-steve-kerr-leads-arizona-to-the-top-of-the-heap-vol-29-no-5/.

Chapter 1: Beirut

5   *They were sure they spotted:* Ann Zwicker Kerr, *Come with Me from Lebanon: An American Family Odyssey* (Syracuse, NY: Syracuse University Press, 1996), 24.

5   *In the Zwicker household:* Ibid., 24–25.

6   *two elementary school students:* For Kerr's life growing up in Santa Monica, Zwicker Kerr, *Come with Me from Lebanon,* 26.

6   *A conversation with:* Ibid., 36.

6   *In August 1954:* Ibid., 37–40.

7   *Elsa at Beirut College for Women:* For background on Stanley Kerr and Elsa Reckman Kerr, see ibid., 26–27; and "Elsa Reckman Kerr, Ex-Dean of Women at School in Beirut," *New York Times,* March 24, 1985.

7   *The first time she spotted him:* Zwicker Kerr, *Come with Me from Lebanon,* 61.

8   *before a recurrence:* Testimony of Dorothy Kerr Jessup, *Susan Kerr van de Ven et al. vs. Islamic Republic of Iran et al.,* U.S. District Court for the District of Columbia, December 19, 2009, court archives, CA 01-1994.

9   *"Never mind":* Ibid., 112.

9   *guests were asked to leave:* For Steve Kerr's birth and first hours, see Zwicker Kerr, *Come with Me from Lebanon,* 143–44.

9   *took Steve for afternoon walks:* Ibid., 146.

10   *Newspapers in English:* Ibid., 17–18.

10   *the same hospital in Santa Monica:* Paul Galloway, "A Separate Peace," *Chicago*

Tribune, October 24, 1993; reprinted as "A Separate Peace: Steve Kerr Has Interest in Mideast Accord," *Daily Oklahoman,* November 6, 1993.

10   *they were thinking of Lebanon:* Susan Kerr van de Ven, *One Family's Response to Terrorism: A Daughter's Memoir* (Syracuse, NY: Syracuse University Press, 2008), 78.

11   *"Whenever we were in L.A.":* John Feinstein, "Kerr Overcomes Tragedy, Injury with Jokes and Jumpers," *Washington Post,* March 6, 1988, https://www.washington post.com/archive/sports/1988/03/06/kerr-overcomes-tragedy-injury-with-jokes-and-jumpers/4aa842c4-fd72-4c92-ba0d-8b8f7f5bfd61/; "A Symbol of Class and Courage," *Capital Times,* March 12, 1988, 13.

11   *"vicious":* Galloway, "A Separate Peace."

11   *Their father finally:* Ibid.

12   *"It was a remarkable sight":* Zwicker Kerr, *Come with Me from Lebanon,* 155.

12   *Ann called learning:* Galloway, "A Separate Peace."

12   *"The food is terrible":* Zwicker Kerr, *Come with Me from Lebanon,* 157.

12   *Steve responded to the news:* Ibid.

12   *especially disappointed:* Melissa Isaacson, *Transition Game: An Inside Look at Life with the Chicago Bulls* (Champaign, IL: Sagamore Publishing, 1994), 173.

12   *The Cairo airport:* Zwicker Kerr, *Come with Me from Lebanon,* 158–59.

13   *If the Kerrs were:* Ibid., 164.

14   *A caller phoned:* David Ottaway, "U.S. College Head Killed in Beirut," *Washington Post,* January 19, 1984, https://www.washingtonpost.com/archive/politics/1984/01/19/us-college-head-killed-in-beirut/2eb94ffd-bc18-4a20-84bf-3bec77287aff/.

14   *"Why did they do it?":* Zwicker Kerr, *Come with Me from Lebanon,* 167–69.

14   *he cried when:* Tom Hoffarth, "Kerr's Life in Basketball Comes Full Circle," *Press-Telegram,* March 17, 2011, https://www.presstelegram.com/2011/03/17/hoffarth-kerrs-life-in-basketball-comes-full-circle/.

14   *riding the Pacific:* Cyrus Saatsaz, "Golden State Warriors Head Coach Steve Kerr Talks about His Passion for Surfing," *The Inertia,* February 19, 2018, https://www.theinertia.com/surf/golden-state-warriors-head-coach-steve-kerr-talks-about-his-passion-for-surfing/.

14   *He briefly played football:* Isaacson, *Transition Game,* 173.

14   *Sticking with basketball led:* Hoffarth, "Kerr's Life in Basketball."

14   *had little contact:* Cunningham interview.

15   *"He hustled":* Author interview with Kiki VanDeWeghe, December 10, 2019.

15   *"He had kind of":* Ibid.

15   *"They were pretty strict":* Hoffarth, "Kerr's Life in Basketball."

16   *Steve reacted to:* Zwicker Kerr, *Come with Me from Lebanon,* 175.

16   *His desire was never:* Ibid.

16   *A nearby grocery store:* Ibid., 177.

16   *Dinner-table conversation:* Kerr van de Ven, *One Family's Response,* 76.

16   *Games often:* Farid Farid, "Steve Kerr and His Mother Talk about the Legacy of His Father's Assassination," *New Yorker,* June 16, 2016, https://www.newyorker.com/news/news-desk/steve-kerr-and-his-mother-talk-about-the-legacy-of-his-fathers-assassination.

17   *riding horses in the desert:* Isaacson, *Transition Game,* 174.

17   *When he scored forty points:* Ian O'Connor, "Steve Kerr Is Tough Enough to Coach," *ESPN,* May 7, 2014, https://www.espn.com/new-york/nba/story/_/id/10895607/golden-state-warriors-steve-kerr-tough-enough-nba-coaching.

17   *"People don't understand":* Feinstein, "Kerr Overcomes Tragedy."

17   *"He's always been":* Farid, "Steve Kerr and His Mother."

17   *one of the team's scorekeepers:* Jeanie Buss, with Steve Springer, *Laker Girl* (Chicago: Triumph Books, 2010), 62.

Chapter 2: Shelly Weather

19   *his midcentury modern:* "Residences of Ronald Reagan," Ronald Reagan Presidential Library, https://www.reaganlibrary.gov/sreference/ronald-reagan-s-residences.

19   *when word came:* John Meroney, "Look Inside Ronald Reagan's Hillside House in Los Angeles," *Architectural Digest* (November 2000), published online November 1, 2005, https://www.architecturaldigest.com/story/reagan-article; John Meroney, "Ronald Reagan in Pacific Palisades," *Architectural Digest* (April 2000): 122.

19   *goals marked by rocks:* Eric Malinowski, *Betaball: How Silicon Valley and Science Built One of the Greatest Basketball Teams in History* (New York: Atria, 2017), 175.

19   *many local families:* Author interview with Ruth Wechsler Mills, August 30, 2019.

19   *"It made me":* "Best of the Axe Files: Steve Kerr" (interview by David Axelrod), *The Axe Files* (podcast), November 23, 2016, https://omny.fm/shows/the-axe-files-with-david-axelrod/best-of-the-axe-files-steve-kerr.

20   *"That's when I saw":* Isaacson, *Transition Game,* 174.

20   *eventually followed by:* Ibid.

21   *Creating a home:* Zwicker Kerr, *Come with Me from Lebanon,* 190.

21   *Ann manufactured a false reality:* Ibid.

21   *"made me nervous":* Ibid., 186.

22   *"I regret to this day":* Testimony of Steve Kerr, *Susan Kerr van de Ven et al. vs. Islamic Republic of Iran et al.,* U.S. District Court for the District of Columbia, December 19, 2002, court archives, CA 01-1994.

22   *"Why did he go":* Ibid.

22   *"Do you think":* Kerr van de Ven, *One Family's Response,* 103.

22   *the oldest Kerr child:* Ibid.

22   *"I bet there's":* Ibid.

22   *"Dad is really president":* Zwicker Kerr, *Come with Me from Lebanon,* 192.

23   *interim president Malcolm was replacing:* "Three Gunmen Kidnapped David Dodge," United Press International, July 19, 1982.

23   *"there's no such thing":* Michael Silver and Steve Kerr, *Tideline,* January 3, 1983, 8.

23   *Another item that school year:* Silver and Kerr, *Tideline,* November 30, 1982.

24   *"Now, with schools":* Kerr, "Releaguing Poses Problems," *Tideline,* April 1, 1982.

24   *"Speaking of the city champion":* Silver and Kerr, *Tideline,* January 3, 1983.

24   *"In class, he seemed":* Author interview with Ruth Wechsler Mills, August 30, 2019.

24   *"didn't need anything":* Anonymous interview with author.

25   *An explanation occasionally followed:* Author interview with Sean Waters, August 15, 2019.

25   *"If he thought":* Ibid.

26   *"You wouldn't believe":* Zwicker Kerr, *Come with Me from Lebanon,* 221–22.

26   *"Almost a mistake-free player":* Chris Ballard, "The Little-Known Book That Shaped the Minds of Steve Kerr and Pete Carroll," *Sports Illustrated,* May 26, 2016, https://www.si.com/nba/2016/05/26/steve-kerr-pete-carroll-nba-playoffs-inner-game-tennis-book.

27   *A "Steve Kerr Timeout":* Author interview with Sean Waters, August 15, 2019.

27   *"He could play":* Author interview with Bob Weinhauer, September 9, 2019.

28 *"you worried about"*: Author interview with Alvin Gentry, December 20, 2019.

28 *"I thought to myself"*: Rick Telander, *In the Year of the Bull: Zen, Air, and the Pursuit of Sacred and Profane Hoops* (New York: Simon & Schuster, 1996), 177.

28 *Arizona's coach:* Lute Olson and David Fisher, *Lute!: The Seasons of My Life* (New York: Thomas Dunne Books, 2006), 95–98.

29 *"That's the kind of man"*: Phil Barber, "Wildcats Kerr, Tolbert, Fraser, McMillan Reunited in Bay Area," *Press Democrat,* November 11, 2017, https://www.press democrat.com/article/sports/barber-wildcats-kerr-tolbert-fraser-mcmillan -reunited-in-bay-area/?sba=AAS&artslide=1.

29 *While Kerr for decades:* Cal State Fullerton "offered me a scholarship," Kerr said in Steve Rivera's *Tales from the Arizona Wildcats Locker Room: A Collection of the Greatest Wildcat Basketball Stories Ever Told* (New York: Sports Publishing, 2013), 118. Arizona was "my one scholarship offer," Kerr said on the day he was introduced as the coach of the Warriors; see "Coach Kerr's Arrival," posted on You-Tube by the Golden State Warriors, May 20, 2014, https://www.youtube.com /watch?v=EZ76cUTrbD4&t=205s. Kerr changed his story other times as well. All that is known for certain is that he initially planned to attend Fullerton, either with a scholarship or as a walk-on.

30 *It was not until:* Olson and Fisher, *Lute!,* 98.

30 *"but it was"*: Ibid.

30 *"There was just something"*: Ibid.

31 *elevate his game:* For the initial Kerr-Olson interaction and arranged pickup game, see ibid., 99.

31 *Malcolm asked his son:* Steve Kerr testimony, *Susan Kerr van de Ven et al. vs. Islamic Republic of Iran et al.*

32 *"If he wants to come"*: Olson and Fisher, *Lute!,* 100.

32 *"life has been"*: Zwicker Kerr, *Come with Me from Lebanon,* 242.

32 *The Kerrs had become:* Kerr van de Ven, *One Family's Response,* 101.

32 *He hiked nearby mountains:* John Branch, "Tragedy Made Steve Kerr See the World beyond the Court," *New York Times,* December 22, 2016, https://www .nytimes.com/2016/12/22/sports/basketball/steve-kerr-golden-state-warriors .html.

32 *"Shelly weather"*: Kerr van de Ven, *One Family's Response,* 140.

32 *"You can never know"*: Rich Dymond, "Beirut Bombing Leaves Scars, Wildcat Says," *Arizona Daily Star,* October 15, 1983, G3.

32 *With the airport instantly shut down:* Zwicker Kerr, *Come with Me from Lebanon,* 244.

33 *Steve finally ended up:* Branch, "Tragedy Made Steve Kerr See the World beyond the Court."

33 *eventually landed in Los Angeles:* Kerr van de Ven, *One Family's Response,* 141.

33 *"Poor Steve!"*: Zwicker Kerr, *Come with Me from Lebanon,* 244.

33 *Malcolm was growing increasingly worried:* Ibid., 272.

Chapter 3: It All Came to an End

35 *"To be honest"*: Chris Ballard, "Steve Kerr's Absence: The True Test of a Leader," *Sports Illustrated,* May 16, 2017, https://www.si.com/nba/2017/05/16/steve-kerr -nba-playoffs-golden-state-warriors-injury-leadership.

35 *"that I couldn't understand"*: Chris Korman, "The Assassination of Steve Kerr's Father and the Unlikely Story of a Champion," *USA Today Sports: For the Win,* June 3, 2015, https://ftw.usatoday.com/2015/06/the-assassination-of-steve-kerrs

-father-and-the-unlikely-story-of-a-champion; "Father's Assassination Shaped Kerr," *Arizona Republic*, June 4, 2015, 9C.

36   *"Honestly, I wasn't"*: Barber, "Wildcats Kerr, Tolbert, Fraser, McMillan Reunited in Bay Area."

36   *telling the Wildcats*: Andrew Keh, "This Teacher Spends Life Being Taught," *New York Times*, November 13, 2014, https://www.nytimes.com/2014/11/14/sports/basketball/warriors-coach-steve-kerrs-style-is-molded-by-many-mentors.html.

36   *"basic hell"*: Steve Kerr, University of Arizona commencement address, May 18, 2004.

36   *"What surprised me"*: Olson and Fisher, *Lute!*, 106.

37   *carrying 2,500 pounds*: Thomas L. Friedman, "Beirut Death Toll at 161 Americans; French Casualties Rise in Bombing; Reagan Insists Marines Will Remain; Buildings Blasted," *New York Times*, October 24, 1983, https://www.nytimes.com/1983/10/24/world/beirut-death-toll-161-americans-french-casualties-rise-bombings-reagan-insists.html.

37   *"All I can remember"*: Robert Fisk, *The Great War for Civilisation: The Conquest of the Middle East* (New York: Vintage Books, 2005), 478.

37   *it shook people awake*: Thomas L. Friedman, *From Beirut to Jerusalem* (New York: Anchor Books, 1989), 202.

37   *About two minutes later*: Friedman, "Beirut Death Toll at 161 Americans."

37   *Rescue workers toiled furiously*: Ibid.

37   *the attack on the American base*: Testimony of Andrew Kerr, *Susan Kerr van de Ven et al. vs. Islamic Republic of Iran et al.*, U.S. District Court for the District of Columbia, December 19, 2002, court archives, CA 01-1994.

37   *Ann heard the explosion*: Zwicker Kerr, *Come with Me from Lebanon*, 265.

38   *Ann and Malcolm spent*: Ibid., 266.

38   *Inspecting new shrapnel marks*: Ibid., 245.

38   *"the nicest people"*: Branch, "Tragedy Made Steve Kerr See the World beyond the Court."

38   *"There is a chaplain"*: Ibid.

39   *Father and son*: Steve Kerr testimony, *Susan Kerr van de Ven et al. vs. Islamic Republic of Iran et al.*

39   *Phoning Ann after leaving*: Zwicker Kerr, *Come with Me from Lebanon*, 270.

39   *learned that some of her students*: Ibid., 268.

39   *Important cable traffic*: Testimony of Richard Murphy, *Susan Kerr van de Ven et al. vs. Islamic Republic of Iran et al.*, U.S. District Court for the District of Columbia, December 19, 2002, court archives, CA 01-1994.

39   *The AUB grounds may have been considered*: Ibid.

39   *but working there*: Gladys Mouro, *An American Nurse amidst Chaos* (Beirut: American University of Beirut Press, 2001), 77.

40   *removing part of the skull*: Ibid., 79.

40   *The* New York Times *man*: Friedman, *From Beirut to Jerusalem*, 213.

40   *The disorder hit*: Andrew Kerr testimony, *Susan Kerr van de Ven et al. vs. Islamic Republic of Iran et al.*

40   *before an estimated 3,000 people*: Rivera, *Tales from the Arizona Wildcats Locker Room*, 73.

40   *"I see why you were"*: Ibid., 74.

41   *With John visiting from Cairo*: O'Connor, "Steve Kerr Is Tough Enough to Coach"; Testimony of John Kerr, *Susan Kerr van de Ven et al. vs. Islamic Republic of Iran et*

al., U.S. District Court for the District of Columbia, December 18, 2002, court archives, CA 01-1994.

41   *"We had the time":* John Kerr testimony, *Susan Kerr van de Ven et al. vs. Islamic Republic of Iran et al.*

41   *they dissected Kerr's three baskets:* Branch, "Tragedy Made Steve Kerr See the World beyond the Court."

41   *Watching Steve in a college game:* O'Connor, "Steve Kerr Is Tough Enough to Coach."

42   *realizing his life:* Albert Hourani, foreword to Zwicker Kerr, *Come with Me from Lebanon,* xvi.

42   *They were concerned:* Zwicker Kerr, *Come with Me from Lebanon,* 282.

42   *"basically nice":* Kerr van de Ven, *One Family's Response,* 114.

42   *he used the escort:* Ibid., 129.

42   *using the detail at all:* Zwicker Kerr, *Come with Me from Lebanon,* 9.

42   *"marked":* Richard Murphy testimony, *Susan Kerr van de Ven et al. vs. Islamic Republic of Iran et al.*

42   *university trustees voted:* Zwicker Kerr, *Come with Me from Lebanon,* 9.

42   *was driven:* Ibid., 5.

43   *"Oh, here he comes now":* Thomas L. Friedman, "University Head Killed in Beirut; Gunmen Escape," *New York Times,* January 19, 1984, https://www.nytimes.com/1984/01/19/world/university-head-killed-in-beirut-gunmen-escape.html.

43   *from inside the stairwell:* Zwicker Kerr, *Come with Me from Lebanon,* 3.

43   *one of the men:* Ottaway, "U.S. College Head Killed in Beirut."

43   *able to get beyond:* Friedman, "University Head Killed in Beirut."

43   *Ann, after teaching:* Zwicker Kerr, *Come with Me from Lebanon,* 4–5.

43   *Rushing there:* Ibid., 5.

44   *the umbrella handle:* Testimony of Ann Kerr, *Susan Kerr van de Ven et al. vs. Islamic Republic of Iran et al.,* U.S. District Court for the District of Columbia, December 18, 2002, court archives, CA 01-1994.

44   *Andrew heard a worker:* Andrew Kerr testimony, *Susan Kerr van de Ven et al. vs. Islamic Republic of Iran et al.*

44   *The youngest Kerr child:* Ibid.

44   *"I want to get":* Zwicker Kerr, *Come with Me from Lebanon,* 7.

45   *"And that lasted":* Andrew Kerr testimony, *Susan Kerr van de Ven et al. vs. Islamic Republic of Iran et al.*

45   *A few days later:* Kerr van de Ven, *One Family's Response,* 142.

45   *Attempts were made:* Zwicker Kerr, *Come with Me from Lebanon,* 7.

45   *"Dad's fate had seemed":* Kerr van de Ven, *One Family's Response,* 159.

45   *Susie knew as soon:* Testimony of Susan Kerr van de Ven, *Susan Kerr van de Ven et al. vs. Islamic Republic of Iran et al.,* U.S. District Court for the District of Columbia, court archives, CA 01-1994.

45   *John was at work:* John Kerr testimony, *Susan Kerr van de Ven et al. vs. Islamic Republic of Iran et al.*

45   *"It all came to an end":* Zwicker Kerr, *Come with Me from Lebanon,* 298.

46   *"impenetrable":* Galloway, "A Separate Peace."

46   *wanting to make sure:* Steve Kerr testimony, *Susan Kerr van de Ven et al. vs. Islamic Republic of Iran et al.*

46   *"sort of hysterical":* Ibid.

46   *ran to the room:* Ibid.

46   *"I was running":* O'Connor, "Steve Kerr Is Tough Enough to Coach."

47   *wishing someone had told:* Rivera, *Tales from the Arizona Wildcats Locker Room*, 120.

47   *raced to Babcock to find:* John Feinstein, *A Season Inside: One Year in College Basket-ball* (New York: Fireside, 1988), 92.

47   *took him to an all-night:* Rivera, *Tales from the Arizona Wildcats Locker Room*, 120.

47   *"To this day":* Paul Rubin, "Steve Kerr's Been Beating the Odds His Whole Life," *Phoenix New Times*, April 24, 2008, https://www.phoenixnewtimes.com/news/steve-kerrs-been-beating-the-odds-his-whole-life-6394407.

47   *in a state of shock:* Olson and Fisher, *Lute!*, 111.

47   *The coach thought:* Eric Malinowski, "Steve Kerr Is the King of Cool: Drama × Joy × Defeat = Destiny on Repeat," *Bleacher Report*, April 19, 2017, https://bleacherreport.com/articles/2704395-steve-kerr-is-the-king-of-cool-drama-x-joy-x-defeat-destiny-on-repeat.

47   *"the only time I can keep":* Howie Kussoy, "Despite Pain of Dad's Murder, Kerr Became a Champion," *New York Post*, April 3, 2014, https://nypost.com/2014/05/03/in-the-wake-of-his-dads-assassination-kerr-became-a-champion/.

47   *Reagan put out a statement:* "Statement on the Assassination of Malcolm Kerr, President of the American University of Beirut," January 18, 1984, Ronald Reagan Presidential Library and Museum, https://www.reaganlibrary.gov/research/speeches/11884b.

48   *before spending the night:* Rivera, *Tales from the Arizona Wildcats Locker Room*, 120.

48   *the caller said:* Ottaway, "U.S. College Head Killed in Beirut."

48   *"added conviction":* Richard Murphy testimony, *Susan Kerr van de Ven et al. vs. Islamic Republic of Iran et al.*

48   *"I watched him move":* Olson and Fisher, *Lute!*, 111.

48   *"This is my family":* Ibid.

48   *expecting Kerr to miss:* Ibid.

48   *"It was the only thing":* Feinstein, *A Season Inside*, 93.

49   *"When he first got there":* Author interview with Bob Weinhauer, September 9, 2019.

49   *Olson offered minimal insight:* Ibid.

49   *He carted the team:* Olson and Fisher, *Lute!*, 105.

49   *trolled campus libraries:* Author interview with Arnie Spanier, February 4, 2020.

50   *Arizona coaches were:* Author interview with Bob Weinhauer, September 9, 2019.

50   *among teammates:* Malinowski, *Betaball*, 179.

50   *Olson's speech to the team:* Olson and Fisher, *Lute!*, 112.

50   *"I was worried for him":* Ibid.

50   *"an explosion of sound":* Ibid.

50   *"It's like a chill":* Author interview with Tom Duddleston, April 7, 2020.

51   *Make Kerr literally feel:* Author interview with Bob Weinhauer, September 9, 2019.

51   *would still hear it:* Steve Rivera and Anthony Gimino, *100 Things Arizona Fans Should Know and Do before They Die* (Chicago: Triumph Books, 2014), 35.

51   *"It might have looked":* Rivera, *Tales from the Arizona Wildcats Locker Room*, 122.

51   *"This was a special situation":* Author interview with Bob Weinhauer, September 9, 2019.

51   *the basic message:* Ibid.

52   *When the media came in:* Author interview with Greg Hansen, August 22, 2019.

52   *"outpouring of affection":* Author interview with Thomas Volgy, March 2, 2020.

52   *"He epitomized":* Rivera, *Tales from the Arizona Wildcats Locker Room*, 115.

52   *Telexes from around the world:* Zwicker Kerr, *Come with Me from Lebanon*, 10; Ann Kerr testimony, *Susan Kerr van de Ven et al. vs. Islamic Republic of Iran et al.*

52 *to pay his respects:* Andrew Kerr testimony, *Susan Kerr van de Ven et al. vs. Islamic Republic of Iran et al.*

52 *an additional heart slash of guilt:* Kerr van de Ven, *One Family's Response,* 91.

52 *"I know he":* Susan Kerr van de Ven testimony, *Susan Kerr van de Ven et al. vs. Islamic Republic of Iran et al.*

52 *Watching others have:* Ibid.

53 *Ann's torment also included:* Kerr van de Ven, *One Family's Response,* 91.

53 *Ann and the children:* Zwicker Kerr, *Come with Me from Lebanon,* 18.

Chapter 4: The Banyan Tree

55 *Ann, John, Andrew:* Zwicker Kerr, *Come with Me from Lebanon,* 14.

55 *The Kerrs and van de Vens:* Ibid., 15.

55 *"The pyramids are nothing":* Ibid.

55 *the final task:* Ibid.

56 *would be the new target:* Ibid.

56 *A group of Ann's students:* Ibid., 20.

56 *"almost an instinctive":* Galloway, "A Separate Peace."

57 *The next day:* Maureen Dowd, "Educator Slain in Beirut Is Mourned in Princeton," *New York Times,* January 30, 1983, https://www.nytimes.com/1984/01/30/nyregion/educator-slain-in-beirut-is-mourned-in-princeton.html.

57 *with four hundred people:* "American University Head Eulogized," *Los Angeles Times,* February 4, 1984, 28.

57 *"immersed myself":* Steve Kerr testimony, *Susan Kerr van de Ven et al. vs. Islamic Republic of Iran et al.*

57 *began showing a preference:* Korman, "The Assassination of Steve Kerr's Father."

57 *"really dealt with it":* Steve Kerr testimony, *Susan Kerr van de Ven et al. vs. Islamic Republic of Iran et al.*

58 *was not noted:* "The Daily Diary of President Ronald Reagan," May 24, 1985, Ronald Reagan Presidential Library and Museum.

58 *dressed in tan slacks:* photo contact sheet, May 24, 1985, Ronald Reagan Presidential Library and Museum.

59 *It likewise helped:* Rivera, *Tales from the Arizona Wildcats Locker Room,* 126.

59 *targeted Olson to replace:* Olson and Fisher, *Lute!,* 121.

59 *After hours of conversation:* Ibid., 122.

60 *Their host in Challans:* Ibid., 124.

60 *retired John Wooden:* Ibid., 128.

61 *Amaker and Bogues had:* Greg Hansen, "Spaniards May Soon Yell, '¡Esteban Kerr!'," *Arizona Daily Star,* July 9, 1986, C1; Greg Hansen, "With Steve Kerr Watching from Tucson, Lute Olson Led Team USA to World Basketball Championship," *Tucson,* May 21, 2020, https://tucson.com/sports/greghansen/greg-hansen-with-steve-kerr-watching-from-tucson-lute-olson-led-team-usa-to-world/article_45ae58ac-c5ad-5f39-b53c-11e680cb4690.html.

61 *"I really didn't know anything":* Hansen, "Spaniards May Soon Yell."

61 *spent about half the ride:* Details of this bus conversation from author interview with Greg Hansen, August 22, 2019.

62 *He hoped to be:* Greg Hansen, "Don't Call Him Opie," *Tucson,* May 25, 2016, https://tucson.com/sports/arizonawildcats/basketball/steve-kerr-dont-call-him-opie/article_614e1934-3a23-5d81-9edc-de336b1ef2a4.html.

62 *had barely disembarked:* Author interview with Greg Hansen, August 22, 2019.

63 *He was solidly:* Hansen, "Opie."

63 *"one of the most horrifying"*: Feinstein, *A Season Inside*, 94.

63 *"To most athletes"*: Hansen, "Don't Call Him Opie."

63 *When he spotted*: Greg Hansen, "Torn Knee Was Lucky Break for Kerr," *Tucson*, June 1, 2015, https://tucson.com/sports/columnists/hansen/hansen-torn-knee-was-lucky-break-for-kerr/article_0075ac0a-531f-5656-80ec-24ff9a63c8ae.html.

64 *When Hansen knocked*: Author interview with Greg Hansen, August 22, 2019.

64 *The words "career ending"*: Hansen, "Don't Call Him Opie."

64 *"I think there's every chance"*: Scott Howard-Cooper, "Healing Process Is Mental for Kerr, Too: He's Haunted by Knee Injury Suffered in World Basketball Championships," *Los Angeles Times*, July 25, 1986, https://www.latimes.com/archives/la-xpm-1986-07-25-sp-119-story.html.

64 *In a ceremony to deliver*: Ibid.

64 *able to watch*: Hansen, "With Steve Kerr Watching from Tucson."

64 *until the game ended*: Howard-Cooper, "Healing Process Is Mental for Kerr, Too."

64 *"I dream about it"*: Ibid.

65 *a timetable that prompted Kerr*: Hansen, "Torn Knee Was Lucky Break for Kerr."

65 *included eight losses*: Adam Doster, "He Could Always Steal: Remembering Kenny Lofton's College Basketball Career," *Deadspin*, January 10, 2013, https://deadspin.com/he-could-always-steal-remembering-kenny-loftons-colleg-5974941.

65 *Later in 1987*: Olson and Fisher, *Lute!*, 143.

65 *"We were close"*: Ibid., 140.

66 *"I'll just have them fire"*: Feinstein, *A Season Inside*, 94.

66 *and would stay*: Olson and Fisher, *Lute!*, 140.

66 *"I keep thinking"*: Jack Rickard, *Tucson Citizen*, date unknown, attributed in Hansen, "Torn Knee Was Lucky Break for Kerr."

66 *his plan to finish*: Sam Smith, "Steve Kerr's Unlikely Journey," *NBA*, June 2, 2016, https://www.nba.com/bulls/history/steve-kerr-unlikely-journey.

66 *and then entering coaching*: Sam Smith, "Steve Kerr Leads with Unique Style," *NBA*, December 6, 2014, https://www.nba.com/bulls/news/steve-kerr-leads-unique-style.

66 *Even after returning*: Author interview with Jay Gonzales, May 7, 2020.

Chapter 5: Steeeeeve Kerrrrr!!!

67 *"I wanted to photocopy"*: Greg Hansen, "30 Years Ago, Lute Olson, Steve Kerr Put Arizona on the Map," *Tucson*, May 15, 2018, https://tucson.com/sports/arizonawildcats/basketball/greg-hansen-30-years-ago-lute-olson-steve-kerr-put-arizona-on-the-map/article_23aefae3-31c2-53d1-b412-3af662c3409d.html.

67 *"A lot of it"*: Jon Gold, "1988 Final Four: The Arizona Wildcats Season That Made Tucson a Basketball Town," *Arizona Daily Star*, March 14, 2018.

67 *losing a recruiting bid*: Shaquille O'Neal, with Jack McCallum, *Shaq Attaq* (New York: Hyperion, 1993), 158.

67 *Kerr and Fraser once discussed*: Olson and Fisher, *Lute!*, 127.

68 *"great"*: Ibid., 146.

68 *If Kerr reclaimed*: Ibid.

68 *"was so locked in"*: Author interview with Mark Hughes, December 31, 2019.

68 *watching Lofton fire*: Gold, "1988 Final Four."

68 *"The best chemistry"*: Eric Prisbell, "Lovable Florida Gulf Coast's Bench Sparks Memories of Arizona Gumbies," *USA Today*, May 28, 2013, https://www.usatoday.com/story/sports/ncaab/2013/03/28/fgcu-bench-celebration-arizona-gumbies/2029449/.

68   *"not that tough"*: Jeff Browne, "Elliott Powers Arizona Past No. 3 Syracuse 80–69," *South Florida Sun-Sentinel*, December 1, 1987, https://www.sun-sentinel.com /news/fl-xpm-1987-12-10-8702100619-story.html.

69   *sent Seikaly running*: Ibid.

69   *"When we came up here"*: Ibid.

69   *"people have completely accepted"*: Feinstein, *A Season Inside*, 95.

69   *a deafening roar*: Jon Gold, "For Arizona Wildcats Legend Sean Elliott, 1988 Final Four Run Was the Start of Something Special," *Tucson*, March 28, 2018, https:// tucson.com/sports/arizonawildcats/basketball/for-arizona-wildcats-legend-sean -elliott-1988-final-four-run-was-the-start-of-something/article_2d2136fc-32c1-11e8 -a22e-f7014807f1c2.html.

69   *a magical time*: Ibid.

69   *"You can tell"*: Olson and Fisher, *Lute!*, 147.

70   *"We do?"*: John Feinstein, *One on One: Behind the Scenes with the Greats of the Game* (New York: Little, Brown and Company, 2011), 208.

70   *inside Carver-Hawkeye Arena*: Olson and Fisher, *Lute!*, 146.

70   *shook a fist*: Feinstein, *A Season Inside*, 118.

70   *It was about 2:00 A.M.*: Author interview with Greg Hansen, August 22, 2019.

70   *By the time*: Author interview with Jay Gonzales, May 7, 2020.

71   *"more than anything"*: Author interview with Quin Snyder, November 1, 2019.

71   *"Yeah, as a matter of fact"*: Feinstein, *A Season Inside*, 198.

71   *Some players, after all, were*: Gold, "For Arizona Wildcats Legend Sean Elliott."

72   *complete the task*: Rivera, *Tales from the Arizona Wildcats Locker Room*, 93.

72   *The school and the conference*: Author interview with Mike Elliott, October 1, 2019.

72   *"Oh my God"*: Author interview with Dick Weiss, December 16, 2019.

72   *the most-requested song*: Bob Young, "UA's Mason Is a Hit Off Court in Tucson," *Arizona Republic*, March 5, 1988, G1.

72   *Tolbert offering bottles*: Author interview with Mike Elliott, October 1, 2019.

72   *"They were having"*: Ibid.

73   *In pink shorts*: Arizona Wildcats Basketball, "Wild about the Cats: 1987–88," https://www.youtube.com/watch?v=204SD7Sk_uc.

73   *"Give Kerr the ball"*: Ibid.

73   *"You have to go back"*: "Recognition is Goal for No. 1 Arizona," *New York Times*, December 25, 1987, https://www.nytimes.com/1987/12/25/sports/the-unknown-no -1-team.html.

73   *spotted around town*: Doster, "He Could Always Steal."

73   *Olson began insisting*: Arthur H. Rotstein, "Steve Kerr Rebounds from Injury to Lead Arizona to Top Spot," *Associated Press*, December 26, 1987, https://apnews .com/e682e9ffd0fdc891de0175b706c8c1d4.

73   *"the glue that holds"*: "Recognition is Goal for No. 1 Arizona," *New York Times*, December 25, 1987.

74   *"the best leader"*: Feinstein, *A Season Inside*, 94.

74   *"You want to know why?"*: Ibid.

74   *He began to consider*: Kerry Eggers, *Jail Blazers: How the Portland Trail Blazers Became the Bad Boys of Basketball* (New York: Sports Publishing, 2018), 238.

74   *"but he has to go"*: Rotstein, "Steve Kerr Rebounds from Injury."

74   *He learned to read*: Feinstein, *A Season Inside*, 88.

74   *"Don't get me wrong"*: Dan Knapp, "Fighting Back from Injury and Personal Tragedy, Steve Kerr Leads Arizona to the Top of the Heap," *People*, February 8, 1988.

75   *He was never a very good*: Feinstein, *A Season Inside*, 196.

75 *"People knew all about him"*: Author interview with Tom Duddleston, April 7, 2020.

75 *"It's nice that people"*: Feinstein, *A Season Inside*, 196.

75 *"I'm trying to enjoy"*: Ibid., 197.

75 *If there was any direction*: Author interview with Joe Lago, March 4, 2020.

75 *Daily Cal staffers*: Ibid.

75 *Cal fans were*: Telander, *In the Year of the Bull*, 176.

75 *wearing straw hats*: Feinstein, *A Season Inside*, 133.

75 *"To the earthy-looking"*: Lee Jenkins, "Steve Kerr: The Warriors' Ringmaster," *Sports Illustrated*, June 8, 2015, https://www.si.com/nba/2015/06/09/steve-kerr -warriors-nba-finals-stephen-curry-ringmaster.

76 *"The only game"*: Feinstein, *A Season Inside*, 320.

76 *"Hey, Kerr"*: Tracy Dodds, "Arizona St. Apologizes to Kerr: Arizona Guard Was Target of Taunts by Fans before Game," *L.A. Times*, March 1, 1988, https://www .latimes.com/archives/la-xpm-1988-03-01-sp-257-story.html; "Fans' Tasteless Heckling Prompts Letter of Apology," *Vancouver Sun*, March 1, 1988, C6.

76 *"Go back to Beirut!"*: Feinstein, *A Season Inside*, 320.

76 *other Arizona State fans*: Author interview with Paul Rubin, October 29, 2019.

76 *believing they were drunk*: Steve Kerr testimony, *Susan Kerr van de Ven et al. vs. Islamic Republic of Iran et al.*

76 *his body shaking*: Dodds, "Arizona St. Apologizes to Kerr."

76 *"the scum of the earth"*: Kussoy, "Despite Pain of Dad's Murder."

77 *Kerr could immediately feel*: Feinstein, *A Season Inside*, 320.

77 *"This time"*: Ibid.

77 *"But I was just so angry"*: Ibid., 322.

77 *Watching on TV*: Author interview Nick Anderson, January 14, 2020.

77 *Hundreds of letters*: Steve Kerr testimony, *Susan Kerr van de Ven et al. vs. Islamic Republic of Iran et al.*

77 *"Dear Steve"*: Dodds, "Arizona St. Apologizes to Kerr."

78 *"We'll be playing"*: Feinstein, *A Season Inside*, 372.

78 *Kerr began to pray*: Ibid., 406.

78 *Kerr was still unsettled*: Ibid., 407–10.

79 *"the greatest feeling"*: Steve Kerr, "Raising Arizona," *The Players' Tribune*, March 28, 2015, https://www.theplayerstribune.com/en-us/articles/steve-kerr-arizona -march-madness.

79 *Returning to Tucson*: Ibid., 416.

79 *appeared at a group news conference*: Ibid., 424.

79 *The Sooners' game plan*: Feinstein, *A Season Inside*, 432.

80 *"These motherfuckers"*: Author interview with Stacey King, December 2, 2019.

80 *he later often said*: Feinstein, *One on One*, 428.

80 *"My mother could have stayed"*: Feinstein, *A Season Inside*, 433.

80 *"This was one of"*: Olson and Fisher, *Lute!*, 158.

80 *The locker room after the game*: Ibid., 157. For the locker-room scene, see Feinstein, *A Season Inside*, 433.

81 *"In the five years"*: Ibid.

81 *brought some in the audience to tears as well*: Author interview with Jay Gonzales, May 7, 2020.

82 *Another USBWA member*: Author interview with Tom Shatel, April 2, 2020.

82 *"I've enjoyed every moment"*: Greg Hansen, "30 Years Ago, Lute Olson, Steve Kerr Put Arizona on the Map," *Tucson*, March 15, 2018, https://tucson.com/sports

/arizonawildcats/basketball/greg-hansen-30-years-ago-lute-olson-steve-kerr-put
-arizona-on-the-map/article_23aefae3-31c2-53d1-b412-3af662c3409d.html.

82 *Kerr appeared to give in:* Author interview with Mike Elliott, October 1, 2019.
82 *"never had a bad practice":* Tom Danehy, "Long Shot," *Tucson Weekly,* February 21, 2008, https://www.tucsonweekly.com/tucson/long-shot/Content?oid=1090515.
82 *"I don't like it":* Knapp, "Fighting Back from Injury and Personal Tragedy."

Chapter 6: This Guy Can't Play

86 *"He was limited somewhat":* Author interview with Wayne Embry, August 26, 2019.
86 *"Half a step slow":* Author interview with Jerry Colangelo, March 10, 2020.
86 *"got better":* Author interview with Bob Weinhauer, September 9, 2019.
86 *He formulated alternatives:* Jenkins, "Steve Kerr: The Warriors' Ringmaster."
87 *He worked an internship:* Author interview with Tom Duddleston, April 7, 2020.
87 *someone pointed out:* Ibid.
87 *Being told in a phone call:* Mike Downs, "Former Cats Chosen in Draft," *Arizona Daily Star,* June 29, 1988, C1.
87 *The draft coverage Kerr had been:* Ibid.
87 *Two months earlier:* Associated Press, "3 Suns Players Are Indicted in Drug Investigation," *New York Times,* April 18, 1987, https://www.nytimes.com/1987/04/18/sports/3-suns-players-are-indicted-in-drug-investigation.html.
87 *Plus,* **Sports Illustrated** *reported:* Armen Keteyian, "Dark Clouds over Sun Country," *Sports Illustrated,* April 27, 1987, https://vault.si.com/vault/1987/04/27/dark-clouds-over-sun-country-the-biggest-drug-bust-ever-in-pro-sports-implicated-11-present-or-former-members-of-the-phoenix-suns.
88 *"probably because they had":* Smith, "Steve Kerr's Unlikely Journey."
88 *"Certainly we were all aware":* Author interview with Jerry Colangelo, March 10, 2020.
89 *Hornacek's early NBA success:* Ibid.
89 *"He was polite":* Robert Albano, "KJ Magnificent 7," *Phoenix* (June 1989): 23.
89 *He developed such a close:* Ibid.
89 *"I'd spot up":* Telander, *In the Year of the Bull,* 178.
89 *Trying to develop:* Ibid.
90 *teammates and opponents took notice:* Author interview with Jim Les, December 11, 2019; author interview with Jeff Turner, January 13, 2020.
90 *Dismissing the idea:* Lowell Cohn, "Shooting the Breeze with Warriors Coach Steve Kerr," *Press Democrat,* February 19, 2015, https://www.pressdemocrat.com/article/sports/lowell-cohn-shooting-the-breeze-with-warriors-coach-steve-kerr/.
90 *"He practiced the shots":* Author interview with Jeff Turner, January 13, 2020.
90 *"one of the guys":* Author interview with Jim Les, December 11, 2019.
90 *He likewise found joy:* Ballard, "The Little-Known Book That Shaped the Minds of Steve Kerr and Pete Carroll."
90 *"I was always":* Ibid.
91 *"He couldn't guard us":* Author interview with Paul Westphal, March 16, 2020.
91 *Kerr was frustrated enough:* David Aldridge, "Coach Steve Kerr More than Willing to Speak Up—and Listen," *NBA,* October 23, 2017, https://www.nba.com/article/2017/10/23/morning-tip-golden-state-warriors-coach-steve-kerr-outspoken-willing-listen.
91 *It didn't help:* Isaacson, *Transition Game,* 184.

91   *"a determined worker"*: Author interview with Tyrone Corbin, January 13, 2020.
91   *"He had to get stronger"*: Author interview with Eddie Johnson, November 19, 2019.
92   *"He had one thing"*: Author interview with Wayne Embry, August 26, 2019.
92   *When Ehlo told:* Author interview with Craig Ehlo, October 1, 2019.
93   *Price went hard at Kerr:* Ibid.
94   *members of the second unit:* Author interview with Paul Mokeski, November 27, 2019.
94   *"When we played together"*: Ibid.
94   *The day Uncle Mo:* Ibid.
94   *"When I got"*: Feinstein, *One on One,* 427.
95   *As a child:* Author interview with Paul Mokeski, November 27, 2019.
95   *he called over one of the writers:* Author interview with Joe Menzer, September 24, 2019.
96   *Unable to drink alcohol:* Author interview with Craig Ehlo, October 1, 2019.
96   *his blackjack strategies:* For details of organizing the trip and the drive, see author interviews with Burt Graeff, September 24, 2019; Craig Ehlo, October 1, 2019; Joe Menzer, September 24, 2019; and Paul Mokeski, November 27, 2019.
96   *"Yes," the dealer responded:* Author interview with Joe Menzer, September 24, 2019.
97   *each punctuated by a solitary:* Author interview with Mike Elliott, October 1, 2019.
97   *Margot asked her new husband:* Steve Kerr testimony, *Susan Kerr van de Ven et al. vs. Islamic Republic of Iran et al.*
98   *"Boy," he was still saying:* Telander, *In the Year of the Bull,* 212.
98   *a move the Bulls felt:* Clifton Brown, "Tired of Sparring, Bulls Prime for Quick Knockout," *New York Times,* May 29, 2992, https://www.nytimes.com/1992/05/29/sports/basketball-tired-of-sparring-bulls-prime-for-quick-knockout.html.
98   **I'm getting this motherfucker:** Author interview with Stacey King, December 2, 2019.
99   *"was bush league"*: Brown, "Tired of Sparring, Bulls Prime for Quick Knockout."
99   *King asserted the fake cover story:* Ibid.
99   *payback was exactly:* Author interview with Stacey King, December 2, 2019.
99   *"You motherfucker!"*: Ibid.
99   *"the only one"*: Ibid.
100 *Strangely, considering the reputation:* Author interview with Pat Williams, August 15, 2018.
100 *Kerr was plainly sweating his future:* Author interview with Joe Menzer, September 24, 2019.
101 *It took Williams:* Author interview with Pat Williams, August 15, 2018.
101 *"This guy can't play"*: Author interview with Rodney Powell, January 13, 2020.
102 *"Yeah, you guys"*: Author interview with Bob Price, October 7, 2019.
102 *"The things that he did"*: Author interview with Nick Anderson, January 14, 2020.
102 *"even though he was young"*: Author interview with Rodney Powell, January 13, 2020.
102 *got a Magic group:* Ibid.
102 *A similar wardrobe repair:* Author interview with Jeff Turner, January 13, 2020.
102 *long before:* Author interview with Pat Williams, August 15, 2018.
103 *still felt like an overpay:* Ibid.
103 *While obviously his famous:* Author interview with Mike Elliott, October 1, 2019.
105 *"He told me"*: Rubin, "Steve Kerr's Been Beating the Odds His Whole Life."

105 *He glanced at Europe:* Isaacson, *Transition Game*, 49.

105 *"I never had any":* Ibid., 185.

106 *but he confided:* Author interview with Jerry Reynolds, December 2, 2019.

106 *"with really nowhere":* Smith, "Steve Kerr's Unlikely Journey."

106 *Jackson assured Kerr:* Isaacson, *Transition Game*, 179.

106 *"We have a non-guaranteed spot":* Smith, "Steve Kerr's Unlikely Journey."

Chapter 7: OKP

107 *"nothing lasts forever":* For Jackson's thoughts and his conversation with Jordan, see Phil Jackson, with Hugh Delehanty, *Eleven Rings: The Soul of Success* (New York: Penguin Press, 2013), 132.

108 *"Boy, it's all about timing":* Author interview with Bill Wennington, December 2, 2019.

108 *"Steve would get":* Smith, "Steve Kerr's Unlikely Journey."

108 *Their Chicago:* Ibid.

108 *Steve and his equipment bag:* Isaacson, *Transition Game*, 184.

108 *Forty-nine wins:* Jackson and Delehanty, *Eleven Rings*, 135.

109 *"the one person":* Roland Lazenby, *Blood on the Horns: The Long Strange Ride of Michael Jordan's Chicago Bulls* (Lenexa, KS: Addax Publishing Group, 1998), 8.

109 *"I think it really":* Roland Lazenby, *Michael Jordan: The Life* (New York: Back Bay Books, 2014), 491.

109 *"He was everybody's":* Ibid.

110 *"What better way":* Jackson and Delehanty, *Eleven Rings*, 134.

111 *Others hummed:* Sam Smith, *The Jordan Rules* (New York: Simon & Schuster, 1992), 36.

111 *"very uncomfortable":* Lazenby, *Michael Jordan: The Life*, 580.

111 *"Can you imagine":* Ibid.

111 *Repeating one of his:* Author interview with Roland Lazenby, August 28, 2019.

112 *"Steve and Phil had":* Author interview with Bill Wennington, December 2, 2019.

112 *"This is a thinking man":* Author interview with Chip Schaefer, December 2, 2019.

113 *Lazenby showed Jackson:* Lazenby interview.

114 *Krause got booed so badly:* Lazenby, *Blood on the Horns*, 45.

114 *"like kids almost":* Lazenby, *Michael Jordan: The Life*, 512.

114 *"He came to practice":* Ibid., 513.

114 *Longley lacked:* Telander, *In the Year of the Bull*, 209.

115 *Will Perdue was:* Smith, *The Jordan Rules*, 32.

115 *Horace Grant "Dummy":* Lazenby, *Blood on the Horns*, 46.

115 *"You're an idiot":* Smith, *The Jordan Rules*, 108.

115 *Jackson considered Grant's psyche:* Telander, *In the Year of the Bull*, 223.

115 *"but he doesn't like":* Ibid., 209.

115 *"just want to":* Ibid.

115 *Pippen was "lost":* Ibid.

115 *Jordan would later:* Michael Silver, "Straight Shooter," *Sports Illustrated*, April 7, 1997, https://vault.si.com/vault/1997/04/07/straight-shooter-after-nine-years-in-the-nba-the-bulls-steve-kerr-is-still-a-hardworking-overachiever.

115 *"Kerr has heart":* Telander, *In the Year of the Bull*, 209.

115 *"may be a good thing":* Lazenby, *Blood on the Horns*, 26.

116 *as Jordan remembered:* Telander, *The Year of the Bull*, 130.

116 *Krause not only:* Ibid., 204.

116 *Finally, after turning down:* J. A. Adande, "Michael Jordan's Famous 'I'm Back'

Fax, 25 Years Later," *ESPN*, March 18, 2015, https://www.espn.com/nba/story/_
/id/12501628/michael-jordan-famous-back-fax-25-years-later.

117 *"We had no idea"*: Lazenby, *Michael Jordan: The Life*, 519.

117 *"would ridicule us"*: Ibid.

118 *Unprompted and without comment*: Author interview with Chip Schaefer, December 2, 2019.

119 *"Since you have"*: Author interview with Charles Grantham, September 6, 2019.

119 *"I got a glimpse"*: Lazenby, *Michael Jordan: The Life*, 528.

120 *"a lot of these guys"*: Ibid., 529.

120 *"Phil's absence definitely led"*: Ibid., 530.

120 *compared it to:* Ibid., 531.

121 *"I had no chance"*: Ibid.

121 *"very shocked"*: Author interview with Stacey King, December 2, 2019.

121 *"Steve fought back"*: Ibid.

121 *Look, Kerr told him:* Author interview with Sam Smith, November 21, 2019.

122 *"everything was still"*: Telander, *In the Year of the Bulls*, 56.

122 *losing the only fistfight:* Lazenby, *Michael Jordan: The Life*, 531.

122 *"By the way"*: Brian Witt, "Steve Kerr Recalls Michael Jordan Fight in Discussing Draymond Green Ban," *NBC Bay Area*, November 13, 2018, https://www.nbcbay area.com/news/sports/steve_kerr_recalls_michael_jordan_fight_in_discussing _draymond_green_ban/166829/.

122 *"helped us tremendously"*: Telander, *In the Year of the Bull*, 210.

122 *"a turning point for the team"*: Blue Shorts, "Phil Jackson: How Michael Jordan and Steve Kerr Came to Blows," *CBS DC*, May 30, 2013, https://washington.cbslocal .com/2013/05/30/how-jordan-kerr-came-to-blows-then-phil-jackson-used-it-to -motivate-the-bulls/.

122 *"Kerr has heart"*: Telander, *In the Year of the Bull*, 209.

123 *"Best team I've ever seen"*: Ibid., 97.

123 *"It's like every move"*: Lazenby, *Michael Jordan: The Life*, 548.

123 *they might be:* Ibid.

124 *"So many guys"*: Telander: *In the Year of the Bull*, 78.

124 *He plotted out:* Ibid., 179.

124 *It wasn't until the playoffs:* Ibid., 97.

124 *"I never knew"*: Ibid.

124 *"I'd be pretty sure"*: Ibid., 205.

125 *usually with basketballs:* Smith, *The Jordan Rules*, 304.

125 *Jordan hadn't flown:* Telander, *In the Year of the Bull*, 207.

125 *Wilmington, North Carolina:* Lazenby, *Michael Jordan: The Life*, 127. Kerr had spoken countless times of his adoration for UCLA growing up.

126 *SuperSonics coach George Karl:* Ibid., 553.

126 *"So that made it"*: Feinstein, *One on One*, 428.

127 *a cigar in one hand and:* Telander, *In the Year of the Bull*, 262.

127 *"is such a fierce competitor"*: Lazenby, *Michael Jordan: The Life*, 553.

Chapter 8: "I'll Be Ready"

129 *the worst of Atlantic City:* Author interview with Chip Schaefer, December 2, 2019.

129 *achieve the goal:* Silver, "Straight Shooter."

129 *approached him:* Jackson and Delehanty, *Eleven Rings*, 173.

129 *"Dennis had sort of been away"*: Silver, "Straight Shooter."

129 *Jackson's only regret:* Jackson and Delehanty, *Eleven Rings*, 173.

130 *Kerr, like Jordan:* Telander, *In the Year of the Bull*, 13.

130 *almost immediately volunteered:* Author interview with Bob Price, October 7, 2019.

130 *exchanged ideas with:* Author interview with Alex Martins, September 23, 2019.

130 *finally informed Kerr:* Author interview with K. C. Johnson.

130 *"Steve understood everything":* Author interview with Roland Lazenby.

131 *Equipment manager John Ligmanowski:* Author interview with John Ligmanowski, December 2, 2019.

131 *"no one else":* Author interview with Bill Wennington, December 2, 2019.

131 *Wennington finally made it official:* Ibid.

132 *Jackson worried about:* Jackson and Delehanty, *Eleven Rings*, 170.

132 *"being a little bit":* Author interview with Bill Wennington, December 2, 2019.

132 *wrote "F.I.":* Eric Freeman, "Steve Kerr Grew a Goatee, Wrote Bad Words on His Shoes While Dealing with Confidence Issues," *Yahoo!Sports*, October 15, 2012, citing *NBA* story by David Aldridge, https://sports.yahoo.com/steve-kerr-grew -goatee-wrote-bad-words-shoes-213119786--nba.html.

132 *"It sounds crazy":* Ibid.

132 *"He was":* Author interview with Bill Wennington, December 2, 2019.

133 *Nearly twenty thousand people:* Michael C. Lewis, *To the Brink: Stockton, Malone and the Utah Jazz's Climb to the Edge of Glory* (New York: Simon & Schuster, 1998), 49.

134 *"because he's so sensitive":* Silver, "Straight Shooter."

134 *a playoff emotional descent:* Anonymous interview with author.

134 *"Why can't I ever":* Terry Pluto, "Bulls' Kerr Waited Entire Life for Chance to Make Clinching Shot," *Akron Beacon Journal*, reprinted in *The Missoulian*, June 17, 1997, D1.

135 *"I'll be ready":* The scene during the time-out and Kerr's statement to Jordan on the bench were captured on video in "Greatest Moments in NBA History—Steve Kerr Winning Shot NBA Finals 1997," October 3, 2014, https://www.youtube .com/watch?v=6uDDA73G5YM.

135 *"I'm far from":* Telander, *In the Year of the Bull*, 180.

136 Oh shit: Author interview with Jeff Hornacek.

136 *Midcourt about twenty rows:* Author interview with Jim Les, December 11, 2019.

136 *Cavaliers general manager:* Author interview with Wayne Embry, August 26, 2019.

136 *In his hometown:* Author interview with Craig Ehlo, October 1, 2019.

137 *"There are certain players":* Author interview with Bob Weinhauer, September 9, 2019.

137 *"Steve's been fighting":* Lazenby, *Michael Jordan: The Life*, 576.

137 *"Tonight Steve Kerr earned":* Ibid., 577.

137 *never felt comfortable:* Jackson and Delehanty, *Eleven Rings*, 1.

138 *He didn't like:* Lazenby, *Michael Jordan: The Life*, 585.

138 *walked away from the podium:* For Kerr's speech at the victory celebration, see "Steve Kerr's Hilarious Story about 1997 Game Winner," posted June 15, 2017, https://www.youtube.com/watch?v=BGTIq4yO-og.

139 *management was trying to trade:* Sam Smith, "Part XVI: The Last Dance for Jordan and the Bulls," *NBA: Bulls*, September 11, 2009, https://www.nba.com/bulls /news/jordanhof_yearfourteen_090911.html.

139 *"There's more bullshit flying":* Lazenby, *Blood on the Horns*, 16.

139 *"In Chicago":* Ibid., 4.

140 *"it's not much of a reward":* For the Bulls in Paris, see David Halberstam, *Playing for Keeps: Michael Jordan and the World He Made* (New York: Random House, 1999), 3.

140 *friends he made in the West:* Andrew Higgins, "Who Will Succeed Kim Jong Il?" *Washington Post,* July 16, 2009, https://www.washingtonpost.com/wp-dyn/content /article/2009/07/15/AR2009071503930_pf.html.

140 *Pak had a collection:* Ibid.

140 *"The finality of it":* Jackson and Delehanty, *Eleven Rings,* 188.

141 *"But in the end":* Phil Jackson with Rick Telander, "The Last Running of the Bulls," *ESPN The Magazine,* May 4, 1998, http://www.espn.com/magazine/vol 1no04jackson.html.

141 *Coleman could have:* Lazenby, *Blood on the Horns,* 184.

141 *"trampoline hands":* Ibid.

142 *"That's one of the things":* Ibid.

142 *Wanting to appreciate:* Lazenby, *Michael Jordan: The Life,* 603.

142 *a special level of importance:* Jackson and Delehanty, *Eleven Rings,* 86.

142 *"very moving":* Ibid., 192.

142 *Kerr was shocked:* Lazenby, *Michael Jordan: The Life,* 603.

142 *His contribution:* Jackson and Delehanty, *Eleven Rings,* 192.

142 *Kerr was one of many:* Lazenby, *Michael Jordan: The Life,* 604.

142 *"I'll never forget":* Jackson with Delehanty, *Eleven Rings,* 192.

143 *"beyond the realm":* Jackson and Telander, "Last Running of the Bulls, Part 4," *ESPN,* July 10, 2012, https://www.espn.com/nba/story/_/page/Mag15lastrunning ofthebullspart4/chicago-bulls-coach-phil-jackson-recounts-historic-1998-season -part-4-espn-magazine-archive.

143 *"That's true desire":* Lewis, *To the Brink,* 264.

143 *"My story is not quite:"* "1998 Chicago Bulls/Michael Jordan—Final Champion-ship Celebration Party—Grant Park," https://www.youtube.com/watch?v=7sa 0J97xooQ.

Chapter 9: Civil Action 01-1994

145 *Kerr reported a session:* Mark Heisler, "NBA Players Show They're Willing to Roll Dice Together," *Los Angeles Times,* October 23, 1998, https://www.latimes.com /archives/la-xpm-1998-oct-23-sp-35402-story.html.

146 *"My agent, Mark Bartelstein":* Sam Smith, "Bulls' Victims Can't Wait to Pour on the Payback," *Chicago Tribune,* January 24, 1999, 5.

146 *"For all the years":* Ibid.

147 *"I hate it":* Gregg Popovich, press conference comments, June 7, 2014, "NBA Fi-nals: Heat v Spurs," *ASAP Sports,* http://www.asapsports.com/show_interview .php?id=99491.

148 *"Timing and detail":* Author interview with Mike Budenholzer, January 10, 2020.

148 *They went from:* Ibid.

149 *"He hated it":* Anonymous interview with author.

149 *Kerr and other players:* Adrian Garcia, "'What if Gregg Popovich Was Fired in 1999?' Former Players, KSAT's Greg Simmons Chime In," *KSAT,* December 29, 2017, https://www.ksat.com/sports/2017/12/29/what-if-gregg-popovich-was-fired -in-1999-former-spurs-players-ksats-greg-simmons-chime-in/.

149 *Johnson viewed Popovich:* Ibid.

150 *after a bad game:* Jackson and Delehanty, *Eleven Rings,* 86.

150 *(retired) David Robinson:* Scott Howard-Cooper, "Robinson Stands Tall," *Sacra-mento Bee,* June 8, 2003, C1.

150 *Jackson listened to Game 3:* Phil Jackson and Charley Rosen, *More Than a Game* (New York: Fireside, 2002), 141–42.

151 *became so disgusted:* Jackson and Delehanty, *Eleven Rings,* 203–4.

152 *"anguishing":* Jackson and Rosen, *More Than a Game,* 194.

152 *"But Steve was also":* Ibid.

152 *Jay Howard's suggestion:* Author interview with Jay Howard, April 1, 2020.

153 *"Well why the":* Ibid.

153 *"He did it instinctively":* Ibid.

154 *The day Popovich:* Hooman Yazdanian, "Steve Kerr Discusses Basketball, Non-violent Protests at Zellerbach Hall," *Daily Californian,* October 7, 2016, https://www.dailycal.org/2016/10/07/steve-kerr-discusses-basketball-non-violent-protest-zellerbach-hall/.

154 *"I think it is more":* Author Q&A with Gregg Popovich, pregame press conference, Chase Center, November 1, 2019.

155 *"We need to do this stuff":* Ibid., 233.

155 *family issue:* Kerr van de Ven, *One Family's Response,* 58.

156 *"time to think about accountability":* Ann Kerr testimony, *Susan Kerr van de Ven et al. vs. Islamic Republic of Iran et al.*

156 *The family agreed:* Kerr van de Ven, *One Family's Response,* 60.

156 *"What if they come":* Ibid., 61.

156 *In that chaotic instant:* Ibid., 62.

157 *"But each of us":* Ibid.

157 *"nonconfrontational by nature":* Ibid., 59.

157 *a very public declaration:* Ibid., 64.

157 *appeared on a local radio show:* Ibid.

157 *Around the same time:* Ibid., 63.

158 *"Anytime you come":* Author interview with Maurice Cheeks, December 19, 2019.

158 *"I knew he was":* Ibid.

158 *When Los Angeles called:* Eggers, *Jail Blazers,* 250.

159 *The time Kerr saw Randolph:* Ibid., 265.

159 *Cheeks conceded his inexperience:* Eggers, *Jail Blazers,* 282.

160 *"added some sanity":* Ibid., 265.

160 *Kerr reported being told:* Ibid., 285.

160 *Kerr was surprised:* Author interview with Bob Whitsitt, November 8, 2019.

160 *being double-crossed:* Author interview with Chris Dudley, November 22, 2019. "There were a few head fakes," Dudley said.

161 *for years remembered:* Author interview with Bob Whitsitt, November 8, 2019. "I talked to both," Whitsitt said. "The agent was telling me he'd love to get back to San Antonio if—*if*—I was going to trade him and was clear that he certainly wasn't requesting a trade or wanting to be traded or any of those things."

161 *"I would trade guys":* Ibid.

162 *When the time came:* Author interview with Bob Price, October 7, 2019.

162 *did not want the attention:* Branch, "Tragedy Made Steve Kerr See the World Beyond the Court."

163 *"the way we are":* Andrew Kerr testimony, *Susan Kerr van de Ven et al. vs. Islamic Republic of Iran et al.*

163 *"My children have each":* Ann Kerr testimony, *Susan Kerr van de Ven et al. vs. Islamic Republic of Iran et al.*

163 *given the somber task at hand:* For Steve Kerr's testimony on the witness stand, see Steve Kerr testimony, *Susan Kerr van de Ven et al. vs. Islamic Republic of Iran et al.*

164 *"I want to say":* Andrew Kerr testimony, *Susan Kerr van de Ven et al. vs. Islamic Republic of Iran et al.*

164 *Jackson concluded the testimony portion:* Thomas Penfield Jackson statement from the bench, *Susan Kerr van de Ven et al. vs. Islamic Republic of Iran et al.*

165 *"Do I really":* Author interview with Greg Simmons, November 13, 2019.

166 *"I've been on ice":* Mike Wise, "'Frozen' Kerr Catches Fire and Lifts Spurs," *New York Times,* May 30, 2003, https://www.nytimes.com/2003/05/30/sports/pro -basketball-frozen-kerr-catches-fire-and-lifts-spurs.html.

166 *"I'm 37":* Associated Press, "Spurs Outscore Mavs 34–9 in Final Quarter," *ESPN,* May 29, 2003, https://www.espn.com/nba/recap?gameId=230529006.

166 *"A lot of people":* Michael Wilbon, "Spurs' Kerr Is a Long-Shot Made Good," *Washington Post,* June 4, 2003.

166 *Kerr stayed with:* Wise, "'Frozen' Kerr Catches Fire and Lifts Spurs."

166 *prompting some Mavericks:* Associated Press, "Spurs Outscore Mavs 34–9 in Final Quarter."

167 *Every time he looked:* Wilbon, "Spurs' Kerr Is a Long-Shot Made Good."

167 *On the Spurs bench:* Author interview with Mike Budenholzer, January 10, 2020.

167 *On the Mavericks bench:* Author interview with Paul Mokeski, November 27, 2019.

167 *his instructions to Dallas defenders:* Ibid.

167 *A fitting finish:* Associated Press, "Spurs Outscore Mavs 34–9 in Final Quarter."

167 *"The greatest feeling ever":* Wise, "'Frozen' Kerr Catches Fire and Lifts Spurs."

167 *When Mokeski congratulated Kerr:* Author interview with Paul Mokeski, November 27, 2019.

167 *Kerr told Popovich:* Associated Press, "Spurs Outscore Mavs 34–9 in Final Quarter."

168 *"residing":* Rubin, "Steve Kerr's Been Beating the Odds His Whole Life."

168 *Kerr radiated:* Author interview with Don Harris, November 23, 2019.

168 *"All I wanted":* Ibid.

168 *the hairs on Kerr's arms:* Ibid.

168 *"a perfect culmination":* Rubin, "Steve Kerr's Been Beating the Odds His Whole Life."

168 *he climbed into bed:* Buck Harvey, "Two Friends Pull Off Two Miracles for Spurs," *San Antonio Express-News,* January 25, 2016, https://www.expressnews.com /sports/spurs/article/Two-friends-pull-off-two-miracles-for-Spurs-6778743.php #photo-7774020.

169 *"This is my 15th year":* Wilbon, "Spurs' Kerr Is a Long-Shot Made Good."

Chapter 10: Speeches and Shouting Matches

171 *"Let's put it":* "Q+A Steve Kerr," *Sports Illustrated,* October 20, 2003, https://vault .si.com/vault/2003/10/20/qa-steve-kerr.

171 *Kerr threw himself into:* Ballard, "Steve Kerr's Absence."

171 *since his youth:* Lee Jenkins, "Steve Kerr: The Warriors' Ringmaster," *Sports Illustrated,* June 8, 2015, https://www.si.com/nba/2015/06/09/steve-kerr-warriors -nba-finals-stephen-curry-ringmaster.

172 *Likins urged an end:* Christine Lagorio, "Commencement: What's in the Air at Graduation?" *New York Times,* April 22, 2007, https://www.nytimes.com/2007 /04/22/education/edlife/toss22.html.

172 *"I think it's great":* Jessica Lee, "Steve Kerr Ready for Grad Speech, Tortillas," *Arizona Daily Wildcat,* May 12, 2004, https://wc.arizona.edu/papers/97/150/01_1 .html.

172 *with his uniform number 25:* It was Kerr's *jersey* that had been retired five and a half years before his commencement address; the school does not retire the

numbers of former stars. That had to be clarified in the summer of 2020 when Arizona added a freshman recruit from Estonia: Kerr Kriisa. Kriisa's father, a former professional player in Europe, was a fan of the Michael Jordan–era Bulls and had named his son after Steve. The younger Kriisa said he had no idea Steve Kerr had played for Arizona until the Wildcats pointed it out during recruiting. Bruce Pascoe, "Arizona Wildcats Freshman Kerr Kriisa Will Wear Same No. 25 as His Namesake, Steve Kerr," *Tucson*, September 5, 2020, https://tucson.com /sports/arizonawildcats/basketball/pascoe/arizona-wildcats-freshman-kerr -kriisa-will-wear-same-no-25-as-his-namesake-steve-kerr/article_ae7a76b8-ef3f -11ea-9c0e-7f8ab78d4ff0.html; Bruce Pascoe, "Big-Name Pickup: Wildcats go to Estonia to Land Recruit Named after Former UA Star Steve Kerr," *Tucson*, April 18, 2020, https://tucson.com/sports/arizonawildcats/basketball/big-name-pickup -wildcats-go-to-estonia-to-land-recruit-named-after-former-ua-star/article _462654ba-3b7f-55a7-8242-2815ccda2b1d.html; "Wildcats Reel in Another Kerr, This One from Estonia," *Arizona Daily Star,* April 19, 2020, C1.

173   *commencement that remained:* Lagorio, "Commencement: What's in the Air at Graduation?"

173   *the most since:* Inger Sandal, "Steve Kerr Admits to Nerves as Commencement Speaker," *Arizona Daily Star,* May 14, 2004, B1.

173   *estimated 25,000 attendees:* Carol Ann Alaimo, "Dreams Come True for UA Graduates," *Arizona Daily Star,* May 16, 2004, B1.

173   *"'is fine with me!'":* The university news service transcribed and posted much of Kerr's commencement address; see University of Arizona, "Steve Kerr's Commencement Speech," May 8, 2004, https://news.arizona.edu/story/steve-kerrs -commencement-speech.

175   *dispatching his Gulfstream:* Olson and Fisher, *Lute!,* 223.

175   *1 percent ownership stake:* Connor Letourneau, "Steve Kerr's 'Whirlwind' as Suns GM: A Shaq Trade, a Firing, Many Lessons," *SFGate,* March 9, 2019, https:// www.sfgate.com/warriors/article/Steve-Kerr-s-whirlwind-as-Suns-GM-A -Shaq-13676560.php.

176   *the approach and dependability:* Author interview with Joe Lago, March 4, 2020.

176   *"He is a unique talent":* Steve Kerr.

176   *"The Warriors are not good":* Steve Kerr.

177   *"Help has arrived":* Ibid.

177   *"Isiah seems to be":* Steve Kerr.

177   *so emotionally invested:* Author interview with Joe Lago, March 4, 2020.

177   *"best atmosphere I've ever":* Kerr press conference, May 20, 2014.

178   *"was the best":* Author interview with David Griffin, December 20, 2019.

178   *Under orders from Sarver:* Anthony Slater, "Why Didn't the Mike D'Antoni–Steve Kerr Partnership Work in Phoenix? It's Complex," The Athletic, May 11, 2018, https://theathletic.com/349207/2018/05/11/why-didnt-the-mike-dantoni-steve -kerr-partnership-work-in-phoenix-its-complex/.

179   *"We've come a long way":* Rubin, "Steve Kerr's Been Beating the Odds His Whole Life."

180   *"Not if he wants":* Ibid.; author interview with Paul Rubin, October 29, 2019. In the interview, Rubin described D'Antoni as turning terse at the question.

180   *and the next day:* Rubin, "Steve Kerr's Been Beating the Odds His Whole Life."

180   *"The only way":* Ibid.

180   *Kerr was shocked:* Ibid.

181   *"I knew this job":* Ibid.

181 *agreeing to Kerr's request:* Author interview with Paul Rubin, October 29, 2019.

182 *"Steve Kerr! Steve Kerr!":* Rubin, "Steve Kerr's Been Beating the Odds His Whole Life."

182 *"He'll feed his kids":* Ibid.

182 *asking rhetorically:* Author interview with Paul Coro, October 23, 2019.

184 *The Suns, Nash said:* Associated Press, "Suns Fire Porter with Team in Stall," *ESPN,* February 16, 2009, https://www.espn.com/nba/news/story?id=3910443.

184 *"Probably the most difficult":* Letourneau, "Steve Kerr's 'Whirlwind' as Suns GM."

184 *Gentry was not surprised:* Author interview with Alvin Gentry, December 20, 2019.

185 *Gentry even considered:* Ibid.

185 *"I was impressed":* Shaquille O'Neal, with Jackie MacMullan, *Shaq Uncut: My Story* (New York: Grand Central Publishing, 2011).

185 *"Steve is one of":* Ibid., 226.

186 *they ranked him second:* Scott Howard-Cooper, "On the Clock: Q&A with Former Golden State Warriors GM Larry Riley," *NBA,* June 6, 2017, https://www.nba.com/article/2017/06/08/clock-larry-riley-golden-state-warriors-drafting-stephen-curry-2009.

186 *Curry reminded him of:* Bay Area Sports Guy, citing story by Marcus Thompson II in the *San Jose Mercury News* (link no longer available), in "Don Nelson: Curry's the next Steve Nash," *Bay Area Sports Guy,* June 27, 2009, http://www.bayareasportsguy.com/don-nelson-currys-the-next-steve-nash/. "I always saw Steve Nash in [Curry], and he is the greatest player I've ever coached," Nelson said. "I've been looking for another one for a long time and this is as close as I've ever seen in a young player. He has that same ability that Steve had. Shooting, passing, knowledge, just the natural things he's done that he's worked on his whole life."

186 *Turning away from:* Howard-Cooper, "On the Clock."

187 *cheering could be heard:* Adam Green, "Former Suns GM: Team Thought It Had a Draft Night Deal with Warriors for Stephen Curry," *Arizona Sports,* March 1, 2013, https://arizonasports.com/story/16570/former-suns-gm-team-thought-it-had-a-draft-night-deal-with-warriors-for-stephen-curry/.

187 *"had his own issues":* O'Neal with MacMullan, *Uncut.*

188 *"I think Steve had":* Anonymous interview with author.

188 *"You can tell with Steve":* Anonymous interview with author.

188 *It was Sarver's idea:* Paul Coro, "Phoenix Suns 'Los Suns' Jerseys Making a Statement," *Arizona Republic,* May 5, 2010, http://archive.azcentral.com/arizonarepublic/news/articles/20100505nba-phoenix-suns-los-suns-jerseys.html.

189 *"I know that":* United Press International, "Obama Cites Phoenix 'Los Suns' Protest," *UPI,* May 5, 2010, https://www.upi.com/Top_News/World-News/2010/05/05/Obama-cites-Phoenix-Los-Suns-protest/44611273101520/.

189 *"I don't think teams":* J. A. Adande, "Phil Jackson on His Future . . . and Leaving Politics in the Past," *ESPN,* May 4, 2010, https://www.espn.com/blog/truehoop/post/_/id/15724/phil-jackson-on-his-future-and-leaving-politics-in-the-past.

189 *Of the eighty-four letters:* Craig Harris, "Political Gesture by Phoenix Suns, a Rarity in Sports, Angers Many Fans," *Arizona Republic,* May 6, 2010, http://archive.azcentral.com/arizonarepublic/news/articles/20100506arizona-immigration-law-phoenix-suns-los-suns-jerseys.html.

189 *"It's hard to imagine":* Coro, "'Los Suns' Jerseys."

189 *"ugly" and "hateful":* Harris, "Political Gesture by Phoenix Suns."

190 *As the clock ticked down:* Author interview with Paul Coro, October 23, 2019.

190 *two unattractive options:* Paul Coro, "Steve Kerr Makes Parting from Phoenix Suns 'Professional, Personal,'" *Arizona Republic,* June 16, 2010. http://archive .azcentral.com/sports/suns/articles/2010/06/16/20100616phoenix-suns-kerr-ON .html.

191 *"I wouldn't say":* Ibid.

191 *"a small part":* Ibid.

191 *"Steve knew he was fine":* Author interview with David Griffin, December 20, 2019.

Chapter 11: In Demand

193 *"a more relaxed":* Author interview with Michael Cage, December 11, 2019.

194 *while watching games on:* Chris Ballard, "Warriors: From One-Dimensional and One-and-Done to NBA Title Favorites," *Sports Illustrated,* February 18, 2015, https://www.si.com/nba/2015/02/19/golden-state-warriors-steve-kerr-stephen -curry-klay-thompson-joe-lacob.

194 *imagining himself preparing:* Steve Kerr, press conference comments, June 3, 2015, "NBA Finals: Cavaliers v Warriors," *ASAP Sports,* http://www.asapsports.com /show_interview.php?id=109709.

194 *would pull:* Ballard, "Warriors: From One-Dimensional and One-and-Done to NBA Title Favorites."

195 *Jackson's insistent behind-the-scenes:* Smith interview.

195 *"I think he thought":* Author interview with Alex Martins, September 23, 2019.

196 *unconventional, the suggestion made sense:* Author interview with Marcus Noland, February 25, 2020.

196 *the present was so treasured:* Anna Fifield, *The Great Successor: The Divinely Perfect Destiny of Brilliant Comrade Kim Jong Un* (New York: PublicAffairs, 2019), 172.

196 *Get Kerr:* Author interview with Marcus Noland, February 25, 2020.

197 *never appeared interested:* Ibid.

197 *"I think he can handle":* Howie Kussoy, "Despite Pain of Dad's Murder, Kerr Became a Champion," *New York Post,* May 3, 2014, https://nypost.com/2014/05/03 /in-the-wake-of-his-dads-assassination-kerr-became-a-champion/.

197 *"knows everything about basketball":* Al Iannazzone, "Toni Kukoc Thinks Steve Kerr Would Be a Fine Coach," *Newsday,* April 18, 2014, https://www.newsday .com/sports/basketball/knicks/toni-kukoc-thinks-steve-kerr-would-be-a-fine -coach-1.7763657.

198 *"It's where his joy":* Author interview with David Griffin, December 20, 2019.

199 *"Steve reads everything":* Bob Raissman, "Marv Albert Told Steve Kerr That It 'Never Ends Well' and 'There Is No Happiness' with Knicks at Garden," *New York Daily News,* May 15, 2014, https://www.nydailynews.com/sports/basketball /knicks/raissman-marv-denies-steered-kerr-knick-job-article-1.1794344.

199 *"It was obligation":* Anonymous interview with author.

200 *"more than likely":* Marc Berman, "Kerr's College Coach Lute Olson Expects Him to Coach Knicks," nypost.com, April 30, 2014. https://nypost.com/2014/04/30 /kerrs-former-college-coach-olson-expects-him-to-coach-knicks/.

200 *Kerr on May 5:* Ian Begley, "Phil Talks Melo, Search for Coach," *ESPN,* May 30, 2014, https://www.espn.com/new-york/nba/story/_/id/11006509/phil-jackson -new-york-knicks-not-losing-sleep-carmelo-anthony-decision.

200 *"very fair":* Fred Kerber, "How Steve Kerr Spurned the Knicks to Find His Haven," *New York Post,* January 10, 2015, https://nypost.com/2015/01/10/kerrs -debut-season-with-warriors-has-been-golden/.

201 *He had a dinner:* Scott Howard-Cooper, "Kerr Gets the Job and Coast He Wanted,"
     Sporting News, October 20, 2014, https://www.sportingnews.com/au/nba/news
     /kerr-gets-the-job-and-coast-he-wanted/1g4avjmy4r44n19nbzcr4i4b5j.
201 *aware he was nearing:* Ibid.
201 *Myers's cell phone rang:* Scott Howard-Cooper, "Warriors Brass Slam Dunks Crit-
     ical Team Decisions," *Sporting News,* May 7, 2015, https://www.sportingnews
     .com/au/nba/news/warriors-brass-slam-dunks-critical-team-decisions/1mhy87
     rzju4rp1058oqyz3pk67.
201 *Joe Lacob's cell phone:* Ibid.
201 *"there was an opening":* Ibid.
202 *"tour de force":* Sam Amick, "Warriors' Ironic Logic for Steve Kerr Replacing
     Mark Jackson," *USA Today,* May 14, 2014, https://www.usatoday.com/story
     /sports/nba/warriors/2014/05/14/steve-kerr-golden-state-head-coach-joe-lacob
     -mark-jackson/9104855/.
202 *he titled one:* Ballard, "Warriors: From One-Dimensional and One-and-Done to
     NBA Title Favorites."
202 *The candidate was soon grilling:* Warriors press conference, May 20, 2014. "That
     was a big part of our conversation," Kerr said. "Anytime a team has success and
     has a good year and the coach is fired, there's questions, right? And so I had a lot
     of questions and I felt like I gained a lot of clarity on the circumstances of the
     situation."
203 *topped the wish list:* Ballard, "Warriors: From One-Dimensional and One-and-
     Done to NBA Title Favorites."
203 *had already spoken:* Malinowski, *Betaball,* 192.
204 *"I told Phil":* Kerber, "How Steve Kerr Spurned the Knicks to Find His Haven."
204 *Jackson additionally softened:* Howard-Cooper, "Kerr Gets the Job and Coast He
     Wanted."
204 *"We all thought":* Ron Kroichick, "Keeping Up with the Kerrs: As Dad Coaches
     Warriors Champs, Kids Hit Courts for Cal," *Cal Alumni Association,* October 26,
     2015, https://alumni.berkeley.edu/california-magazine/just-in/2016-06-05/keeping
     -kerrs-dad-coaches-warriors-champs-kids-hit-courts-cal.
204 *"He's a total":* Hooman Yazdanian, "Maddy Kerr Talks Volleyball, Steve Kerr,"
     Daily Californian, July 13, 2015, https://www.dailycal.org/2015/07/13/maddy
     -kerr-talks-volleyball-steve-kerr/.
204 *"two biggest factors":* Kroichick, "Keeping Up with the Kerrs."
205 *"willing to put in":* Associated Press, "Steve Kerr Starts Warriors Job No One
     Saw Coming," *New York Post,* May 20, 2014, https://nypost.com/2014/05/20/steve
     -kerr-warriors-begin-once-unlikely-partnership/.
205 *"Look," Lacob said:* Amick, "Warriors' Ironic Logic for Steve Kerr Replacing Mark
     Jackson."
205 *"Steve was a no-brainer":* Jacob Bourne, "Gregg Popovich Says It Was 'Easy to See'
     Steve Kerr Would Become Coach," *Bleacher Report,* November 11, 2014, https://
     bleacherreport.com/articles/2264566-gregg-popovich-says-it-was-easy-to-see
     -steve-kerr-would-become-coach."

Chapter 12: Strength in Words
207 *pushed back from:* All flight times from Qantas are taken from Twitter message to
     author, February 28, 2020.
207 *and $13,213.60 in airfare:* Itinerary acquired by author.
208 *"He's an incredible guy":* Howard Beck, "Kerr and Draymond's Relationship

Nearly Destroyed Warriors; Now It Fuels Them," *Bleacher Report*, May 24, 2018, https://bleacherreport.com/articles/2777471.

208 *He knows what he's doing:* Author interview with Mychal Thompson, February 1, 2020.

208 *In conversation with Curry:* Melissa Rohlin, "Steve Kerr and Gregg Popovich Open Up about Their Relationship," *Mercury News*, March 7, 2018, https://www.mercurynews.com/2018/03/07/gregg-popovich-and-steve-kerr-open-up-about-their-relationship/.

208 *he told Barnes on the phone:* Author interview with Harrison Barnes, November 19, 2019.

208 *the Warriors merely needed:* Andre Iguodala, with Carvell Wallace, *The Sixth Man* (New York: Penguin Random House/Blue Rider Press, 2019), 171.

209 *"We're the lucky ones":* Fred Kerber, "What about the Verbal Agreement? How Close Kerr, Knicks Were," *New York Post*, January 10, 2015, https://nypost.com/2015/01/10/what-about-the-verbal-agreement-how-close-kerr-knicks-were/.

209 *Tannenbaum arranged a meeting:* Antonio Gonzalez, "Almost Colleagues, Kerr and Blatt are Rare Rookies in Finals," *Associated Press*, May 30, 2015, https://apnews.com/2b4b04bc2c1845f387a72d5f446c1b20.

210 *Walton did not, however:* Author interview with Luke Walton, January 6, 2020.

210 *"We knew each other":* Ibid.

210 *were going to be good:* Steve Kerr, press conference comments, June 3, 2015, "NBA Finals: Cavaliers v Warriors."

211 *Kerr so quickly felt:* Scott Howard-Cooper, "With Hard Work and Laid-Back Attitude, Kerr Finds Groove," *NBA*, June 3, 2015, http://archive.nba.com/2015/news/features/scott_howard_cooper/06/02/steve-kerr/index.html.

211 *Later in the off-season:* Ibid.

211 *"He's not a guy":* Author interview with Alvin Gentry, December 20, 2019.

212 *He even spent:* Ballard, "Steve Kerr's Absence."

212 *couldn't help but think:* Jeff McDonald, "All-Star Coaches Fell off Spurs' Coaching Tree," *San Antonio Express-News*, February 13, 2015, https://www.expressnews.com/sports/spurs/article/All-Star-coaches-fell-off-Spurs-coaching-tree-6080132.php.

212 *"Give me one of":* Ballard, "Steve Kerr's Absence."

212 *Putting together an introductory video:* Steve Kerr, press conference comments, June 3, 2016, "NBA Finals: Cavaliers v Warriors," *ASAP Sports,* http://www.asapsports.com/show_interview.php?id=119875.

212 *"I'm the greatest":* Baxter Holmes, "The Charcuterie Board That Revolutionized Basketball," *ESPN*, October 11, 2017, http://www.espn.com/espn/feature/story/_/page/enterpriseWarriors/how-steve-kerr-revolutionized-golden-state-warriors-offense-charcuterie-board.

213 *"he had us laughing":* Andrew Keh, "This Teacher Spends Life Being Taught," *New York Times*, November 11, 2014, https://www.nytimes.com/2014/11/14/sports/basketball/warriors-coach-steve-kerrs-style-is-molded-by-many-mentors.html.

213 *"Cotton Fitzsimmons and":* Ibid.

213 *prepared for his debut:* Ibid.

214 *"This is a":* Ballard, "Steve Kerr's Absence."

214 *former Sacramento guard:* Author interview with Doug Christie, November 19, 2019.

215 *"I thought it set":* Steve Kerr, postgame press conference comments, June 11, 2015,

"NBA Finals: Cavaliers v Warriors," *ASAP Sports*, http://www.asapsports.com /show_interview.php?id=110190.

215 *"plays of insanity"*: David Aldridge, "New Coach Kerr, Warriors Look to Get Stronger Together," *NBA*, November 17, 2014, http://archive.nba.com/2014 /news/features/david_aldridge/11/17/morning-tip-steve-kerr-adjusting-to -coaching-golden-state-warriors-role-of-injuries-for-derrick-rose-and-superstars -q-and-a-with-joe-johnson/index.html.

215 *"This is an interesting"*: Ballard, "Steve Kerr's Absence."

215 *"But let me tell you"*: Author interview with Alvin Gentry, December 20, 2019.

216 *He would return:* Ramona Shelburne, "Steve Kerr Has Suffered More than You Will Ever Know," *ESPN*, April 6, 2016, https://www.espn.com/nba/story/_/id /15148955/on-top-nba-world-steve-kerr-found-struggling-just-stand.

216 *After practice in Oakland:* Lowell Cohn, "The Steve Kerr Basketball Fans Don't Know," *Press Democrat*, March 24, 2016, https://legacy.pressdemocrat.com /sports/5421799-181/lowell-cohn-a-glimpse-into.

216 *"He was just giddy"*: Shelburne, "Steve Kerr Has Suffered More than You Will Ever Know."

217 *question the success:* Phil Jackson (@PhilJackson11), "NBA analysts give me some diagnostics on how 3pt oriented teams are faring this playoffs . . . seriously, how's it going?" Twitter, May 10, 2015, https://twitter.com/philjackson11/status /597453125297917953?lang=en.

217 *he also appreciated:* David Aldridge, "Coach Steve Kerr More than Willing to Speak Up—and Listen, Too," *NBA*, October 23, 2017, https://www.nba.com/article /2017/10/23/morning-tip-golden-state-warriors-coach-steve-kerr-outspoken -willing-listen?curator=SportsREDEF.

218 *"The pressure is like"*: Kerr press conference, June 9, 2015, "NBA Finals: Cavaliers v Warriors," *ASAP Sports*, http://www.asapsports.com/show_interview.php ?id=110071.

219 *The suggestion to shrink:* Steve Kerr, press conference comments, June 13, 2015, "NBA Finals: Cavaliers v Warrior," *ASAP Sports*, http://www.asapsports.com /show_interview.php?id=110222.

219 *Kerr also recalled:* Buck Harvey, "Popovich Influenced Kerr, and Will Again," *Express News*, June 1, 2016, https://www.expressnews.com/sports/columnists /buck_harvey/article/Popovich-influenced-Kerr-and-will-again-7958077.php.

219 *"Well," Kerr said:* Steve Kerr, press conference comments, June 13, 2015, "NBA Finals: Cavaliers v Warriors,"

220 *"looked like San Antonio"*: Author interview with Jerry West, November 15, 2019.

220 *Kerr also found:* Steve Kerr, press conference comments, February 10, 2020.

220 *The locker room was:* Steve Kerr, press conference comments, June 16, 2015, "NBA Finals: Cavaliers v Warriors," *ASAP Sports*, http://www.asapsports.com/show _interview.php?id=110339.

Chapter 13: Agony

223 *By the time he arrived:* Shelburne, "Steve Kerr Has Suffered More than You Will Ever Know."

223 *He was, he said:* Anonymous interview with author.

224 *to avoid falling:* Jackie MacMullan, "What a Title Will Never Fix for Steve Kerr and Bob Myers," *ESPN*, June 27, 2016, https://www.espn.com/nba/story/_/id /16182445/tragic-bonds-tie-steve-kerr-bob-myers-together; Shelburne, "Steve Kerr Has Suffered More than You Will Ever Know."

224 *Eight days later:* MacMullan, "What a Title Will Never Fix for Steve Kerr and Bob Myers."

224 *"We don't anticipate":* Golden State Warriors statement, October 1, 2015.

225 *Jackson needed to have:* Jackson and Rosen, *More Than a Game,* 45.

225 *"I don't want to see":* Author interview with Bill Walton.

225 *was talking to Kerr:* Author interview with Luke Walton, January 6, 2020.

226 *"certain similarities between":* Scott Howard-Cooper, "Are Warriors Comparable to Showtime Lakers?" *NBA,* December 24, 2015, http://archive.nba.com/2015/news/features/scott_howard_cooper/12/24/cavs-warriors-preview-showtime-lakers/index.html.

226 *without mentioning it publicly:* Scott Howard-Cooper, "Still Not Fully Recovered, Kerr Just Grateful to Be Back," *NBA,* May 20, 2016, https://www.nba.com/2016/news/05/19/health-woes-gives-kerr-perspective/.

226 *"Bob, I just don't know":* MacMullan, "What a Title Will Never Fix for Steve Kerr and Bob Myers."

227 *In Portland:* Shelburne, "Steve Kerr Has Suffered More than You Will Ever Know."

227 *approach Kerr:* Author interview with Jamison Webb, April 13, 2020.

227 *Excitedly agreeing:* Ibid.

227 *Kerr waited until:* Ibid.

228 *"the crowd that night":* Ibid.

228 *"I needed the job":* Howard-Cooper, "Still Not Fully Recovered, Kerr Just Grateful to Be Back."

228 *"incredibly shy":* Ballard, "Steve Kerr's Absence."

229 *"Now, it is rare":* White House transcript, February 4, 2016.

230 *accepted an invitation:* Marcus Thompson II, *KD: Kevin Durant's Relentless Pursuit to Be the Greatest* (New York: Atria, 2019), 125.

230 *"I wouldn't equate":* Howard-Cooper, "Still Not Fully Recovered, Kerr Just Grateful to Be Back."

230 *"I don't think I would":* Ibid.

231 *entered the visitors' locker room:* Author interview with Marcus Thompson II, December 27, 2019.

231 *Curry was calm:* Ibid.

232 *"It was like":* Ibid.

233 *"I can't believe":* Smith, "Steve Kerr's Unlikely Journey."

233 *sent her to:* Farid Farid, "Steve Kerr and His Mother Talk about the Legacy of His Father's Assassination," *New Yorker,* June 16, 2016, https://www.newyorker.com/news/news-desk/steve-kerr-and-his-mother-talk-about-the-legacy-of-his-fathers-assassination.

233 *wounded:* Jacey Fortin, "No Civilians Were Hit by Police Gunfire at Pulse Nightclub Shooting, Authorities Say," *New York Times,* February 13, 2019, https://www.nytimes.com/2019/02/13/us/pulse-nightclub-orlando-officer-gunfire.html; Gregor Aisch, Larry Buchanan, Joe Burgess, Ford Fessenden, Josh Keller, K. K. Rebecca Lai, Iaryna Mykhyalyshyn, Haeyoun Park, Adam Pearce, Yuliya Parshina-Kottassergio, Pecanha Anjali Singhvi, Derek Watkins, and Karen Yourish, "What Happened inside the Orlando Nightclub," *New York Times,* June 12, 2016, https://www.nytimes.com/interactive/2016/06/12/us/what-happened-at-the-orlando-nightclub-shooting.html.

233 *"for lack of a better":* MacMullan, "What a Title Will Never Fix for Steve Kerr and Bob Myers."

234 *bowed his head:* Farid, "Steve Kerr and His Mother."
234 *Kerr found himself trying:* David Aldridge, "'This Is a Time to Step Back': Steve Kerr Plans, Following Phil & Pop's Example," The Athletic, July 15, 2020, https://theathletic.com/1929210/2020/07/15/this-is-a-time-to-step-back-steve-kerr-plans-following-phil-pops-example/.
234 *"Sometimes it works out":* Monte Poole, "Kerr Laments Game 7 Loss, Would 'Definitely' Change Some Decisions," NBC Sports, June 24, 2016, citing Kerr interview on KNBR, https://www.nbcsports.com/bayarea/warriors/kerr-laments-game-7-loss-would-definitely-change-some-decisions.
235 *Kerr handled it so well:* Michelle Smith, "Warriors' Steve Kerr and UConn's Geno Auriemma Trade Insights and Quips at Cal Fundraiser," ESPN, December 21, 2018. https://www.espn.com/womens-college-basketball/story/_/id/25591239/warriors-steve-kerr-uconn-geno-auriemma-trade-insights-quips-cal-fundraiser.
235 *"You know":* "Joe Lacob: Michael Jordan Not Impressed with Warriors' Record 73-Win Season," ESPN, February 8, 2017, citing Lacob interview on 95.7 FM The Game, https://www.espn.com/nba/story/_/id/18644571/golden-state-warriors-owner-says-michael-jordan-not-impressed-record-73-win-season.
235 *"He's fantastic":* Ibid.
236 *"Can I mention one more thing?":* Steve Kerr, interview by Tim Kawakami, The TK Show, June 24, 2016, https://soundcloud.com/tkshow/steve-kerr (at 37:29).
236 *Maybe, Kawakami figured:* Author interview with Tim Kawakami, February 7, 2020.
236 *The moment struck:* Ibid.

Chapter 14: The Fury of a Patient Man
237 *Klay Thompson arrived:* Tim Kawakami, "'Why Do You Want Me?' An Oral History of Kevin Durant's July 2016 Hamptons Meeting with the Warriors," The Athletic, June 3, 2018, https://theathletic.com/353318/2018/06/03/why-do-you-want-me-an-oral-history-of-kevin-durants-july-2016-hamptons-meeting-with-the-warriors/.
237 *to allow agent Rich Kleiman:* Ibid.
237 *More specifically:* Malika Andrews and Marc Stein, "Inside the Hamptons House Where Kevin Durant Hosted NBA Suitors in 2016," New York Times, May 16, 2018, https://www.nytimes.com/2018/05/16/sports/warriors-hamptons.html.
238 *the contingent disembarked:* Iguodala and Wallace, The Sixth Man, 198.
238 *"Everybody was in":* Kawakami, "'Why Do You Want Me?' An Oral History."
238 *Durant wanting confirmation:* Ibid.
238 *"Bob and I each said":* Ibid.
238 *"He's just so cool":* Iguodala and Wallace, The Sixth Man, 168.
239 *"I was already sold":* Kawakami, "'Why Do You Want Me?' An Oral History."
239 *Green later revealed:* Lee Jenkins, "'I'm Ready': The Text That Started the Warriors' Dynasty," Sports Illustrated, June 12, 2017, https://www.si.com/nba/2017/06/12/golden-state-warriors-kevin-durant-nba-championship-draymond-green-text.
239 *"We're not getting him":* Scott Howard-Cooper, "Durant Signing Still Sinking in for Golden State's Myers," NBA, July 13, 2016, http://archive.nba.com/2016/news/features/scott_howard_cooper/07/12/qa-golden-state-warriors-gm-bob-myers/index.html.
239 *Myers jokingly wondered:* Ibid.
239 *when he got the good news:* Ibid.
239 *Kerr found out:* Kawakami, "'Why Do You Want Me?' An Oral History."

239 *"Well, I haven't"*: Warriors press conference to introduce Kevin Durant, July 7, 2016, *ASAP Sports*, http://www.asapsports.com/show_conference.php?id=121122.

240 *as a suppository*: Author interview with Monte Poole, December 30, 2019.

240 *painkillers*: Chris Haynes, "Steve Kerr Says He Used Marijuana for Back Pain, Hopes Leagues Soften Stance," *ESPN*, December 2, 2016, quoting Kerr on CSN Bay Area podcast, https://www.espn.com/nba/story/_/id/18190785/steve-kerr -says-used-marijuana-back-pain-hopes-leagues-soften-stance.

240 *acupuncture*: Jack McCallum, *Golden Days: West's Lakers, Steph's Warriors, and the California Dreamers Who Reinvented Basketball* (New York: Ballantine Books, 2017), 270.

240 *"skittish" and "nervous"*: Jenkins, "'I'm Ready': The Text That Started the War-riors' Dynasty."

240 *"head was spinning"*: Aldridge, "Coach Steve Kerr More Than Willing to Speak Up."

240 *"you can get"*: McCallum, *Golden Days*, 217.

240 *was appalled*: David Jones, "Steve Kerr Has Something to Say about Donald Trump's Immigration Policy That's Worth Hearing," *PennLive: Patriot News*, January 30, 2017, https://www.pennlive.com/sports/2017/01/steve_kerr_donald _trump_immigr.html.

241 *"Pissed at the world"*: Beck, "Kerr and Draymond's Relationship Nearly De-stroyed the Warriors."

241 *Kerr handed*: Ibid.

241 *"Yes, I should be"*: McCallum, *Golden Days*, 289.

241 *"I do what master say"*: Marc J. Spears, "Andre Iguodala's 'Master' Comments Dis-respect the Experience of Actual Slaves," *The Undefeated*, March 11, 2017, https:// theundefeated.com/features/andre-iguodala-master-golden-state-warriors/.

241 *"he has a very cryptic"*: Ethan Sherwood Strauss, "Andre Iguodala Fined $10K for Racially Charged Remarks," *ESPN*, March 13, 2017, https://www.espn.com/nba /story/_/id/18900881/golden-state-warriors-andre-iguodala-fined-racial-remarks.

242 *"It was a devastating thing"*: Lazenby, *Michael Jordan: The Life*, 503.

242 *"the biggest mistake"*: Kerr, Yahoo via Lago email.

242 *suddenly flared*: Scott Cacciola, "Steve Kerr Returns to Coach Warriors in Game 2 of the NBA Finals," *New York Times*, June 4, 2017, https://www.nytimes .com/2017/06/04/sports/basketball/golden-state-warriors-steve-kerr.html.

242 *Walking with Kerr to lunch*: Ballard, "Steve Kerr's Absence."

242 *"For years, Kerr looked"*: Ibid.

242 *"Oh my God"*: Author interview with Jerry West, November 15, 2019.

242 *management considered ordering*: Tim Kawakami, "Steve Kerr Is Feeling as Good as He's Felt in a Long While, Just When the Warriors Need Him at His Best," The Athletic, January 2, 2019, https://theathletic.com/563832/2019/01/02/kawakami -steve-kerr-is-feeling-as-good-as-hes-felt-in-a-long-while-just-when-the-warriors -need-him-at-his-best/.

243 *"settle in"*: Scott Cacciola, "After Steve Kerr's Halftime Speech, the Warriors Rally Past the Spurs," *New York Times*, May 14, 2017, https://www.nytimes .com/2017/05/14/sports/basketball/nba-playoffs-warriors-steve-kerr.html.

243 *"Apparently it was not"*: Steve Kerr, pregame press conference comments, June 4, 2017, "NBA Finals: Cleveland v Golden State," *ASAP Sports*, http://www.asap sports.com/show_interview.php?id=130522.

244 *"I'm going to pull out"*: Ibid.

244 *tears in his eyes*: Malinowski, *Betaball*, 333.

244 *Iguodala told him*: Iguodala and Wallace, *The Sixth Man*, 237.

244 *"Winning is fantastic"*: Steve Kerr, postgame press conference comments, June 12, 2017, "NBA Finals: Cleveland v Golden State," *ASAP Sports*, http://www .asapsports.com/show_interview.php?id=131024.

244 *the best Golden State roster*: Wes Goldberg, "Steve Kerr Says Warriors Were at Their Best in 2017: 'No Question,'" *Mercury News*, March 28, 2020, https://www .mercurynews.com/2020/03/28/steve-kerr-says-warriors-were-at-their-best-in -2017-no-question/.

244 *"I, like many"*: Tim Kawakami, "Talking with Steve Kerr: On a Trump White House Visit, Cavs' 'Steph Curry Rules,' and More," transcription of highlights from *The TK Show*, June 26, 2017, https://www.mercurynews.com/2017/06/26 /steve-kerr-podcast-transcript-on-the-white-house-adjusting-to-clevelands-steph -curry-rules-and-much-more/.

245 *Commissioner Adam Silver*: Cork Gaines, "Steve Kerr and Adam Silver Both Wanted the Warriors to Go to the White House for a Specific Reason—But Now It Doesn't Seem Possible," *Business Insider*, September 24, 2017, http://static3 .businessinsider.com/steve-kerr-adam-silver-warriors-visit-white-house-2017-9.

245 *decided before the season*: Monte Poole, "Sources: Warriors Prepared to Make Political Statement against Trump," *NBC Sports*, June 13, 2017, https://www .nbcsports.com/bayarea/warriors/sources-warriors-prepared-make-political -statement-against-trump.

245 *"Here it is"*: Steve Kerr, as told to Chris Ballard, "Mr. President: You Represent All of Us. Don't Divide Us. Bring Us Together," *Sports Illustrated*, September 24, 2017, https://www.si.com/nba/2017/09/24/steve-kerr-warriors-donald-trump-white -house-stephen-curry.

245 *"Would we have gone?"*: Ibid.

246 *Kerr likewise tagged Trump:* Ibid.

246 *"There's no need"*: Ibid.

246 *she learned from:* Tim Kawakami, "Transcript: Warriors Coach Steve Kerr (Actually, His Wife Margot) on His Moods—'Beware the Fury of a Patient Man,'" The Athletic, October 2, 2018, https://theathletic.com/558330/2018/10/02/transcript -warriors-coach-steve-kerr-actually-his-wife-margot-on-his-moods-beware-the -fury-of-a-patient-man/.

246 *Both Kerrs would reference:* Ibid.

246 *Once, he took offense:* Author interview with Tim Kawakami, February 7, 2020.

247 *"Tolbert told me"*: Ibid.

247 *"I think some people"*: Aldridge, "Coach Steve Kerr More Than Willing to Speak Up."

247 *He again advocated:* Ibid.

247 *"I really wasn't"*: Ibid.

247 *"all the time"*: Ibid.

248 *was a contrast:* Author interview with Damion Thomas, November 13, 2019.

248 *along with the kids:* Brian McNally, "In Lieu of White House Visit, Warriors Take Kids to Museum," *AP*, February 28, 2018, https://apnews.com/9cda9396a81f4d66b d0ab098feb07163/In-lieu-of-White-House-visit,%20-Warriors-take-kids-to -museum.

248 *Despite a general dislike:* Tim Kawakami, "Steve Kerr on His Love of Premier League Soccer, Mo Salah, and (Occasionally) Swearing on Live TV," The Athletic, May 15, 2019, https://athletique.com/979963/2019/05/15/kawakami-steve-kerr -on-his-love-of-premier-league-soccer-mo-salah-and-occassionally-swearing-on -live-tv/.

248 *"as excited to be there"*: Author interview with Damion Thomas, November 13, 2019.

248 *Thomas took note:* Ibid.

249 *"You're not going"*: McNally, "In Lieu of White House Visit, Warriors Take Kids to Museum."

249 *"we're kind of busy today"*: Janie McCauley, "Warriors' Kerr Questioned about Not Attending Clark Rally," *AP*, March 31, 2018, https://apnews.com/977794a6f50e 45fab64b65657195b6a2.

250 *"accusatory if you'd like"*: "Kerr Talks about Why He Couldn't Attend Stephon Clark Rally," *Mercury News*, March 31, 2018, https://www.youtube.com /watch?v=XX3CMYiKnU4.

250 *"had a bad vibe"*: Chris Ballard, "There's No Franchise in Sports Quite Like the Golden State Warriors," *Sports Illustrated*, December 12, 2018, https://www .si.com/nba/2018/12/12/golden-state-warriors-2018-sportsperson-of-the-year -inside-the-organization.

250 *"was starting to drift"*: Steve Kerr, "Steve Kerr on 25 Years with the Secret (and Why Curry's Warriors Couldn't Keep It)" (interview by Bill Simmons), *Book of Basketball 2.0* (podcast), November 5, 2019, https://podcasts.apple.com/us/podcast /book-of-basketball-2-0/id1483525141?i=1000455983343 (audio at 64:00).

250 *"showed the wear and tear"*: Kit Rachlis, "The Road to Dynasty," *California Sunday*, September 19, 2018, https://story.californiasunday.com/steve-kerr-phil-jackson.

250 *berated the Warriors so badly:* Ibid.

250 *"We pat him down"*: Anthony Slater (@anthonyVslater), "Gregg Popovich, joking, on Steve Kerr's son, who is an intern in San Antonio: 'We pat him down every day after work,'" Twitter, November 2, 2017, https://twitter.com/anthonyVslater /status/926211663963049986.

251 *"That's when I knew"*: Ethan Strauss, "A Title Defense for the Warriors and a Called Shot for Kerr," The Athletic, June 9, 2018, https://theathletic.com/386306 /2018/06/09/a-title-defense-for-the-warriors-and-a-called-shot-for-steve-kerr/.

251 *approached the few remaining players:* Author interview with Marcus Thompson II, December 27, 2019.

251 *words were infused:* Author interview with Marcus Thompson II, December 27, 2019.

251 *"Look," Kerr told:* Strauss, "A Title Defense for the Warriors."

252 *"just saw something"*: Ibid.

252 *"You thought I was crazy"*: Strauss, "A Title Defense for the Warriors."

253 *"I've learned kind of how"*: Tim Kawakami, "Steve Kerr's Improving Health, the Sustainability of the Big Four, and Everything That Was Underlined by This Warriors Title Run," The Athletic, March 10, 2018, https://theathletic.com /387384/2018/06/10/kawakami-steve-kerrs-improving-health-the-sustainability-of -the-big-four-and-everything-else-that-was-underlined-by-this-warriors-title-run/.

253 *"First of all"*: Karl Buscheck, "Steve Kerr Plays It Cool on Draft Night and Gets His Wing," *957FM: The Game*, June 21, 2018 (no link available).

253 *The family traveled in Europe:* Anthony Slater, "Steve Kerr on the Warriors' Mindset Heading into Training Camp, Integrating DeMarcus Cousins and More," The Athletic, September 20, 2018, https://theathletic.com/537679/2018/09/20 /steve-kerr-on-the-warriors-mindset-heading-into-training-camp-integrating -demarcus-cousins-and-more/.

253 *"So I am doing better"*: Kawakami, "Warriors Coach Steve Kerr (Actually, His Wife Margot) on His Moods."

254 *They agreed on Kerr:* Author interview with Jerry Colangelo, March 10, 2020.
254 *return of the same:* Rachlis, "The Road to Dynasty."
255 *When Jackson chose:* Lazenby, *Blood on the Horns,* 248.
255 *"One of the things":* Rachlis, "The Road to Dynasty."
256 *Kerr saw it as:* Kerr, "Steve Kerr on 25 Years with the Secret" (Simmons interview) by Simmons, *Book of Basketball 2.0.*
256 *took a lead role:* Ballard, "There's No Franchise in Sports Quite Like the Golden State Warriors."
256 *Kerr told Mike Brown:* "Steve Kerr CAUGHT Saying 'I'm So F-Ing SICK of Draymond' after TRASH Loss to Suns!" *The Fumble,* March 11, 2019, https://www.youtube.com/watch?v=BRUs53MYKLc.
256 *"I thought we move":* Anthony Slater (@anthonyVslater), "Kevin Durant asked [during a March 5, 2019, press conference] about Kerr saying the team needed to play with more anger: 'I thought we moved off joy. Now anger? I disagree with that one,'" Twitter, March 6, 2019, https://twitter.com/anthonyVslater/status/1103181567256518657.
256 *"an incredible opportunity":* K. C. Johnson, "Steve Kerr Stays Positive, Keeps Perspective with New Warriors' Challenge," *NBC Sports,* December 5, 2019, https://www.nbcsports.com/chicago/bulls/steve-kerr-stays-positive-keeps-perspective-new-warriors-challenge.
257 *Curry called it:* Sopan Deb, "Stephen Curry Finally Gets Some Rest (but Only from Basketball)," *New York Times,* June 21, 2019, https://www.nytimes.com/2019/06/21/sports/stephen-curry-finals-durant-politics.html.
257 *"Holy shit":* Kerr, "Steve Kerr on 25 Years with the Secret" (Simmons interview).
257 *Kerr's favorite game:* Ibid.
258 *The carnage of Virginia Beach:* Steve Kerr, pregame press conference comments, June 2, 2019, "NBA Finals: Warriors v Raptors," *ASAP Sports,* http://www.asapsports.com/show_interview.php?id=150442.
258 *"The insanity of it all":* Sean Gregory, "The Golden State Warriors Revolutionized the NBA. Now They Plan to Keep the Dynasty Dream Alive," *Time,* June 18, 2019, https://time.com/5608475/golden-state-warriors/.
258 *A 2003 letter:* Ibid.
258 *"I don't have one":* Ibid.
259 *"I just told the team":* Steve Kerr, postgame press conference comments, June 10, 2019, "NBA Finals: Warriors v Raptors," *ASAP Sports,* http://www.asapsports.com/show_interview.php?id=150937.
259 *"bizarre":* Ibid.
259 *"and connected with our staff":* Chris Ballard, "Inside the Warriors' New Reality and Their Uncertain Future," *Sports Illustrated,* June 15, 2019, https://www.si.com/nba/2019/06/15/golden-state-warriors-steve-kerr-kevin-durant-klay-thompson-stephen-curry-nba-finals-uncertain-future-free-agency-rumors.
259 *"I don't know how":* Ibid.
260 *"Maybe go to Italy":* Tim Kawakami, "Sadness, Exhaustion, Pride, and the Possible Inevitable End of the Warriors Dynasty," The Athletic, June 14, 2019, https://theathletic.com/1027479/2019/06/14/kawakami-sadness-exhaustion-pride-and-the-possible-inevitable-end-of-the-warriors-dynasty/.

Chapter 15: Tremendous Forces at Play

261 *"It feels unfair":* Jackie MacMullan, "'You Can't Plan beyond Next Year': Coaching in an NBA Where Stars Call the Shots," *ESPN,* August 1, 2019, https://www.espn

.com/nba/story/_/id/27282369/you-plan-next-year-coaching-nba-where-stars
-call-shots.

262   *"Not to him specifically"*: Author interview with Jerry Colangelo, March 10, 2020.

262   *"We can't fix"*: Ben Golliver, "Gregg Popovich and Steve Kerr, Two Vocal Trump
Critics, Hope Team USA Is a 'Unifying' Force,'" *Washington Post*, August 6, 2019,
https://www.washingtonpost.com/sports/2019/08/06/gregg-popovich-steve
-kerr-two-vocal-trump-critics-hope-team-usa-is-unifying-force/.

262   *Popovich that he had previously labeled:* Ibid.

262   *"gutless leadership"*: Mark Medina, "Steve Kerr: 'Somebody Could Walk in the
Door in the Gym Right Now and Start Spraying Us with an AR15,'" *Mercury
News*, August 5, 2019, https://www.mercurynews.com/2019/08/05/steve-kerr
-somebody-could-walk-in-the-door-in-the-gym-right-now-and-start-spraying-us
-with-an-ar15/.

263   *"Somebody could walk in"*: Ibid.

263   *"I'm proud to represent"*: Golliver, "Gregg Popovich and Steve Kerr, Two Vocal
Trump Critics."

263   *"One, just the team"*: Author interview with Harrison Barnes, November 19, 2019.

263   *"For sure"*: Ibid.

263   *"It was wonderful"*: Gregg Popovich, pregame comments, November 1, 2019.

264   *in his eyes:* "Already a World Cup Champion, USA Assistant Coach Steve Kerr
Looking for Second Title in China," *FIBA.basketball*, September 6, 2019, http://
www.fiba.basketball/basketballworldcup/2019/news/already-a-world-cup
-champion-usa-assistant-coach-steve-kerr-looking-for-second-title-in-china. "I'm
getting to watch Pop up close for the first time," Kerr said. "I played for him but
I've never coached with him. The experience has been fantastic."

264   *"Well, I'm excited"*: Steve Kerr, press conference comments, September 30, 2019,
"Golden State Warriors Media Conference," *ASAP Sports*, http://www.asapsports
.com/show_conference.php?id=154024.

265   *billions invested:* Jeff Zillgitt and Mark Medina, "As Impasse over Pro-Hong Kong
Tweet Simmers, What's at Stake for the NBA in China?" usatoday.com, October 9, 2019.

265   *"bizarre international story"*: Jason Owens, "Outspoken Warriors Coach Steve
Kerr No Comments NBA's China Controversy," *Yahoo!Sports*, October 7, 2019,
https://sports.yahoo.com/outspoken-warriors-coach-steve-kerr-no-comments
-nb-as-china-controversy-043403491.html.

266   *"And yet to our own country"*: Ibid.

266   *Trump reaffirmed:* Donald J. Trump (@realDonaldTrump), "So funny to watch
Steve Kerr grovel and pander when asked a simple question about China. He
chocked, and looks weak and pathetic. Don't want him at the White House!"
Twitter, October 11, 2019, https://twitter.com/realDonaldTrump/status/11828
59828386885633.

266   *as he would acknowledge:* Candace Buckner (@CandaceDBuckner), "With the
NBA addressing severed ties w/ a Chinese bkb camp, I wanted to share this from
Steve Kerr I'm working on a piece abt coaches & their role in speaking up & Kerr,
usually outspoken, admitted he didn't like his comments re: China last yr I think
this is honest reflection," Twitter, July 24, 2020, https://twitter.com/CandaceD
Buckner/status/1286713767619891205.

267   *"Raymond and I were just"*: Steve Kerr, pregame press conference comments, October 10, 2019.

267   *"Does anyone want"*: Ibid.

267   *"It's hard for me":* Ibid.

267   *"Wow":* Ibid.

267   *a $78 parking ticket:* Steve Kerr, postgame press conference comments, October 10, 2019.

268   *Relocating across the Bay Bridge:* Anthony Slater, "Why Did the Warriors Choose Marquese Chriss over Alfonzo McKinnie? Age and Immediate Need," The Athletic, October 18, 2019. https://theathletic.com/1305205/2019/10/18/why -did-the-warriors-choose-marquese-chriss-over-alfonzo-mckinnie-age-and -immediate-need/

268   *$125.9 million in combined salary:* Anthony Slater (@anthonyVslater), "Combined salary of the Warriors seven currently inactive players: $125.9 million. Combined salary of the nine remaining active players: $12.5 million (plus two two-way contracts)," Twitter, November 2, 2019, https://twitter.com/anthonyVslater/status /1190765407692455936.

268   *seats with a face value:* Darren Rovell (@darrenrovell), "You can buy a club access (food & drink included ticket) with seats 5 rows off the wood for the fourth ever Warriors regular season home game at the Chase Center tonight for $400. These seats have a $950 face value & come with a $55K PSL," Twitter, November 2, 2019, https://twitter.com/darrenrovell/status/1190656097650171905.

268   *It took only until:* Kerr postgame press conference comments, October 11, 2019.

268   *Shootarounds went from:* Mark Medina, "First to Worst: How Warriors Coach Steve Kerr Keeps Positive Attitude with Golden State," *USA Today,* November 19, 2019, https://www.usatoday.com/story/sports/nba/2019/11/19/steve-kerr -warriors-cant-lose-hope/4196254002/.

268   *"There would be nights":* Ibid.

268   *"This is more the reality":* Steve Kerr, postgame press conference comments, October 24, 2019.

269   *"I do believe in karma":* Anonymous interview with author.

269   *"Kerr always did things":* Ric Bucher, "Warriors No More," *Bleacher Report,* November 8, 2019, https://bleacherreport.com/articles/2861577-warriors-no-more.

269   *Watching from Los Angeles:* Author interview with Jerry West, November 15, 2019.

269   *Similarly wondering about:* Author interview with Craig Ehlo, October 1, 2019.

269   *"Steve is not stressed out":* Author interview with Stacey King, December 2, 2019.

269   *"He's a grown man":* Popovich.

270   *"I think he's doing":* Author interview with Luke Walton, January 6, 2020.

270   *"Steve has done":* Rick Carlisle, January 14, 2020.

270   *"fun"* and *"a different challenge":* Kerr Shootaround, January 6, 2020.

Bibliography

Brennan, Karen. *Being with Rachel: A Story of Memory and Survival*. New York: W. W. Norton & Company, 2002.

Buss, Jeanie, with Steve Springer. *Laker Girl*. Chicago: Triumph Books, 2010.

Eggers, Kerry. *Jail Blazers: How the Portland Trail Blazers Became the Bad Boys of Basketball*. New York: Sports Publishing, 2018.

Feinstein, John. *A Season Inside: One Year in College Basketball*. New York: Fireside, 1988.

———. *One on One: Behind the Scenes with the Greats in the Game*. New York: Little, Brown and Company, 2011.

Fifield, Anna. *The Great Successor: The Divinely Perfect Destiny of Brilliant Comrade Kim Jong Un*. New York: PublicAffairs, 2019.

Fisk, Robert. *The Great War for Civilisation: The Conquest of the Middle East*. New York: Vintage Books, 2005.

Friedman, Thomas L. *From Beirut to Jerusalem*. New York: Anchor Books, 1989.

Gallwey, W. Timothy. *The Inner Game of Tennis* [1974], rev. ed. New York: Random House, 1977.

Halberstam, David. *Playing for Keeps: Michael Jordan and the World He Made*. New York: Random House, 1999.

Iguodala, Andre, with Carvell Wallace. *The Sixth Man: A Memoir*. New York: Penguin Random House/Blue Rider Press, 2019.

Isaacson, Melissa. *Transition Game: An Inside Look at Life with the Chicago Bulls*. Champaign, IL: Sagamore Publishing, 1994.

Jackson, Phil, with Hugh Delehanty. *Eleven Rings: The Soul of Success*. New York: Penguin Press, 2013.

Jackson, Phil, and Charley Rosen. *More Than a Game*. New York: Fireside, 2002.

Jenkins, Bruce, Rusty Simmons, Scott Ostler, Bob Fitzgerald, and Tim Roye. *Strength in Numbers: The Official Championship Commemorative Book*. San Diego: Skybox Press, 2015.

Lazenby, Roland. *Blood on the Horns: The Long Strange Ride of Michael Jordan's Chicago Bulls*. Lenexa, KS: Addax Publishing Group, 1998.

———. *Mad Game: The NBA Education of Kobe Bryant*. Lincolnwood, IL: Masters Press, 2000.

———. *Michael Jordan: The Life*. New York: Back Bay Books, 2014.

Lewis, Michael C. *To the Brink: Stockton, Malone, and the Utah Jazz's Climb to the Edge of Glory*. New York: Simon & Schuster, 1998.

Malinowski, Erik. *Betaball: How Silicon Valley and Science Built One of the Greatest Basketball Teams in History*. New York: Atria Paperback, 2017.

McCallum, Jack. *Golden Days: West's Lakers, Steph's Warriors, and the California Dreamers Who Reinvented Basketball*. New York: Ballantine Books, 2017.

Menzer, Joe, and Burt Graeff. *Cavs from Fitch to Fratello: The Sometimes Miraculous, Often Hilarious Wild Ride of the Cleveland Cavaliers*. New York: Sports Publishing, 1994.

Mouro, Gladys. *An American Nurse Amidst Chaos*. Beirut: American University of Beirut Press, 2001.

Olson, Lute, and David Fisher. *Lute!: The Seasons of My Life*. New York: Thomas Dunne Books, 2006.

O'Neal, Shaquille, with Jackie MacMullan. *Shaq Uncut: My Story*. New York: Grand Central Publishing, 2011.

O'Neal, Shaquille, with Jack McCallum. *Shaq Attaq!* New York: Hyperion, 1993.

Peet Carrington, Anne, and Børre Ludvigsen, eds. *Fill the Bathtub!* Al Mashriq, 2011.

Rich, Rosa La Sorte. *Crossing Boundaries: Beirut and Beyond, Remembering 1964–68*. Self-published, 2005.

Rivera, Steve. *Tales from the Arizona Wildcats Locker Room: A Collection of the Greatest Wildcat Stories Ever Told*. New York: Sports Publishing, 2013.

Rivera, Steve, and Anthony Gimino. *100 Things Arizona Fans Should Know and Do before They Die*. Chicago: Triumph Books, 2014.

Smith, Eddie. *The Cornerstone of Arizona Basketball: The Eddie Smith Story*. CreateSpace Independent Publishing Platform, 2013.

Smith, Sam. *The Jordan Rules*. New York: Simon & Schuster, 1992.

Stockton, John, with Kerry L. Pickett. *Assisted: An Autobiography*. Salt Lake City: Shadow Mountain, 2013.

Telander, Rick. *In the Year of the Bull: Zen, Air, and the Pursuit of Sacred and Profane Hoops*. New York: Simon & Schuster, 1996.

Thompson, Marcus, II. *Golden: The Miraculous Rise of Steph Curry*. New York: Touchstone, 2017.

———. *KD: Kevin Durant's Relentless Pursuit to Be the Greatest*. New York: Atria Books, 2019.

Van de Ven, Susan Kerr. *One Family's Response to Terrorism: A Daughter's Memoir*. Syracuse, NY: Syracuse University Press, 2008.

Zwicker Kerr, Ann. *Come with Me from Lebanon: An American Family Odyssey*. Syracuse, NY: Syracuse University Press, 1994.

Index

Virginia Beach shooting of 2019, 257–58
Volgy, Thomas, 52

Wallace, Rasheed, 160
Walton, Bill, 224–25
Walton, Luke, 210–11, 224–25, 227, 233,
    242–43
Ward, Joe, 88
Washington Bullets, 132–33
Washington Huskies, 78
Washington Post, 70, 75
Washington State Cougars, 71, 78, 92
Washington Wizards, 165, 195, 201, 229,
    248
Waters, Sean, 25
Webb, Jamison, 227–28
Webber, Chris, 214
Weinhauer, Bob, 27–28, 49–52, 86, 137
Weiss, Dick, 72
Welts, Rick, 253
Wennington, Bill, 108, 112, 124, 130,
    131–32, 140, 141–42, 146
West, Jerry, 111, 220, 226, 258, 269
Westbrook, Russell, 209, 231–32, 238, 257
Westphal, Paul, 91
What Really Happened to the Class of '65?
    (TV show), 19

Whitaker, Forest, 19
White House, 58, 229–30, 244–46,
    248–49
Whitsitt, Bob, 160–61, 177, 178, 192
Wiggins, Andrew, 271
"Wild About the Cats" (rap), 71–73, 97
Wilkens, Lenny, 92, 93, 169, 174, 177,
    205, 213
Williams, John, 98
Williams, Pat, 100–101
Williams, Reggie, 95
Williams, Scott, 124
Williams, Ted, 166, 167–68, 172
Williams, Walt, 166
Willis, Kevin, 161
Winter, Morice Fredrick "Tex," 109, 127,
    214, 232
Wooden, John, 15, 21, 60, 232, 258
World War II, 5–6, 37
Worthy, James, 111, 176
Wright, Jay, 254
Wynn, Steve, 262

Yahoo!Sports, 175, 176–78, 242

Zwicker, John, 5–6, 20
Zwicker, Susan, 5–6, 20